# The Psychology of Sex

*By the same authors*

THE EXPERIMENTAL STUDY OF FREUDIAN THEORIES
KNOW YOUR OWN PERSONALITY
A TEXTBOOK OF HUMAN PSYCHOLOGY
THE PSYCHOLOGICAL BASIS OF IDEOLOGY

# The Psychology of Sex

H.J. Eysenck
and
Glenn Wilson

J.M. Dent & Sons Ltd

London, Toronto and Melbourne

First published 1979


Phototypeset in VIP Times by
D.P. Media Ltd, Hitchin, Hertfordshire
Printed in Great Britain by
Billing & Sons Ltd, London, Guildford & Worcester for
J.M. Dent & Sons Ltd
Aldine House, Welbeck Street, London

British Library Cataloguing in Publication Data

Eysenck, Hans Jürgen
The psychology of sex.
1. Sex (Psychology)
I. Title II. Wilson, Glenn Daniel
155.3 BF692

ISBN 0-460-04332-3

# Contents

# Acknowledgments

The authors would like to thank the following for permission to reproduce or quote from their surveys and questionnaires in this book: John Alan Lee for 'Twenty Questions About Your Love Relationship' which appeared in *Lovestyles*, published by J.M. Dent & Sons Ltd; D. Nias for material from 'Husband-Wife Similarities' which appeared in *Social Science* 1977, **52**, 206–11; D. Kipnis, P.J. Castell, M. Gergen and D. Manch for the 'Marital Power Questionnaire'; Plenum Publishing Corporation for Ellen Vance and Nathaniel Wagner's 'Written descriptions of orgasm: A study of Sex Differences' which appeared in *Archives of Sexual Behavior* 1976, **5**, 87–98.

# 1 Why another book on sex?

Since Havelock Ellis published his famous seven-volume *Studies in the Psychology of Sex* at the turn of the century, there has been an ever-increasing outpouring of books on the subject. Many of these have been of the 'do-it-yourself' variety, telling people how to have bigger and better orgasms; others have dealt with sex therapy, or how to get over one's hang-ups. Neither genre has been very helpful, for various reasons which we shall deal with presently. Our book is rather different: it aims to look at certain questions and problems in the field of human sexuality, and to tell the reader concisely and, we hope, in an entertaining manner what science has to say about them. For although science has learned a great deal about sexual behaviour since Havelock Ellis' time, curiously little of this knowledge has trickled through to the man in the street. Perhaps writers have been too busy advising him on what to do, and how to do it; perhaps psychologists and physiologists have been too worried about their image to write for popular consumption. Whatever the reason, there appears to be a gap in the popular literature, and here we aim to fill it, with a concise account of current scientific evidence on such topics as male-female differences and personality differences in relation to sexual behaviour, courtship, love, marriage and divorce, sexual fantasy, arousal and deviation, orgasm difficulties and treatment of sexual disorders.

The material is largely factual, being based mostly on surveys and experiments. Little attention is given to speculative theories, such as those of Freud, and there is a minimum of moral and political philosophy, although the social implications of some of the findings are discussed. But this is not a text-book, so we have not documented all the thousands of references we have consulted. We have quoted some of the more readable secondary sources, and many of these contain further references for anyone interested in pursuing the subject in more detail.

Why are the do-it-yourself sex manuals and therapy books of so little use to those who are likely to consult them? For one thing, there seems to be an underlying assumption in most of these books that human beings are fundamentally alike, and that they will all be happy once they have achieved the same degree of sexual fulfilment. There is a second assumption that this fulfilment is essentially of a physical nature, and a third assumption, to the effect that by reading books everyone can reach the same degree of expertise in the sexual field. 'Unhappy in bed?' these books seem to ask – 'then ginger up your sex life with a bit of "69", get going on those simultaneous orgasms, and everything in the garden will be lovely. Perhaps you will have to throw in a bit of mate-swapping, or start on some of those kinky habits, but never worry – practice makes perfect.' Unfortunately life is more complex and complicated than that.

Consider first of all human diversity. The French novelist Simenon boasted recently that he had slept with 10,000 women, i.e. a new one every 50 hours; yet the philosopher Kant never slept with a woman at all! A certain Mlle Dubois, who lived just before the French Revolution, made a catalogue of her lovers over a twenty-year period: it totalled 16,527 individuals, or three a day. On the other hand there are spinsters and nuns who never have intercourse at all. The Boston Strangler, according to his wife's testimony, insisted on having intercourse nineteen times a day; other men have intercourse only once a week, or even more rarely. Catherine the Great advocated having sexual relations six times a day and apparently followed her own advice. King Lapetakaka II considered it his duty to deflower every native maiden in Tonga, and even at the age of eighty (when Captain Cook visited him) he was performing his appointed task eight to ten times a day. In our own society, men and women on the average have intercourse two to three times a week (less often as they get older), but this figure hides a great deal of variability: some 5 per cent have intercourse more than once a day, another 5 per cent only once a fortnight, or even less frequently. Nothing is more obvious to the student of human sexuality, therefore, than the tremendous variability shown in everything that pertains to its expression; and frequency of intercourse is only one example. We have emphasized human diversity in this book; we have, we hope, convincingly shown that men and women are fundamentally (i.e. physiologically and genetically) different in their sexual, as well as in their social attitudes and behaviours. We have also shown that, within each sex, personality – itself genetically determined – powerfully influences the way men and women deal with the problems raised by the sexual drive. These differences are almost completely neglected by the usual run of books on sex, but unless we pay attention to them we are never likely to achieve sexual contentment and happiness.

There is more to human diversity than variations in the frequency of intercourse. Preferences for 'tits versus bums', as the newspapers so inelegantly call them, are related to personality; so are puritan versus permissive attitudes. How these different attitudes grow, and to what extent they are anchored in genetic predispositions, is an important question for the research psychologist, and the answers have many important consequences for us all. The very meaning of 'sexual fulfilment' differs for different people; where one woman searches desperately for the man who can give her multiple orgasms, another will look rather for a loving and caring relationship, and never mind the frequency of orgasms. Maybe it is because the latter search is the more difficult that books on sex seem to concentrate on the former requirement, and give advice entirely on the best way of achieving it. Whatever the reason, this emphasis has contributed to the misleading impression that the psychological side is less important than the purely physical – which has led many people into unhappiness and dissatisfaction with their love lives. The one-sided stress on physical sex so characteristic of our culture, as well as our sex books, is self-defeating and ultimately destructive of what is characteristically human in the relationship between men and women.

Can it at least be said that 'do-it-yourself' books on sexual techniques are successful in what they aim to achieve? The answer must be that such success is at best very doubtful. Making love is at least as complex and difficult an activity as playing tennis, or golf; we cannot learn either game simply by reading books about it, and it is very doubtful that reading books on how to make love will improve one's performance either. Perhaps a book can direct one's attention to very obvious faults and errors, but even this does not always, or even usually, lead to the eradication of these errors. How many golfers have cured their habit of slicing the ball into the rough by reading a book? How many tennis players have corrected their faulty service in that way? Why then should we assume without proof that we can correct ingrained habits of doing the wrong thing when making love by reading a book? Indeed, making love well is probably even more difficult than playing golf or tennis really well. These games are controlled by the cortex, the cerebellum and the central nervous system, i.e. a combination which is subject to voluntary control, and hence to rational guidance and learning. The physiology of sexual reactions is governed by the autonomic nervous system, so called because it is largely independent of the voluntary control of the central nervous system; to gain control over such an independent and wilful apparatus is a more complicated affair than it appears to be at first sight. To be told what to do is quite another story from actually doing it; books on sex may give you ideas, but they will not help you very much in improving your performance, and by holding out false hopes, they may mislead the reader and breed disappointment and frustration. Sex therapy books, too, can outline possible methods of correcting such disabling faults as frigidity, impotence and premature ejaculation but, again, it needs a therapist actually to supervise the treatment – few people succeed in doing it by themselves.

Many sex books seem to take it for granted that everyone can become a great lover; this is as absurd as to imagine that everyone can play tennis like Laver, or Connors, or Borg. Casanovas, like sport stars, are born, not made; coaching can improve a person's game, but if he is not born with the proper hand-eye coordination, stamina and temperament, he is unlikely to emerge from the great mass of mediocre players. Tennis can be fun, even for amateurs; in fact, they probably enjoy their games as much as the professionals. The same is probably true of sex. One does not have to be a sexual athlete to enjoy oneself – indeed, the sexual athlete always has something to prove, and may fail to enjoy his acrobatic acts in any sense other than as sporting achievements. It may be possible to have sex hanging from the chandelier, or under water, or standing on one's head, but this is not to say that it will be more enjoyable than having it in bed, in the 'missionary position'. The sexual act can express many other needs and aims than the purely sexual; it is the final common pathway of a large number of emotions, desires, motivations, instincts and drives. To regard it as a sporting achievement and nothing else is to be blind to its complexity, its beauty and its human meaning. By seeming to encourage such a one-sided approach, the sex manuals may be doing a disservice to their readers.

There is no doubt, of course, that sex does present us with many problems, and that neurosis and sex are intimately connected – although not all neuroses have a sexual basis, as has so frequently and erroneously been asserted. A large number of problems arise from the simple logistics of sex, as the Polish mathematician and philosopher Mosciewitzky pointed out quite forcefully. He took as his example physical attraction, to which we shall return in a later chapter where we shall consider the empirical studies carried out on this subject. Mosciewitzky remained on the theoretical level throughout. He started by looking at the large number of different physical features which must be considered in declaring a woman 'beautiful' (or a man 'dishy', of course; what is sauce for the gander is sauce for the goose). There are the nose, the ears, the hair, the lips, the shape of the head, the size and shape of the breasts and buttocks, the legs, the abdomen, the quality of the skin and the waist – to name just a baker's dozen. Let us assume that there are ten degrees of perfection for each, and that these different features are unrelated (which is true to an extent). It would take $10^{13}$ women, or one in a hundred million million, to find one perfect woman – that is to say, many thousand times more women than are alive now, or ever lived on the planet Earth throughout its history! Add to this an equal number of psychological traits (because the perfect woman is obviously not to be defined exclusively in physical terms), and it becomes clear that the perfect woman never has existed, and never will – and neither does, or will, the perfect man.

Of course the whole argument is put forth partly with tongue in cheek, but it does illustrate a profound truth, namely, that there is never a sufficient number of really desirable women and men available to satisfy the needs and desires of men and women seeking partners. This conclusion would be little affected if we decided that on the Mosciewitzky scale ten units are too many, and five or even three, would suffice; or that the baker's dozen of attributes included too much, and that fewer would do. Equally, we need not jib at the fact that different men may like different types of women; as we shall see later, there is sufficient agreement on what constitutes the attractive girl to produce tremendous competition. In this sexual competition, marriage constitutes a restrictive practice; this is why people both decry it, and yet don't seem able to live without it!

In addition to the logistic problems outlined above, we have the added complication that some of the more shapely and physically desirable people are taken out of the ordinary matrimonial stakes: the girls may take up careers as film starlets, models, go-go dancers or prostitutes; the men may become gigolos, film stars, turn homosexual, etc. And what is true of the body is also true of the mind. Many outstanding women do not marry, and neither do many outstanding men – thus three out of four leading philosophers have remained celibate. Clearly, the position is desperate.

There is an additional consideration which affects men particularly. The period of optimum physical bloom is much shorter for women than for men; roughly speaking, men are sexually desirable for women for almost twice as long as women are for men. Of course it is realized that physical appeal is not all, and that for many people love tides them over the gradual decline in physical appeal of their partners; nevertheless, for possibly even more people this physical decline in the appeal of their partner, accompanied by general satiation, leads to boredom and ultimately either to a cessation of sexual passion, or to desire seeking a new direction. In a slightly lesser way the same considerations affect women, too, of course; men also lose their sex appeal as they get older and time often destroys their desirability. With these logistic problems to think about we hardly require Freudian complexes to explain the fact that there are few people who are not anxious about their sexual adequacy, upset about their lowly status in the sex-appeal race or worried about their love life. When we add the complications of psychological factors to those produced by sheer physical appeal (or its lack!), it will be clear why sexual causes so often figure in the histories of our neurotic patients.

Quite apart from actual neurosis, there are many problems to be found even in the most normal type of marriage. Kinsey asserted that upper income people have fewer sexual problems than the rest of the population, but a recent survey of a hundred couples aged about thirty-five who had the happiest, most comfortable marriages that the researchers could find – made up of predominantly white, Christian, well-educated and middle class people – found that three-quarters of the women and half the men had one or more sex problems, ranging from difficulty in reaching orgasm to a general lack of interest in sex. In spite of this, 86 per cent of the women and 85 per cent of the men rated their sex lives as very or moderately satisfying. Most of the hundred had been married at least five years and had an average of two children; none were undergoing any kind of sexual or marital treatment. Yet 63 per cent of the women reported a physical problem. The most common complaints, experienced by almost half the women, were difficulty in getting 'turned on' and in achieving orgasm. Of the men, some 40 per cent reported a physical problem, by far the most frequent being premature ejaculation, which was complained about by 36 per cent; difficulties in maintaining an erection occurred only in 9 per cent. Psychological problems were both more frequent and, especially for women, more important in how satisfying they found their sex life: 77 per cent of the women reported problems in this area. Most common was an inability to relax (47 per cent), followed by too little foreplay (38 per cent), disinterest (35 per cent), and inconvenient timing.

Each person was asked to report not just his or her problems, but also those of their partner. Wives were mainly accurate in seeing their husbands' problems, but the men tended to underestimate their wives' difficulties. For example, less than half of the men whose wives had trouble staying excited during sex recognized this problem. It is clear that even among the most favoured there are physical and psychological sexual problems which, while they do not cause partners to rate their marriages as unhappy, nevertheless give rise to complaints.

In addition to logistical, behavioural and psychological problems there are also physical ones. As an example to be looked at in more detail later, the ancient parent of all modern sex manuals, the *Kama Sutra*, produced a rather odd typology based on the size of the male and female sex-organs; men and women were divided into three classes according to this standard, and it was laid down that large should only mate with large, small with small, and intermediate with intermediate – all other matings were fraught with difficulty! This of course is absurd; except in the most extreme cases, size of the sex organs is really quite irrelevant to the adequacy of sexual matings, or the satisfaction produced by them. However, the fact that men are bigger and stronger than women has certainly produced many problems; the large number of battered wives, the increasing incidence of rape, and the physical aggression so characteristic of males are evidence for the fact that man has defined the roles of the sexes in a very unfair and unilateral manner. A recent study showed that 80 per cent of female students had experienced some form of unwanted and unprovoked physical aggression, from the mild (a pinched bottom, or a kiss forced on them) to the extreme (rape, violence).

These weight differences are not peculiar to humans; they are found to an equal extent in baboons and other mammals. There are, admittedly, occasional exceptions, but these occur usually among animals far removed from *homo sapiens*. Among spiders, for instance, there are species where the female is very much larger than the male, and has the somewhat uncivil habit of eating her sex partner after making love (if that is the appropriate term in the case of spiders). We shall be dealing with sex differences in personality and sexual behaviour in the next chapter; here let us merely note that the differences in size and strength do, for too many women, constitute an inescapable limitation on equality; nothing can excuse the abuse of physical strength which has enslaved millions of women over thousands of years, but equally nothing can argue away the existence of this difference.

The assumption is often made that what 'consenting adults' do is their own affair, and that they know best what they like and don't like. Intuitively obvious as this seems, it is nevertheless very doubtful if it is true. Take one study which went beyond looking at what the couple were actually doing, and asked them whether they liked what they were doing. The outcome of the study was very salutary. Manual genital manipulation of the male by the female, for instance, was enjoyed by 94 per cent of the men, but only 64 per cent of the women; similarly, mutual genital manipulation was enjoyed by 96 per cent of the men, but only 69 per cent of the women. Fellatio (oral sex) was enjoyed by almost all the participating males, but only just over 50 per cent of the participating females! Typically, few men know what their partners really think of the practices they indulge in, and the 'consent' is often really a form of duress – 'suck me off, or I'll go somewhere else!' The *machismo* implicit in such attitudes is world-wide, and may be an innate masculine pattern; we shall look carefully at the evidence for such biological differences between men and women.

If at times male and female conduct seems almost predetermined by biology, at other times sexual behaviour seems almost infinitely modifiable by social imperatives and constraints. The Chinese government seems to have succeeded very largely in suppressing the sexual impulse, frowning as it does on marriage before the late twenties, and disapproving even more of premarital sex; many observers have acknowledged the success of the Party's attempt to reduce sex to a relatively unimportant drive compared with the social and political imperatives favoured by the government. Typical of the Chinese attitude is this quotation from the *Peking Workers' Daily*: 'Love between man and woman . . . consumes energy and wastes time. On the other hand, love of the Party and of the Chairman Mao-Tse-Tung, takes no time at all, and is in itself a powerful tonic.' Such a view would clearly not go down well in Soho, even though there is no reason to suppose that the Chinese so addressed, and the inhabitants of Soho, are genetically any different from each other. Clearly both social and biological factors have to be considered; it is a token of immaturity to embrace one set of causes to the exclusion of the other. We shall try to give a balanced account, dealing with both environmental and genetic causes. A good example of the complementary roles played by these two sets of determinants is given by the change in height observed in recent years among Japanese males and females. There has been a marked increase in height over the past twenty years or so, due probably to better food, the elimination of certain habits which stunted the growth and produced a bowing of the legs (such as carrying babies in slings on the back of the mother), and other similar causes. This shift was clearly due to environmental causes, just as are the differences between Chinese sexual habits now and a hundred years ago. But within each of the two periods being compared, the major part of the differences observed between tall and short, sexually active and inactive, was due largely to genetic causes; the differences between tall and short Japanese today are only in small part due to environmental factors.

Our book does not aim to teach any lessons, persuade the reader of any great truth, or urge him or her to change in any way. We have aimed to instruct and entertain; the ways of a man with a maid are interesting, but also amusing. As Lord Chesterfield said about sexual intercourse: 'The pleasure is momentary, the position ridiculous and the expense damnable'. Nevertheless, there seems a good chance that it will continue to be enjoyed and also to give rise to problems – problems which are rather different from those dealt with in the do-it-yourself books. As Chesterton once said: 'It isn't that they can't see the solution. It is that they can't see the problem.' We hope to elucidate *en passant* some of the problems; we are not rash enough to offer any solutions!

It will be seen that there is very little in this book that touches upon Freud or psychoanalysis, in spite of the widespread rumour that Freud invented sex. The reason is very simple – Freud is as little relevant to modern research into sex as is Havelock Ellis; both are historical figures whose work has not stood the test of time. We have devoted a whole book to *The Experimental Study of Freudian Theories*, and do not propose to duplicate this examination here; readers who wish to see in detail why we feel that Freud has little to say to us nowadays, in spite of his historical importance in changing the climate from Victorianism to permissiveness, may with advantage consult our previous book.

What has happened since then to change the approach to the psychology of sex? Three things, in the main. In the first place, Kinsey taught us that if we want to know what people think and do, the best way of finding out is to ask them. Simple as the advice may seem, there are many difficulties – difficulties of sampling (finding groups of people willing to answer your questions, without biasing the replies), difficulties in controlling for lying, evasions and misunderstanding, difficulties in interpretation of answers (you may ask questions about orgasm, say, but did your female respondents mean by the word what you mean?), and many more. Most middle class people fail to understand that many working class people do not use terms which to the academic seem obvious, and considerable research has to go into the framing of questions which are intelligible to all. An actual investigation that came to grief because of neglect of this point may illustrate the difficulties involved.

A large-scale study was done in America to investigate the hypothesis that women married to circumcised men suffer less frequently than others from cancer of the womb. Large numbers of women were interviewed, and were asked, among other things, about whether their husbands had been circumcised or not. When all the questionnaires and interview results were in, a meeting was held to decide on the precise method of analysis. At that moment a psychologist who had been invited as a consultant spoke up and said: 'But did these women *know* whether their husbands had been circumcised or not?' Loud laughter followed because the other members of the committee did not realize that a term such as 'circumcision' might not be intelligible to, say, a working class wife who had left school at an early age.

The psychologist finally convinced his colleagues that a small-scale study might be advisable, and interviewers went round to ask a number of women about circumcision of their husbands, then went on to find out just what these women thought circumcision meant. The outcome of this little study was an eye-opener to many people on the committee: many of the less well-educated women had no idea what circumcision meant, and thought it might have something to do with castration! Others again did know what circumcision meant, but had never seen their husbands in the nude, and really had no idea whether they were circumcised or not. In the end the whole study had to be repeated, with explicit guidance to each interviewee as to just what the term 'circumcision' meant. Difficulties of this kind can be overcome, at least to a large extent, and there is no doubt that we have learnt a great deal through interview studies of the kind begun by Kinsey. Even so, it is advisable to keep one's critical powder dry!

In the second place, we have learned to take our questions into the psychological laboratory, and subject them to experimental study proper. Whereas Kinsey would *ask* his respondents about their degree of sexual arousal upon seeing pornographic films – and the replies certainly do tell us something about the people questioned, though it is difficult to sort out what is genuine in their replies, what simply traditional, and what is produced because the man or woman questioned believes that this is what you, the experimenter, wish to hear – nowadays we would take our subject into the laboratory, sit him or her in front of a screen, and show a particular pornographic film. In this way we can standardize the stimuli involved in the experiment, rather than having to rely on the chance events of the subject's past life. We would then take psychophysiological recordings of our subject's reactions to the film. Some of these reactions would be directly sexual, i.e. changes in the state of our subject's penis or vagina, which can be measured very accurately. We can put a strain gauge around the penis and measure precisely the degree of erection produced by our film. In the case of a woman, we can measure the temperature of the *labia* (with sexual excitement, the temperature increases). We can show that these physiological measures agree well with verbal statements about the degrees of sexual arousal experienced; thus we have a check on the accuracy and validity of both verbal and psychophysiological measures. Another thing we can do is to measure the general degree of arousal of the subject, other than the specifically sexual response; we can monitor the heartbeat, breathing rate, electric conductivity of the skin and many other indices of arousal. In this way we can get some idea of the subject's interest in what is shown, his or her emotional reaction, disgust, etc. There are of course all sorts of problems in this type of work, from ethical to technical, but on the whole the trouble taken over laboratory studies has been well worthwhile; they complement the Kinsey-type purely verbal studies, and extend the bounds of our knowledge beyond them.

In the third place, we have learned to look at animals, interpret their sexual behaviour, and relate it to ours – particularly when we look at the behaviour of our closest cousins, the apes. There are many different kinds of comparisons that can be made between animals and ourselves, ranging from the purely physical to the behavioural. Man, of course, is unique in the animal kingdom, not only for his powers of speech, and other attributes that make him *homo sapiens*, but also for certain features of his sexuality. Unlike most species, humans have no closed sexual seasons, and the female is as ready and able as the male to indulge in sex at most times during adulthood. We are also unique in copulating simply for pleasure – female animals do not usually experience those spasms of intense sensation we call orgasm; this is reserved for their male partners. These are some of the differences that must be borne in mind before we can draw any reasonable conclusions from animal data.

Humans are also rather outstanding as regards penis length. The average male has an erect penis of just over 6 in. in length and 4 in. in girth, when measured just below the tip; the majority are between 5 and 7 in. long, with a very few extending to 8 in., or as small as 4 in. The normal penis grows by about one-third of its resting length under conditions of sexual excitement, but the amount of increase is in part a function of its resting length: the larger the resting member, the smaller the increase.

We are familiar with these statistics, if only from personal experience, but we do tend to have entirely the wrong ideas about other animals. We think that chimpanzees, and particularly gorillas, have vastly superior organs to ourselves, but this is quite untrue. The chimpanzee has a small pink spike, and the gorilla, whose weight may be the equivalent of that of three fully grown men, has an erection only one-third as long as a man's, amounting to no more than 2 in. or so. Furthermore, the gorilla is by no means as lustful as he is often portrayed. George Schaller, an American zoologist, closely observed mountain gorillas in their natural habitat in the Congo; in 466 hours of observation only two copulations were noted!

Other animals, however, certainly do excel the human as far as size of penis is concerned. That of a stallion may extend to 2 ft, that of a bull giraffe to 30 in.; and that of a fully grown elephant may be close to 5 ft long, and 60 lb. in weight – plus 10 lb. testicles. The elephant is also characterized by having a strong set of muscles embedded in his penis which enables it to move around and search for the cow's vaginal orifice. All this splendid equipment, however, seems rather wasted. Cows only agree to copulation for two or three days in the middle of their three-week oestrus cycles, and immediately after insemination they become pregnant which, together with looking after the baby, makes them inaccessible for a further three or four years!

Duration of copulation is another source of complaint for elephants, as compared with man. For African elephants, copulation lasts less than a minute; Asian elephants are even less well off. One scientist carefully timed the mating behaviour of elephants in Sri Lanka; on the average, bulls spent 23.06 seconds on top of their mistresses, with the agitated penis jerking around searching for the vagina of his partner; once lodged therein, orgasm came within 9.2 seconds. (The reasons for this short duration are of course related to the fact that an elephant carries a weight close to the limits of its supporting skeleton and the added weight of the bull places an enormous strain on the cow's body structure.)

For size, then, the elephant is outstanding, surpassed only by the whale which has a penis about 8 ft in length. But for actual performance it takes a lot to beat the ram. A ram in his prime can cover some thirty ewes in four days. If we reckon that he mounts each ewe twenty-five times, he will be carrying out his sexual functions no less than 750 times, ejaculating on some 200 occasions. Bulls also do rather well; one animal is reported to have ejaculated seventy-seven times in a six-hour sex session.

Lions, too, deserve a mention. A fertile lioness will copulate about every fifteen minutes for between two and three days; many lions may indulge in intercourse nearly a hundred times a day. On one occasion a lion was observed for two-and-a-half days in the Serengeti; during the first day he copulated seventy-four times with one female and twelve times with another. On the second day he copulated sixty-two times, and during the last half day another nine times. During the course of this period, therefore, the lion copulated altogether 157 times with an average interval of twenty-one minutes between mounts. In a Dresden zoo, a pair of lions copulated some 360 times over a period of eight days.

However, for the record breaking performances we have to go to the smaller rodents. Gerbils are pretty near the top; a pair of Shaw's jirds was found to indulge in 224 mountings during the course of one hour, although of course not every one resulted in the release of sperms. These rodents go for frequency of copulation, rather than length; each jird's copulation lasted only about 3 seconds on the average. Other animals go for length rather than frequency. Thus the male kowari can stay mounted for up to three hours, and Stewart's marsupial mouse can prolong the sex act for twelve hours. Snails have been timed up to twelve hours, with a pair of diamond-backed rattlesnakes staying entwined for twenty-two hours and forty minutes. Agoutis, the South American rodents, have been found to extend the sex act to twenty-four hours and more – with butterflies holding the record, having been timed as remaining locked together in intercourse for a whole week! Both for frequency and for length of copulation, therefore, some animals leave man standing.

In a sense these are all oddities; they do not throw much light on human behaviour. The position changes when we come to types of sexual conduct which show unmistakeable links between animals and ourselves. The so-called Coolidge effect is one example. Male rats, when placed with female rats, will indulge in mounting and intromission at a gradually falling rate; the longer the same female is segregated with the same male, the lower will become the rate of mounting. If the female is then replaced with another one, the rate of mounting immediately increases. Rats, too, get tired of their sex partners and bored with the same recurring activity, just like humans. Note also that, just as with humans, there are individual differences: some rats get tired of their partners more quickly than others.

Another similarity between animal and human behaviour is the frequency with which male animals collect a number of females around them in harem fashion; this is particularly so among the apes. Human males, too, whenever they have a chance to do so, seem to indulge in similar practices. However, it is easy to misinterpret the apparent power relations in such groups. Among certain species of apes, such as the Gelada baboons, the females require that the male should pay certain types of attention to them, in particular that they should take part in grooming activities. With a large harem this may keep the unfortunate male busy for a very large part of his time and, indeed, set the limit to the size of his harem. (In the same way, of course, the human male has to earn the money to keep his harem, and this also sets limits to the number of inmates.) Female baboons who are not satisfied with the amount of grooming they get from their lord and master have the opportunity to steal away and join another harem; thus power does not reside entirely in the male, for the females too have their share of influence. Early observers missed these subtle interconnections, and gave quite the wrong picture of the social life of apes and monkeys. The more we get to know about it, the more it resembles *mutatis mutandis*, the human condition; our evolutionary cousins enable us to see ourselves more clearly perhaps than if we simply look at human behaviour through the usual glasses of prejudice, special pleading and imagination.

Through interviews and questionnaires, through experimental investigations, and through comparative studies of animals, therefore, psychologists have been able to transcend the very limited knowledge available to early writers in the field of human sexuality, and to give us a more realistic and scientific picture.

In this book we have picked out subjects which we thought would interest most readers, and we have concentrated on topics where sufficient scientific knowledge was available to make conclusions possible and reasonable. We have not tried to deal with the many complexities that arise, or the problems which even a well-performed experiment raises; this is not a text-book, where such procedural discussions might be more appropriate. We have tried to satisfy ourselves that the conclusions drawn are supported by a critical review of all the data; and we have used data more to illustrate the conclusions than to prove them. Readers who are doubtful about this process will have to go back to the original sources; there really is no other way. Popularization in science is an important service that the practising scientist has to perform if he wishes the people – who after all pay his salary – to be well informed. But popularization stops well short of the detailed critical discussion that one finds in the experimental literature. We believe that our facts are not likely to be challenged, or our conclusions disputed, by anyone who has worked in the fields covered; opposition may of course arise on ideological grounds, but unless this can be supported by new and additional facts, we don't think it should be taken very seriously. Ideological commitments shift and change; the early universal permissiveness in the sexual field that characterized the Russian Revolution soon turned into a Victorian regime that was only outdone, as far as Puritanism was concerned, by the Communism of Red China. Clearly communism can identify with equal ease with opposite extremes on this continuum; so can other ideologies. We have written this book without any sort of ideological commitment, and we hope that the reader will enjoy it in the same spirit.

## References

ELLIS, H., *Studies in the Psychology of Sex*. New York: Random House, 1936.
EYSENCK, H.J., *Sex and Personality*. London: Open Books, 1976.
GORER, G., *Sex and Marriage in England Today*. London: Nelson, 1971.
KINSEY, A.C., *Sexual Behaviour in the Human Male*. New York: W.H. Saunders, 1948.
KINSEY, A.C., *Sexual Behaviour in the Human Female*. New York: W.H. Saunders, 1953.
MASTERS, W.H. & JOHNSON, V.E., *Human Sexual Response*. London: Churchill, 1966.
SEYMOUR-SMITH, M., *Sex and Society*. London: Hodder and Stoughton, 1975.
SPARKS, J., *The Sexual Connection*. London: David and Charles, 1977.

# 2 Male and female: the eternal difference

When Professor Higgins asks the rhetorical question, 'Why can't a woman be like a man?' in *My Fair Lady*, the musical based on Shaw's *Pygmalion*, many people nowadays answer that surely she can – and is. Equality of the sexes is not only taken for granted; it is even ordained by law. But the law only concerns itself with legal rights, with employment practices, and similar problems; what is seriously put forward by many feminists is that men and women are really alike in every respect – except of course the *petite difference*, for which we are all profoundly grateful, and the ability of women to bear children. How does such a belief square with the fact that men and women, in their everyday social and sexual behaviour, seem so greatly different? How can such a belief be reconciled with the reality of male dominance, female submissiveness? Why is it that girls play with dolls, boys with toy soldiers? If men and women are truly alike, then how does it come about that men are ever the pursuers, women the pursued; that men are much more impersonal in their love-making, women much more romantic; that men like pornography, women become prostitutes, rather than the other way about? Is the notion of equality, meaning identity in all important aspects, perhaps wrong, and should we rather embrace a belief in equality of social status, value to the community and civic rights, together with diversity of abilities, personalities and behaviour patterns? Do men and women perhaps have different needs as well as different abilities; different instincts as well as different ways of acting; different ways of manifesting their common humanity as well as different reactions to similar situations? In particular, do men and women fundamentally really have similar or identical attitudes to sex, reactions to sexual stimuli and behaviour patterns directed towards the other sex? Or are there important and biologically founded differences in sexual conduct which contrast male and female sexual behaviour?

Feminists have answered this question by appealing to the concept of *social modelling*. Society, so they say, has a model of male and female behaviour which is incorporated into the way we bring up our children; from infancy the little girl learns to be modest, submissive and kind; she learns to play with dolls, cook and wash dishes; whereas the boy learns to be dominant, aggressive and hard, to play with soldiers, play football and fight. This process of modelling is continued all through life: indoctrination, brain-washing, and conditioning continue almost from birth until old age, and consequently boys and girls learn their apportioned station in life, and behave differently because they have been taught to behave according to these imposed sex-roles. Men and women only differ in so far as society decrees that they should differ; were society to decree a change in roles, such a change would be speedily forthcoming. There is no biological foundation to the observed differences; all are culturally determined.

Fortunately we do not have to rely on belief, persuasion and common sense in order to answer the question of why a woman is not like a man: there is by now much relevant evidence from psychological, anthropological and biological science to enable us to give an unequivocal answer. The question being such a fundamental one for any reasonable understanding of the sexual behaviour of human beings, their hang-ups and their satisfactions, we will look at all these sources of evidence in turn; it is the fact that they all agree in ruling out an exclusively environmentalist answer to our question, in terms of modelling, imitation and conditioning, that makes us believe that there is a strong, underlying biological source for the widely differing sexual attitudes and behaviours we observe when we look at men and women (Wesley & Wesley, 1977).

First, however, it may be worthwhile to document the actual differences in sexual attitudes between men and women in our society. Consider the forty questions in the Masculinity-Femininity questionnaire printed below; all relate to sexual behaviour, and all show marked differences in the answers provided by men and women. The questionnaire was administered to almost one thousand British men and the same number of British women: the percentage of 'Yes' answers given by men and women to various questions is indicated in the questionnaire, as are the differences between the frequency of the

'Yes' answers between the two sexes. (A + sign preceding the difference score indicates that the men answered the question in the affirmative more frequently, while a − sign indicates that the women did so.) Readers can obtain their own scores by answering the forty questions for themselves. Each 'Yes' answer to a + question, and each 'No' answer to a − question counts one point. The lowest (most feminine) score is obviously nought, the highest (most masculine) score is forty; hardly anyone is ever likely to get such extreme scores, of course.

Masculinity-Femininity Scale

| | | *M* | *F* | *Diff.* |
|---|---|---|---|---|
| (1) | Sex without love ('impersonal sex') is highly unsatisfactory. | 43 | 60 | −17 |
| (2) | Conditions have to be just right to get me excited sexually. | 15 | 42 | −27 |
| (3) | Sometimes it has been a problem to control my sex feelings. | 50 | 38 | +12 |
| (4) | I get pleasant feelings from touching my sexual parts. | 81 | 66 | +15 |
| (5) | I do not need to respect a sex partner, or love him/her, in order to enjoy petting and/or intercourse with him/her. | 43 | 26 | +17 |
| (6) | Sexual feelings are sometimes unpleasant to me. | 6 | 11 | −5 |
| (7) | It doesn't take much to get me excited sexually. | 75 | 44 | +31 |
| (8) | I think about sex almost every day. | 87 | 61 | +26 |
| (9) | I get excited sexually very easily. | 68 | 40 | +28 |
| (10) | The thought of a sex orgy is disgusting to me. | 15 | 40 | −25 |
| (11) | I find the thought of a coloured sex partner particularly exciting. | 32 | 11 | +21 |
| (12) | I like to look at sexy pictures. | 80 | 45 | +35 |
| (13) | My conscience bothers me too much. | 13 | 20 | −7 |
| (14) | I enjoy petting. | 95 | 88 | +7 |
| (15) | Seeing a person nude doesn't interest me. | 6 | 28 | −22 |
| (16) | Sometimes the woman should be sexually aggressive. | 95 | 88 | +7 |
| (17) | I believe in taking my pleasures where I find them. | 34 | 19 | +15 |
| (18) | Young people should be allowed out at night without being too closely checked. | 69 | 54 | +15 |

| | | *M* | *F* | *Diff.* |
|---|---|---|---|---|
| (19) | I would particularly protect my children from contact with sex. | 6 | 12 | −6 |
| (20) | I like to look to pictures of nudes. | 84 | 44 | +40 |
| (21) | If I had the chance to see people making love, without being seen, I would take it. | 67 | 37 | +30 |
| (22) | Pornographic writings should be freely allowed to be published. | 74 | 55 | +19 |
| (23) | Prostitution should be legally permitted. | 82 | 63 | +19 |
| (24) | I had some bad sex experiences when I was young. | 13 | 20 | −7 |
| (25) | There should be no censorship, on sexual grounds, of plays and films. | 73 | 53 | +20 |
| (26) | Sex is far and away my greatest pleasure. | 35 | 26 | +9 |
| (27) | Absolute faithfulness to one partner throughout life is nearly as silly as celibacy. | 41 | 28 | +13 |
| (28) | The present preoccupation with sex in our society has been largely created by films, newspapers, television and advertising. | 45 | 54 | −9 |
| (29) | I would enjoy watching my usual partner having intercourse with someone else. | 18 | 6 | +12 |
| (30) | I would vote for a law that permitted polygamy. | 31 | 11 | +20 |
| (31) | Even though one is having regular intercourse, masturbation is good for a change. | 55 | 39 | +16 |
| (32) | I would prefer to have a new sex partner every night. | 7 | 2 | +5 |
| (33) | Sex is more exciting with a stranger. | 21 | 7 | +14 |
| (34) | To me few things are more important than sex. | 44 | 26 | +18 |
| (35) | Sex is not all that important to me. | 11 | 19 | −8 |
| (36) | Group sex appeals to me. | 33 | 10 | +23 |
| (37) | The thought of an illicit relationship excites me. | 52 | 32 | +20 |
| (38) | I prefer my partner to dictate the rules of the sexual game. | 9 | 37 | −28 |
| (39) | The idea of 'wife swapping' is extremely distasteful to me. | 37 | 63 | −26 |
| (40) | Some forms of love-making are disgusting to me. | 15 | 30 | −15 |

The distribution of scores obtained from our sample is plotted in Figure 1; it has been smoothed to eliminate chance irregularities. As will be seen, the men have much higher scores on the average than the women; twenty-six as compared with nineteen. There is also a good deal of overlap: 8 per cent of the women have scores above the mean of the men, and similarly 8 per cent of the men have scores below the mean of the women. This kind of result has been found in other countries also, and is typical of conditions in the Western world; unfortunately no such studies have been carried out in the USSR, or in China, but results from Japan suggest that similar results would be found in these countries also. Anthropological studies suggest that, in so far as we can apply these questions meaningfully in other cultures, conditions are fairly universal in making men more impersonal in their sexual behaviour, more easily excited, more pleasure-oriented, less inhibited sexually, more permissive, more attracted by illicit sexual practices, less easily disgusted, more highly sexed, more interested in nudity and voyeurism, in prostitution and in pornography. The fact of overlap between the two sexes makes all of this a less-than-universal observation; we would expect in any culture that some women would show 'typical' male behaviour and attitudes, and some men 'typical' female behaviour and attitudes. But this fact should not blind us to the existence of large, systematic sex differences, practically universal in all civilized societies, and extending back through recorded history – ancient Greece and Rome, to judge by what is known about sexual lives there, were not very different in this respect from our own modern societies.

It is important not to overinterpret the data presented. Consider for instance the questions concerning pornography; these show that women are much less keen on such items than men, and have much less interest in them. This does not mean that women are less *aroused* by erotica than men, as Kinsey had suggested on the basis of his large-scale interviews on sexual matters. Direct evidence from laboratory studies in which men and women are shown explicit sexual films, and are then questioned on their physiological and psychological responses, and may also be subjected to direct measurement of penile erection or vaginal lubrication, has shown that both sexes respond fairly equally to such stimuli. Nor does it seem true that women respond more to love themes, men to purely libidinal themes.

There does seem to be some evidence that men respond more to visual pornography, women to written pornography, but even here the final word has not yet been spoken. What is clear, however, is that although women may *respond* physiologically and psychologically as strongly as men to erotica, their *evaluation* is very different: they show much more disgust and dislike, would prefer to have such exhibitions censored and report much less enjoyment. This may seem paradoxical, but need not be so. Among men, too, there is a dissociation between arousal and enjoyment; many men are aroused by pornography, but experience disgust, guilt and other negative emotions – so much so that they would prefer not to be aroused in this fashion. Some men and even more frequently women experience

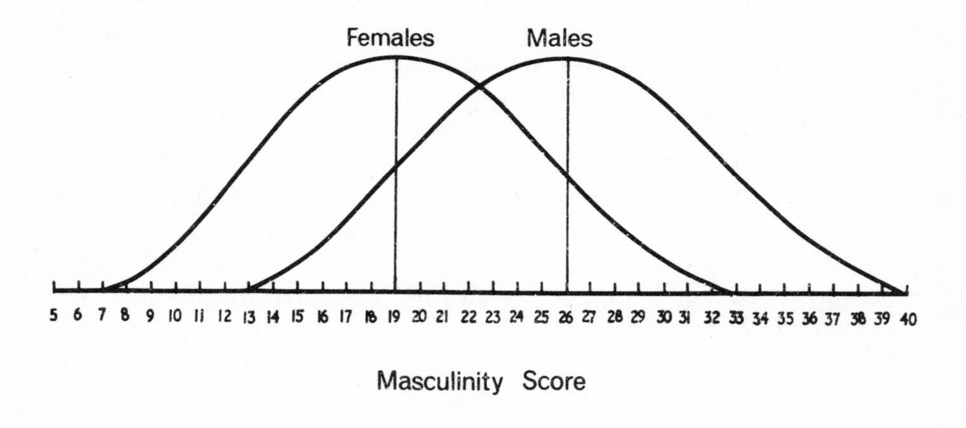


Figure 1 Scores of men and women on masculinity-femininity of sex attitudes inventory

signs of sexual arousal as a threat, and prefer to withdraw; physical arousal is only one of many different reactions to erotica, and others may be psychologically more important. We all react in a similar fashion to a cold shower, but while some like it, others loathe it – psychological reactions are not predetermined by physiological ones!

The differences within the male and female groups are perhaps as interesting as are the differences between the groups; the difference between the groups amounts to something like seven points on our scale, while the differences between extremes within the male or the female groups amount to something like twice that amount. In other words, the differences *within* each sex are much larger than the differences which obtain on the average *between* the sexes; these within-sex differences are connected intimately with personality, and will be dealt with in the next chapter. We may, however, note here that these differences are strongly determined by genetic factors, as is indicated by a large-scale study of identical and fraternal twins (Eysenck, 1976). Identical twins are genetically identical, being the outcome of the splitting of a single ovum, fertilized by a single sperm; fraternal twins on the average only share 50 per cent identical heredity, being the outcome of two ova fertilized around the same time by two sperms. Consequently any trait which is largely determined by genetic factors will be manifested in a similar fashion by identical twins; fraternal twins will be much less alike, only sharing 50 per cent identical heredity. These facts can be used to estimate the amount of heritability of a given trait, and also to construct models of inheritance which give us information on such factors as assortative mating (like marrying like), dominance of the trait over its opposite, and the like.

When the necessary calculations are done, it is found that well over half the total amount of variability in respect to 'masculine' and 'feminine' sexual attitudes and behaviours within each sex is due to genetic causes; this finding should be qualified by stating that the contribution of environmental factors is larger for women than for men. It would certainly tally with popular folklore if sexual attitudes in this respect were determined more strongly by cultural and familial pressures in women, while men were less inhibited by such pressures, and variation in them were more an expression of their genotype. Evidence was found of significant influence of family upbringing and tradition on women, though not on men; this again agrees well enough with popular stereotypes. The whole picture is of course more complex, but there can be little doubt about the influence of genetic factors in relation to these sexual attitudes and behaviours – though of course it would not be sensible to disregard the equally important influence of environmental factors, particularly on females. It is not necessary to decide between genetic and environmental influences in an either-or fashion: both are required to produce the observed behaviour, and to disregard one is as inadvisable and unscientific as to disregard the other. What is needed is always a detailed, quantitative attempt to construct a proper scientific model which incorporates both types of factors. If we have laid more stress on the genetic contribution, this is largely because so many writers in recent years have overemphasized the contribution of environment, family and society, and have overlooked completely the genetic component.

Of the complementary importance of cultural factors there can, therefore, be no doubt (Beach, 1977). The anthropological literature demonstrates tremendous differences between one social group and another. Some societies believe in monogamy; more are polygynous, that is to say, it is possible and regarded as desirable for a man to have more than one wife at one time; a very few societies are polyandrous, i.e. a wife may have more than one husband simultaneously. But this great variety of laws and customs is somewhat misleading. Note the prevalence of polygyny, and the almost complete lack of polyandry; as with most mammalian species it is the male who is lord over a number of females, an *harem* principle translated from lions and apes into human society! Even where monogamy is the rule, it is more frequently the males who indulge in extramarital activities, whether with prostitutes or mistresses. Thus in spite of apparent differences there are compelling similarities between societies which suggest a biological foundation for these observed similarities.

Another indication of the masculine stress on impersonal sexual satisfaction and enjoyment is the fact that in most of these societies for which we have data, it is reported that men take the initiative and, without extended foreplay, proceed vigorously to satisfy themselves and achieve climax, without much regard for allowing the woman concerned to achieve orgasm also. 'Again and again, there are reports that coitus is primarily completed in terms of the man's passions and pleasure, with scant attention paid to the woman's response. If women do experience orgasm, they do so passively.' (Beach, 1977, page 149.) Our own bad habits in this respect are not, as some critics have maintained, the result of Christian teaching or capitalist determination; these practices are pretty universal all over the world. They are usually associated with the equally widespread belief that man's sexuality is greater and stronger than that of women; again a belief which is echoed in our own society, and in the responses of men and women to our questionnaire.

Many of the differences that are observed between different cultures mirror differences which can be found even within our own. Thus the continuum going from extreme puritanism to extreme permissiveness in our society can be duplicated by noting differences between societies. As extremes of puritanism we may cite the rural Inis Beag Society in Ireland (Beach, 1977), where the ethos negates sexuality completely, and all forms of sexual behaviour are apparently infrequent. Similarly, the Manus, who live in Papua-New Guinea, considered intercourse between husband and wife to be sinful and degrading, to be undertaken only in strict secrecy. Women considered coitus to be an abomination which they had to endure, while the easily aroused sexuality of men was regarded as brutish. At the other extreme of permissiveness, we have the Polynesian cultures of the central Pacific, where even infantile and juvenile expressions of sexuality were considered normal and healthy. Adolescents of both sexes were encouraged to indulge in masturbation and premarital intercourse, and marital and extramarital intercourse were openly discussed and practised.

Even within the same society, there can be a rapid transition from one extreme to the other. Puritanism and Restoration provide a good example. Clearly there was no change in the genetic constitution of the population, but there was a marked change in their sexual behaviour when one replaced the other. Going back to our Figure 1, one might say that governments can push the distributions of attitudes and behaviours in one direction or the other, but whatever the mean value achieved, there will still be differences between men and women, and there will still be differences within each group. There is thus an important interplay between social and biological factors in determining conduct; man is a biosocial organism, and it would be foolish to disregard the contribution of either biology or society. Both must be taken into account in any realistic appraisal of our sexual behaviour.

What are the main reasons which compel us to posit biological determinants? One reason has already been mentioned: it is the pretty universal discovery of certain uniformities in human societies, and even animal societies. In the majority of these, men govern the roost, are allowed to enjoy the favours of several wives; have the freedom to express their sexuality freely, and regardless of the desires or wishes of women; are regarded as more highly sexed; and constitute the dominant sex generally. This dominance of course extends well beyond the sexual sphere. Patriarchy, i.e. the system of social organization in which the overwhelming number of upper positions in the social hierarchy is occupied by males, is universal in all human societies; while some earlier writers believed that they had discovered societies in which matriarchy was practised, these beliefs have in fact been shown to be erroneous (Goldberg, 1977).

Our own Western society, and in particular the social organization of the USA, probably comes nearest to a matriarchy, but, as Goldberg points out:

> For all the brave words and clenched fists, there are now fewer women in Congress than there were ten years ago. I do not attach any particular significance to the decrease; the number of women in power is so small that it is doubtful that this fluctuation has any real meaning. . . . There are so few women in positions of power and leadership in the financial and business world. . . . The political distribution of the sexes is no different in any other society. . . . In Sweden all thirteen of the Ministers with Portfolio are men. In Cuba twenty of the twenty-one Ministers and all fifteen Members of the Political Bureau and the Secretariat of the Communist Party are men. In Israel eighteen of the nineteen Cabinet Ministers are men and well over 90 per cent of the Parliament are male. In Communist China, which has been committed to equalization since the revolution, thirteen of the fourteen leaders of the Standing Committee of the National Peoples' Congress, all seventeen members of the State Council, and all sixty-seven Heads of the General Ministries are men. . . . In the Soviet Union, where even the theories of biology tend to deny the relevance of biology to behaviour, 96.9 per cent of the members of the Central Committee are men.

Patriarchy refers to hierarchical social arrangements; Goldberg goes further and argues that male *dominance* is equally universal, defining dominance here as dealing with male-female personal encounters and relationships, 'the feelings acknowledged by the emotions of both men and women that general authority in face-to-face and familial relationships ultimately resides in the male.' He points out:

> I realize that this is not the most gracious way of defining male dominance, but it is the most accurate. As with patriarchy, male dominance is universal; no society has ever failed to conform its expectations of men and women, and the social roles relevant to these expectations, to the feeling of men and women that it is the male who 'takes the lead'.

We thus have widespread evidence, from the study of many hundreds of different cultures, indicating the universality of social and sexual behaviours associated with the male and female sex respectively, which would be difficult to explain in cultural or environmentalist terms; as Cicero said, '*Numquam naturam mos vinceret; est enim ea semper invicta*' (Custom will never conquer nature, for it is always she who remains unconquered). We should perhaps add at this point that to state these facts is not to approve of the situation; facts remain facts whether we like them or not. Many men, from John Stuart Mill onwards, have joined with women to deplore the universal dominance of men over women, and most people will welcome the steps that have been taken to secure greater equality for women before the law and in society generally. What are we arguing here is that their search for equality is likely to encounter great difficulties when it comes up against biological reality, and that equality in the sense of identity, rather than of equal but different value, may be destined to remain a *fata morgana* (Lloyd & Archer, 1976).

It is easy thus to demonstrate the greater sexual and social dominance of the male in all existing human societies (and in many animal societies as well); does biology provide a convenient mechanism which can be shown to determine the types of behaviour in question? This is the crucial problem, and the answer must be in the affirmative. In order to discuss the evidence we must first of all say a few words about the differences between gonadal, hormonal and morphologic sex. The gonads (i.e. testis or ovaries) do not directly dictate the developmental fate of the bodily structures, but do so by way of the hormones they release. The most important of the hormones involved is a testicular androgen or male hormone, namely *testosterone*. Circulating in the blood stream, this male sex hormone dictates the developmental programme of the external sexual organs, and also has a masculinizing influence on the brain. When testosterone is added to the blood stream of a genetic female foetus during a critical period of development, the girl will be born with masculinized sex organs; such a discrepancy between gonadal and hormonal sex thus leads to a grotesque morphological mix-up of male and female characteristics. This condition of prenatal masculinization is in most cases due to one of two causes.

On a number of occasions in the past, it was inadvertently induced by hormonal drugs given to the mother to prevent a miscarriage. These hormones belong to a recently synthesized group of steroids which were related in chemical structure to androgens but were, in biological action, substitutes for pregnancy hormones (progesterone) and hence were named *progestines*. When these progestines were first synthesized it was not known that certain of them would, under certain circumstances, exert a masculinizing influence on a female foetus, and thus in the 1950s a small number of girl babies showing this masculinization were born. Some of these girls would be born with a penis, regarded as boys with undescended testicles, and brought up as boys. Other babies, with only incomplete masculinization of the clitoris, would be regarded as girls although some surgical adjustment of the external genitalia might be required. At the age of puberty the girl's ovaries would function normally, totally feminize the body and induce menstruation. It is these girls, brought up normally and with the full pressure of society to behave as girls, who are of interest to us, because the progestine would have indelibly affected their psychological makeup, and would have it made more masculine. This masculinization, if our theory is correct, should influence their sexual and social behaviour.

Progestine-induced masculinization is an artefact of human interference; the adrenogenital syndrome, however, is an abnormality of development which occurs quite naturally in a small number of cases. In these cases, the adrenal glands function defectively, the defect already beginning in foetal life. The primary defect is a genetic one which prevents the adrenal glands from synthesizing the proper hormone, cortisol, and instead releasing an androgen, i.e. a male sex hormone, which enters into the blood stream of the foetus, masculinizing it to a certain extent. When the diagnosis is promptly established in the neonate the child is allowed to grow up as a girl, some minor vaginal surgery being needed, but above all, hormonal regulation from birth onwards is possible by treatment with cortisone to prevent postnatal continuance of developmental masculinization. In other words, the girl receives masculine hormone as a foetus but is then allowed to grow up anatomically, physiologically and psychologically as a girl, with all the social pressures which are exerted on girls. The interest here again is in the social and sexual behaviour of these girls in later life. Just like the girls masculinized by progestines, the adrenogenital syndrome girls constitute an interesting experiment made by nature. Society treats them just like all other girls, and the pressure therefore is the same as that which most girls experience; is this sufficient to make their behaviour 'feminine'? The biologist would predict that the answer would be no; the influence of the male hormone which they received in the foetal stage should be sufficient to render their behaviour masculine in many ways. Here then we seem to have two crucial experiments: what is the outcome?

The behaviour of the girls was compared with that of a control group of normal girls matched on the basis of age, intelligence quotient, socioeconomic background and race. The masculinized girls, in the first place, differed from their controls in regarding themselves as tomboys. Nine of the ten girls with the progestine-induced syndrome and eleven of the fifteen with the adrenogenital syndrome claimed they were tomboys, and this was confirmed by the mother, and was recognized and accepted by playmates and friends. In this they differed very significantly from the control group girls. In addition to this masculine, tomboy behaviour, many of the girls would rather have been born a boy, had there been a choice, and others were ambivalent. In this, too, they differed from the normal girls.

The masculinized girls showed a high level of physical energy expenditure, demonstrated in vigorous outdoor play, games and sports generally considered typical of boys. (In this they seem to resemble prenatally masculinized female rhesus monkeys, who indulged in typically masculine rough-and-tumble play.) Team games with a ball, such as neighbourhood football and baseball, were a favourite with the masculinized girls, and many preferred boys as playmates. J. Money, who carried out these studies, formulated the generalization that dominance, assertion and striving for position in the dominance hierarchy of childhood was a variable which most distinguished the masculinized girls from the others.

It is interesting that differences also appeared in relation to clothing and adornment. The masculinized girls preferred utilitarian and functional clothing, as compared with the chic, pretty or fashionably feminine. They preferred slacks and shorts to dresses, and also showed less interest in accessories like jewellery, perfume and hairstyling.

The masculinized girls differed from the controls in their preferences for toys: they were indifferent to dolls, or openly neglectful of them, and preferred cars, trucks and guns, and other toys traditionally associated with boys. Later on, this lack of interest in dolls became a lack of interest in infants; they did not enjoy doing things for the care of babies and did not anticipate doing such things, even as paid babysitters, in the future. Some girls even disliked handling little babies and believed they could not do this well. The control girls of course behaved very differently in this respect! Many of the androgenized girls stated that they would rather not have children, and even those who did not reject this idea were rather perfunctory and matter of fact in their anticipation of motherhood, lacking the enthusiasm of the control girls.

The choice between career and marriage produced another marked difference between the control girls and the masculinized girls. The masculinized girls preferred careers to marriage, or else wanted to combine a career with marriage, whereas the control girls favoured marriage, and regarded marriage as the most important thing in their future. Here again, then, we have typically masculine preferences emerging in the biologically masculinized girls.

Similar findings to those mentioned were made in androgenized girls who were studied before cortisone therapy was discovered; they showed identical developments along the lines of tomboyism and the other variables discussed.

Little has been said about similar experiments with animals, where of course androgen can be injected, and androgen-containing drugs be given, in a way which would not be permissible with humans. Here results have in general been very similar, and in fact even more convincing. Thus among rats, mice, and many other mammals, the administration of testosterone is related not only to sexual differentiation but to dominance itself. Females treated with testosterone during the crucial period just after birth develop a dominant tendency as adults. In rhesus monkeys it has been found that males mount more than females do, and that males progress from keeping both feet on the ground while they mount to using their feet in climbing onto the female. Normally female monkeys do not do this, but foetally masculinized females do. There would be little point in discussing the very large animal literature here; suffice it to say that the evidence is pretty conclusive that male hormones play a large part in governing animal as well as human social and sexual behaviour, and directing it in a masculine or feminine fashion.

It should be noted, in addition to the facts already mentioned, that the modelling of sex roles by society does have a powerful effect on the later development of these masculinized girls. It would be idle to deny the importance of social factors of this kind, just as it would be idle to deny the importance of the hormonal and other biological factors. Neither in isolation can determine behaviour; they always act together, and it would be unrealistic to stress the importance of one above the other. It is possible to generalize that for animals lower in the phyletic scale biological factors are more important, whereas for the higher mammals, and particularly man, social factors are relatively speaking more important. This is undoubtedly true, but we should never leave out of account either factor in dealing with biological organisms (Levine, 1972).

It is important to realize that the contribution to masculine or feminine behaviour of testosterone has been ante-natal; it is at a crucial period of the development in utero of the foetus that the masculinizing action of the androgen takes place. Levels of testosterone determined at adolescence or adulthood are much more difficult to interpret. It would not be true to say, as seems on commonsense grounds most likely, that the more androgen is secreted in the male, and the more oestrogen is secreted in the female, the more masculine or feminine that person will be; the evidence rules out such a grossly oversimplified idea. Libido seems to be determined in both men and women by androgens; in other words, women with a greater supply of male hormone are more likely to be highly sexed than are women with more oestrogen! This agrees well with our findings as shown in Figure 1: it is the women who show a rather masculine outlook who are more 'feminist' in their behaviour. Altogether, androgen levels in a given person differ so much from occasion to occasion that means are not very reliable, and hence comparisons between individuals are of doubtful value, particularly when the androgen level is only determined once. Sexual activity is not only determined in part by androgen level, but in turn influences androgen level in the future! Nevertheless, there seems little doubt that within a given person sexual activity will be found correlated with androgen level – more sexual activity when the level is high, less when it is low. Oestrogen does not seem to be correlated with active sexual behaviour to any marked extent; it is the androgen which is important. The evidence also strongly suggests that aggression, hostility and fighting behaviour are all related to androgen level – the more androgen, the more aggressive the person! Thus both sexual behaviour and social conduct are influenced by a person's hormones, along lines which are in good accord with the stereotyped views propagated by society; clearly these stereotypes are not entirely based on prejudice, but have a good biological foundation.

Before leaving the question of biological determination of human conduct, however, brief mention must at least be made of the important work of a German physician, Dr W. Schlegel (1966). The ante-natal androgen hormone level in the foetus appears to determine the shape of the pelvis. As is well known, males tend to have a funnel-shaped pelvis, narrow at the bottom, while females tend to have a tube-shaped pelvis, relatively broad at the bottom. The size of the pelvic outlet is of obvious importance in childbirth, and thus selection through evolution may have produced this difference. However, the shape of the pelvis differs from person to person within each sex. Thus there are some males with tube-shaped pelvises and some women with funnel-shaped pelvises. Figure 2 shows the distribution of pelvic shape in men and women; what is measured is the width of the outlet, with the narrower measures characterizing the male, the wider measurements the female. The similarity of this graph with that shown in Figure 1 is unmistakeable although of course now the men are on the left, the women on the right. If pelvic shape is determined by ante-natal androgen secretion, and if later sexual and social behaviour is also determined by ante-natal androgen secretion, then one would expect to find correlations within each sex between behaviour and pelvic shape. This is precisely what Schlegel did find. Men and women with funnel-shaped (male-type) pelvises tended to behave in a masculine manner, while men and women with tube-shaped (female-type) pelvises tended to behave in a feminine manner. Masculine type pelvis correlated with leadership, an active sexual role, dominance and preference for younger sex partners, in men and women alike. Feminine type pelvis correlated with empathy, suggestibility and compliance, as well as preference for older sex partners. In other words, behaviour in both sexes seems to be determined by the same hormonal factors which orginally produced skeletal features of the pelvis, namely androgen secretion at the foetal stage. Schlegel even studied cows (whose pelvic outlets are more easily observed than are those of human subjects!) and found that cows with narrow outlets, i.e. funnel-shaped pelvises, tended to mount other cows and generally behave in a more masculine manner! Truly, the ways of nature are wondrous to behold.

It is interesting to note that Schlegel found two further correlates of

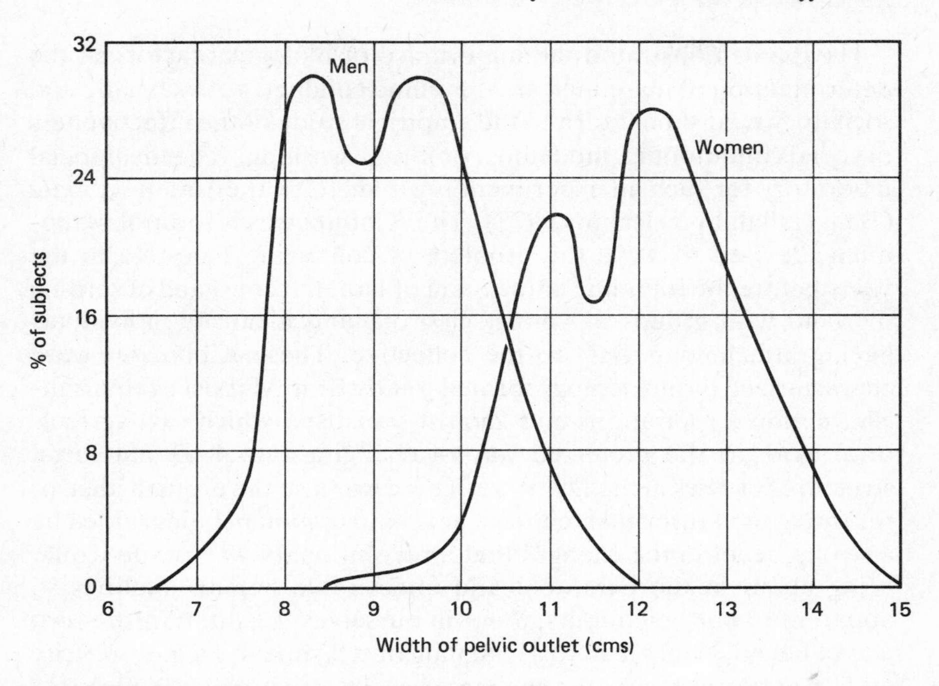


Figure 2 Distributions of pelvis shapes for men and women

pelvic shape. Homosexual males tended to have feminine-type pelvises; this is perhaps not entirely unexpected, in view of the fact that a genetic component has been demonstrated to exist in predisposition to homosexual conduct. (It may be relevant to note that homosexual women have higher levels of testosterone in the blood than do heterosexual women; the amount of testosterone in the blood plasma averaged 38 per cent higher for the homosexual women than for the heterosexuals. In contrast, for homosexual men the testosterone level is slightly below that for heterosexual men; it is highest for men who combine homo- with heterosexuality.) He also found that men and women concordant for pelvic shape (i.e. men with masculine-type pelvis, women with feminine-type pelvis) were much less likely to be divorced than men and women discordant for pelvic shape (i.e. men with feminine-type pelvis, women with masculine-type pelvis). This finding suggests fascinating vistas of computer-dating organizations and marriage guidance officials adding pelvic shape to their other data and advising clients accordingly!

Having demonstrated the importance of biological factors in the determination of masculine and feminine conduct, both sexually and socially, we must next turn to the empirical study of the effectiveness of social conditioning, modelling, or 'brain-washing'. The ideal social laboratory for such an experiment is provided by the Israeli Kibbutz (Beit-Hallahmi & Rabin, 1977). The Kibbutz was a form of settlement, devised to solve the problem of colonizing Palestine in the years before the founding of the State of Israel. It consisted of settling the land with groups of young, vigorous and idealistic individuals having attachments only to the collective. These Kibbutzim were characterized by an ideology formed jointly from Marxist egalitarianism, national aspirations and Zionist socialism, which saw agricultural work as the preferred way of changing the abnormal social structures of Jews in the Diaspora. There was also the utopian ideal of returning to nature and creating a new kind of human being, aided by a strong belief in the changes that a revolutionary way of life would bring about in the persistent and undesirable human qualities so apparent in our neighbours, if not in ourselves. Egalitarianism, so it was believed, would lead to a lessening of selfishness, greater security and greater generosity; the changes in social structure were expected to lead to psychological changes in the individuals concerned.

Of particular importance in the development of the Kibbutz was the ideology of child-rearing. This stressed communal practices, the aim of which was to work against individualism and identification with the family unit. It was believed that experts in child-rearing would be able to inculcate the ideology of the Kibbutz better and more strongly than would be possible if this task were left to the parents. Thus parents were relegated to a second place as agents of socialization, and nurses, teachers and peer groups were regarded as more important. Parents thus spent little time with their children, who were effectively brought up by a variety of caretakers, called *metapelets*.

The obvious rebellion against traditional family patterns was accompanied by a move towards equality between the sexes and the abolition of traditional sex roles, particularly in the area of work. Workers in the Kibbutz considered the ideal of equality between the sexes, and the breakdown of traditional sex roles, as one part of their struggle against the traditions of an unjust world. An outcome of this was the attempt to dismantle the traditional bourgeois family, which, with its close mother-child ties, was seen as promoting selfishness and individualism. Thus the three major aims of the Kibbutz were the destruction of traditional family patterns, the introduction of socialism and the stress on equality between the sexes, both at work and in relation to society. These ideological conceptions were inculcated into the Kibbutz children as they grew up, in a tremendous effort toward indoctrination and even 'brain-washing' – no contrary voices were tolerated. What was the outcome of all this effort?

The new generation, brought up in a small-scale society which stressed ideals contrary to those of our own, reverted strongly to the patterns of sexual and social behaviour consciously rejected by their parents. During the past fifteen years there has been a marked trend towards closer parent-child contact and a more individual type of caretaking behaviour. Communal sleeping arrangements have been introduced into most of the right-wing and some of the moderate Kibbutz, with only some of the left-wing groups remaining 'orthodox'. These family-based sleeping arrangements have succeeded in abolishing the most unique aspect of child-rearing in the Kibbutz, i.e. multiple mothering at an early age. These changes in child-rearing have been accompanied by growing conservatism in economic, political, ideological and psychological areas. There has been an obvious movement away from socialism, and a trend in the direction of a 'consumerist' lifestyle.

Similar changes have taken place in the ideals of sexual equality and sharing of work:

> Recent developments in the Kibbutz show a pattern of consistent movement towards more traditional patterns of sex roles, marriage and family life, and a clear revival of the traditional division of labour between the sexes. . . . There is a clear polarization of work between men and women, with men predominantly in production and women predominantly in communal services. Women are involved in the same types of job that fit the traditional female role, except that most of these jobs serve the community, not just the family. . . . Women are almost excluded from agricultural field work or industrial jobs. (Beit-Hallahmi and Rabin, 1977).

These are important findings. Here we have a group selfconsciously setting out to change the traditional sexual roles of women in the direction of absolute equality at work, as well as in child-rearing and home management. The children in these relatively isolated communes grow up under conditions where the sexual roles which they are taught, and which they see modelled by their parents, are not the traditional ones, but are largely those of the idealized egalitarianism which informed the early settlers. If modelling, conditioning and indoctrination generally have such profound effects on people as is commonly believed, then we would imagine that the children would grow up even more convinced of the correctness of these new models, and would indoctrinate their children accordingly. Nothing of the kind is found. The children have reverted very largely to the traditional patterns, with women doing women's work, insisting on looking after their children, and generally departing from the complete egalitarianism in which they were brought up. No doubt one must bear in mind the influence of the larger community (the Kibbutz was always a minority movement in Israel), but nevertheless the self-conscious feelings of superiority which the Kibbutz inculcated in its members might have been expected to produce an ever greater loyalty to the ideals of the movement as it came under attack from outside.

If this is the best that persuasion, example, modelling, and outright indoctrination can do, then clearly feminists who believe in the complete equality (meaning identity) of men and women have a hard row to hoe. Obviously there are biological factors which pull back men and women from social practices contrary to nature, and which insist that men and women have different roles to play as dictated in part at least by nature. No doubt considerable changes can be made in human conduct by society, and no doubt many such changes are desirable and necessary in order to achieve a greater degree of justice for women, who throughout the centuries have been the losers in the power game. As far as sexual behaviour is concerned, however, and other aspects of social conduct also, there is no doubt that there are limitations to what can be achieved, and it may be surmised that for many women the loss in giving up the joys of child-rearing are greater than the gains in equality. We conclude that the many differences observed between men and women, not only in our society, but almost universally, are real and have a fundamental biological basis. Any proper understanding of sexual behaviour must bear this in mind.

Sex dictates not only the various differences in social and sexual behaviour we have noted; it also gives rise to differences in personality and intellect. It is beyond the current brief to go into these topics in great detail. They have been treated at great length by Maccoby and Jacklin (1975). It has been found, in many different studies, that on the whole men are more extraverted, i.e. sociable, risk-taking, impulsive, happy-go-lucky and carefree, while women are more introverted, i.e. the opposite in all these respects. Similarly, women are more emotional and show much greater tendency to develop neurotic troubles of one kind or another, i.e. anxieties, worries, depression, etc. These general personality differences make good sense from the point of view of evolution. Women, as the mothers of the next generation, and as physically weaker on the whole than the men, would naturally be expected to develop stronger emotions of fear and anxiety, predisposing them to avoid danger, whereas man the hunter and warrior would be useless in this task if he were prevented from undertaking dangerous actions by such emotions. Similarly the need for close peer support in war and hunting would lead to the development of a stronger tendency to pair-bonding and sociability generally in men, and the various other extraverted tendencies too can be seen in the same light. It is interesting to note that in most mammals similar differences between males and females also tend to appear, although there are one or two exceptions. Thus here too biology and evolution seem to have decreed that men and women should differ in predetermined and important ways as far as personality is concerned. We shall return to this point in the next chapter.

As far as intellectual capacities are concerned, it is well known that men and women have equal capacity; IQ measures undertaken on many different samples have not found any differences between men and women. However, there are differences as far as certain special abilities are concerned, and these again are very much what one would have expected biologically in terms of the role of the woman as mother, and the man as warrior and hunter. The main differences between the sexes are in the development of speech and verbal communication, where girls and women tend to be superior, and visuo-spatial ability and orientation, where males tend to be superior. The role of the mother, having to communicate to her babies and younger children the rules of the society, as well as to ensure their social and language development, makes it desirable that women should be fluent linguistically, and able to undertake this communication successfully; nothing in the role of the male seems to necessitate such a special development of linguistic skills. On the other hand, man, being away from home a good deal of the time, and having to find his way through woods and countryside, is required to develop his skills in orientation and visuo-spatial behaviour which are not required by the women whose life is largely bounded by the home and the village. Obviously these explanations in terms of evolution of the observed differences between the sexes are to some degree speculative, but they do make sense, and indeed there is even evidence that in the higher animals similar sex differences can be observed. This seems to rule out the possibility of environmental influences and modelling having played an all-important part in their development.

The perspective given by these biological and social experiments, converging as they do on the assertion that biological factors and genetic influences are basic to an understanding of sex roles, both socially and sexually, may help us in gaining some insight into the relation between these two apparently conflicting sets of forces, i.e. the biological and the environmental. What seems to be happening is perhaps something like this. Sexual reproduction, and the facts of the survival of the fittest, dictate that women, who in primitive societies are incapacitated over long periods of conceiving, carrying and having babies, should develop maternal instincts which cause them to take delight in these tasks, and to enjoy watching over the development of the babies they have brought into the world; were it not so, then the human race would have died out long ago! Presumably the four million years or so that have seen the evolution of *homo sapiens* have ensured that women who did not share these genetic propensities had fewer surviving children than those who did, thus firmly enshrining these instincts in the female of the human race.

At the same time, the male, not being weighed down by these duties and responsibilities, had other tasks to perform – such as searching for food, or fighting aggressors and enemies generally, whether human or animal. Again, evolution over all these millions of years, would make sure that those most fit to survive, and to endow the largest possible number of children with their genes, would be those who most assiduously performed the typical masculine role. All this biological pressure towards specificity of masculine and feminine roles, genetically enshrined in our chromosomes and handed on from generation to generation, would of course not have begun when *homo sapiens* first separated out from apes and monkeys; it would be the burden of all mammalian history, stretching back over many more aeons. Hence the similarities between our own social and sexual behaviours, and those shown by apes, monkeys, and even lower animals.

We have made appeal to evolution to account for the many asymmetries in male-female relations which crop up in all cultures, and also among most mammals; this appeal can be made even more precise by reference to the concept of the 'selfish gene', i.e. the notion that man is in effect nothing more than a carrier of a set of genes, the preservation of which determines all his major activities. Natural selection, the basis of Darwinian evolution, is a process of reproductive competition among members of a given species, and the attributes of an organism (including behaviour) which make a positive contribution to success in this competition are ultimately selected for. This leads on to the thought that organisms must have evolved *strategies* which maximize their reproductive success, and it may be useful to look at the differential sexual behaviours in this light. This way of considering the problem has been common among biologists at least since the classical studies of the British geneticist A.J. Bateman on fruit flies in the early 1940s.

It is clear that mothers typically contribute more nurture to each offspring, both pre-natal and post-natal, both in point of time and in point of substance, than do fathers. Males also have an infinite number (almost) of sperms, while women have a very restricted supply of ova. Thus a female's reproductive potential is limited in two ways – capacity to provide nurture, and availability of ova. A male, on the other hand, can beget many more children than any one female can bear. Thus males gain from having many mates (polygyny), while females have nothing to gain from having multiple mates (polyandry). Males, investing little in each offspring, have everything to gain from sowing their seeds as widely as possible; hence they compete for the opportunity to fertilize women. Females invest considerably more in each offspring, and hence are predisposed to exhibit greater selectivity in their choice of mates. Men, of course, do invest parentally to some extent, and hence it is in their interest to protect themselves against *cuckoldry*, which would involve them in investing in the genes of other men! Males thus are much more involved in securing the fidelity of their mates than are females – if the male has intercourse outside marriage, this does not affect the security of his mate's genes embodied in her offspring. Note how neatly this explanation accounts for the greater promiscuity and impersonal sex attitude of males, to which we drew attention at the beginning of this chapter. Several large-scale surveys, in different countries, have shown that some 50 per cent of men, but only some 25 per cent of women, said they would like to indulge in extramarital sex. We may recall in this connection the Coolidge effect, i.e. the tendency in rats and other mammals for the exhausted male to renew its sexual interests when new partners are provided. Females do not show this effect; for them, the duration of sexual receptivity is *shortened* by copulation.

In human society, this concern with cuckoldry has usually shown itself in legal provisions which consider female sexual unfaithfulness much more serious than male. Furthermore, men are much more likely to seek divorce on grounds of adultery than women, although in actual fact men are much the more adulterous sex! Infidelity was twice as prevalent among the men in Kinsey's study as among the women, yet it was a major factor in divorce twice as frequently for men than women – a four-fold disproportion, along the lines expected from the evolutionary argument. Female adultery faces men with the presence of 'bastards' in his house, and the duty and responsibility to care for them and bring them up; male adultery at most leads to a withdrawl of the male's time, society and sexual energy from the wife. There is here thus a biological asymmetry, corresponding to the social asymmetries noted.

We can account along similar lines for the greater discrimination in sexual matters of females, as compared with males. In animals, the task of species recognition, and the avoidance of hybrid matings, is usually undertaken by females – it is they who lose more time and energy in a mismatch than does the male. In many species (e.g. crabs and ducks), females recognize appropriate males at first sight, but males have to learn to recognize females of their own kind. Thus male butterflies have been known to court falling leaves, and male frogs to mount galoshes. In a similar way, most sexual perversions in humans are the (almost) sole prerogative of males – fetishists, transvestites, exhibitionists, voyeurs, sadomasochists, necrophiliacs, frotteurs and the like are almost always men, and with most of the other categories (e.g. homosexuality, transsexualism, bestiality and pedophilia) men outnumber women to a marked degree. Men simply can afford to waste their seed, without reducing the number of offspring available to women impregnated by other, more willing males. If women wasted their reproductive potential in a similar manner, the danger to the species would be much greater.

If women are more choosey about their mates than are men, who tend to adopt the doctrine that 'all cats are grey at night', then this too is an evolutionary feature already found in animals. Mate quality is more important for the female than for the male, precisely because she invests so much more in the nurture of the offspring. This is so not only in mammals, but also in birds and insects; males are made to make gifts and other types of commitment, and the female only responds gradually to male courtship, thus protecting herself from philanderers whose parental duties elsewhere might lead them to abscond and neglect their implied support for her brood. It is for the same reason, one must presume, that financial provision is so important to females in selecting a mate among humans.

Society, in order to survive, has adopted the principle that these 'natural' tendencies should not be left to the accidents of genetic transmission and segregation alone, but that these biological determinants should be aided by precept and modelling; thus social norms in the vast majority of all societies we know have emphasized social and sexual roles very much in line with those which instinct dictated in any case. We thus have society and nature working in harmony, rather than fighting against each other. The fact that all successful and surviving societies have taken this course suggests that if there had ever been any that took a different and contrary course, then these would have perished in the struggle for survival. History certainly records no memory of them.

If this brief and inevitably speculative account of the development of sex roles is anything like accurate, what does it portend for the future? We must not make the mistake of imagining that because something has been biologically useful in the past, therefore we must without criticism or opposition accept it as a guiding principle for the future. Nature 'red in tooth and claw', has certainly been a hard task master in the past, and has shaped human behaviour in ways that are unacceptable, and that none of us can tolerate without a loss of common humanity – wars, pillage and rape; racism, ethnocentrism and xenophobia have been the laws of nature enshrined in our so-called civilized behaviour. It does not take a major prophet to foretell that unless we manage to overcome these trends we are not likely as a species to survive the next hundred years – if indeed we do not succeed in taking all creation with us into oblivion! There have certainly been hopeful signs that biological evolution is not the only guide for our behaviour, and that social evolution, i.e. the development of new and more promising types of conduct, can successfully take its place.

In saying therefore that our present-day masculine and feminine roles are deeply embedded in our biological nature is not to say categorically that no change can ever be brought about in this state of affairs. What is suggested is rather that such a change would be extremely difficult to produce, and that at the moment we certainly do not know how to effect it. Whether it is desirable to change the state of affairs that is acceptable and often deeply fulfilling for both men and women is of course another question; it is not a factual one, and therefore is not one which we feel able to answer. Certainly the majority of women seem to delight in the feminine role, just as the majority of men delight in the male role; whether it is desirable to deprive them of this delight in the uncertain hope that both might find satisfaction in some form of unisex culture and role-playing activity seems very doubtful to us, but of course a decision on questions of this kind must be left to the individual.

## References

BEACH, F.A., *Human Sexuality in Four Perspectives.* London: Johns Hopkins University Press, 1977.

BEIT-HALLAHMI, B & RABIN, A.I., 'The Kibbutz as a social experiment and as a child-rearing laboratory', *American Psychologist,* 1977, **32**, 532–41.

EYSENCK, H.J., *Sex and Personality.* London: Open Books, 1976.

GOLDBERG, S., *The Inevitability of Patriarchy.* London: Temple-Smith, 1977.

LEVINE, S. (ed.), *Hormones and Behaviour.* London: Academic Press, 1972.

LLOYD, B. & ARCHER, J., *Exploring Sex Differences.* London: Academic Press, 1976.

MACCOBY, E.E. & JACKLIN, C.M., *The Psychology of Sex Differences.* Stanford: University Press, 1975.

MONEY, J. & EHRHARDT, A.A., *Man and Woman, Boy and Girl.* London: Johns Hopkins University Press, 1972.

SCHLEGEL, W.S., *Die Sexualinstinkte des Menschen.* München: Rütten Verlag, 1966.

WESLEY, F. & WESLEY, C., *Sex-Role Psychology.* New York: Human Sciences Press, 1977.

# 3 Sex and personality

In Chapter 2 we discussed in some detail the differences between males and females, as far as sexual behaviour and attitudes are concerned; in this chapter we shall go on to consider the many differences which appear within each sex, and which are associated with personality. To illustrate the kinds of differences which appear, and the sorts of studies which have been carried out in order to measure them, we may start with some theories of Freud as to the kinds of persons who might prefer women with large breasts, as opposed to the kinds of persons who might prefer women with small breasts. The Freudian theory of orality (i.e. that some people get stuck at the stage of development which centres on oral behaviour) leads to the clear hypothesis that men showing dependency should prefer large-breasted women. Dependency, as a personality variable, is believed by Freudians to be closely related to fixation at the oral stage of development, and consequently we may test the Freudian hypothesis by looking at the actual breast-size preferences of men who are, or who are not, dependent in that sense. When preferences for pictures of women with different sizes of breasts were ascertained for some 169 male students, it was found that there was indeed a relationship between dependency and size of breast preferred, but it was in the opposite direction to that demanded by the Freudian theory: men who were dependent preferred women with smaller breasts!

In another study, Nancy Hirschberg (1979) used preference judgements derived from nude female silhouettes, arranged as in Figure 3. Fifteen such silhouettes were constructed so that each silhouette varied independently on one of three body parts (breasts, buttocks or legs) and each part assumed one of five possible sizes, from large through moderately large, standard, and moderately small to small. All possible pairs of silhouettes were shown to the subjects, and for each pair the subject had to indicate which member of the pair he preferred, on a seven-point rating scale as shown in the Figure. It was found that the men who preferred the large-breasted figures dated frequently, had masculine interests and read sports magazines; they had a need for heterosexual contact and for exhibitionism (saying witty things and being the centre of attention). They read *Playboy* magazine, were independent and somewhat egocentric. Men who preferred the smaller-breasted females indicated lack of orality, in

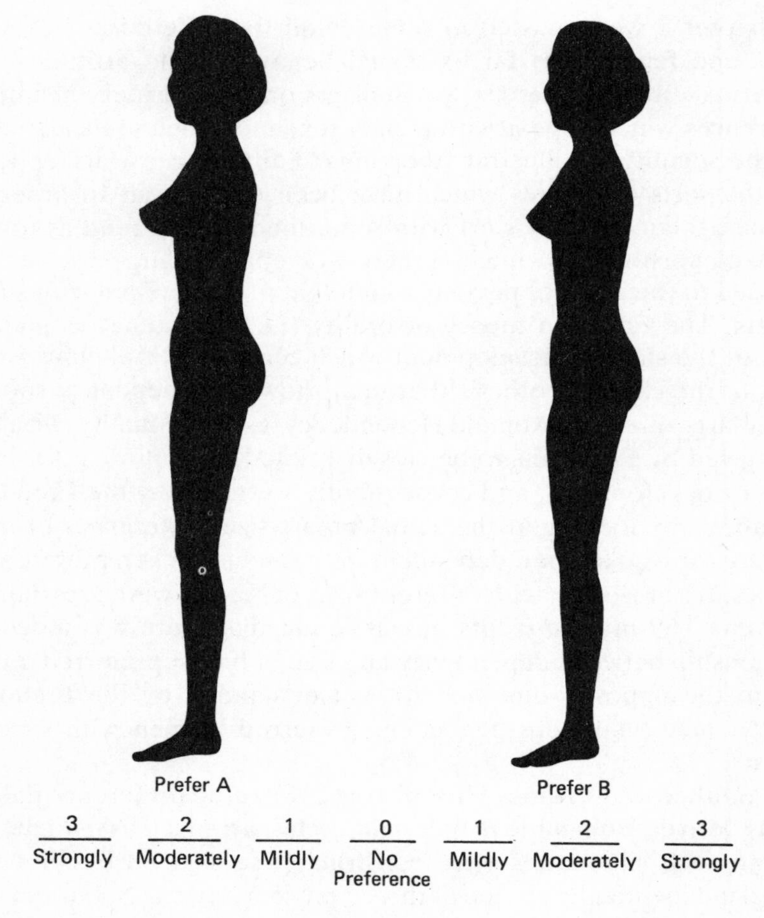


Figure 3 A silhouette comparison of the kind used by Hirschberg

that they did not smoke or drink. Such men also held fundamentalist religious beliefs and were mildly depressed. As we shall see later, the personality structure of the men who liked large-breasted women was similar to that of the extravert, that of the men preferring smaller-breasted women to that of the introvert. Several other studies since have directly attacked this question, and have shown that indeed extraverts tend to prefer large-breasted women, introverts smaller-breasted ones. Why this should be so we shall discuss in a minute; here let us merely note the fact itself (Eysenck, 1972).

What are large-breasted and small-breasted women like, as far as personality is concerned? Hirschberg had 144 female undergraduates photographed nude in three poses: front, sideways, and from the back. These women were also administered two personality questionnaires, and their photographs were measured for the same body parts that were manipulated in the silhouette study mentioned above, i.e. breast size, buttock size and leg size. Women with large breasts emerged as being undersocialized, undependable, impulsive, lacking in control, flexible and adventuresome – in other words they showed all the characteristics of the extravert! Thus it would seem that extraverted males like the physical appearance of extraverted females, which is perhaps just as well. (It is interesting to note that women with large buttocks were introverted, non-participative socially, had feelings of guilt, were self-abasing and seemed generally to be the opposite of women with large breasts. It had previously been found that men who liked large buttocks were also self-abasing, had feelings of guilt, were socially dependent and had a high need for order – again we find that introverted men like women who have the physical appearance associated with introversion.)

Matching men and women according to their physical and mental attributes has of course been the aim of match-makers throughout history, right up to modern computer-dating organizations; size of breasts and buttocks, or extraversion-introversion, are only some of the indices which have been used. The earliest example comes from the *Kama Sutra* of Vatsyayana, the great Indian classic of the technique and art of love and love-making – although to judge by this example the advice give there is of doubtful value! In this original guide to sex, we are told that:

> Man is divided into three classes, viz., the hare man, the bull man, and the horse man, according to the size of his *lingam*. Women also, according to

> the *epeth* of her *yoni*, is either a female deer, a mare, or a female elephant. There are thus three equal unions between persons of corresponding dimensions, and there are six unequal unions, when the dimensions do not correspond.

Having established this typology, the *Kama Sutra* goes on to state that: 'Amongst all these, equal unions are the best'; the remainder are given various values according to the differences in size of lingam and yoni. In actual fact, of course, the size of both these instruments of sexual passion is largely irrelevant to satisfactory sexual performance. The yoni will stretch, if necessary, and the lingam needs only to reach beyond the clitoris to produce satisfactory orgasms; only in really extreme cases is there any problem.

The *Kama Sutra* is on safer ground, as we shall see, when it goes on to say that 'there are also nine kinds of union according to the force of passion or carnal desire (libido)', with men and women being graded into 'those with small, middling, or intense desire'. It appears, although this is nowhere stated, that corresponding degrees of passion get on best together. And as a third principle of classification, we are told that 'according to time there are three kinds of men and women, viz., the short-timed, the moderately-timed, and the long-timed, and of these as in the previous statements, there are nine kinds of union'. Presumably here also corresponding couples, whose speed of reaching orgasm is similar, are best suited. The *Kama Sutra* concludes that 'there being thus nine kinds of union with regard to dimensions, force of passion, and time, respectively, by making combinations of them, innumerable kinds of union would be produced. Therefore in each particular kind of sexual union, men should use such means as they may think suitable for the occasion.' The second part of this statement does not seem to follow from the first, and the first is wrong in any case: the number of possible combinations is not infinite, but is simply $9^3$, or 729. However, the *Kama Sutra* did recognize that there are important individual differences within each sex, both with regard to physical and psychological dimensions, and this recognition is fully borne out by modern research.

Having looked in detail at one particular source of difference within the male sex, i.e. preferences for women with large or small breasts, and large or small buttocks, and having noted the important part played by personality in creating these preferences, we must next turn to a more detailed discussion of personality and sexual behaviour and attitudes generally. This discussion should in the end give us a clue as to why the observed relations between personality and liking for large or small breasts are as they are.

We therefore next go on to look at the relationships between personality, within each sex, with sexual attitudes and behaviour. It has been found that these relations are very similar for men and women, and consequently in most cases we will simply quote general findings, without differentiating between males and females. The discovery that male extraverts, say, and female extraverts behave in a very similar manner, as compared with male and female introverts, adds considerably to our conviction that the data are meaningful, consistent and replicable. Before turning to the results let us first of all have a look at theoretical predictions as to the kind of thing we would expect to find. The first personality variable to be looked at is extraversion/introversion, using these terms in the now accepted behavioural sense, i.e. based on the fact that some people (extraverts) are more sociable, impulsive, physically active, talkative, carefree, easygoing, hopeful, histrionic and hot-headed than are others (introverts) who are more thoughtful, serious, unsociable, high principled, controlled in their behaviour and generally less outgoing. Of course extraverts and introverts are not separate 'types' in the sense that everybody is either the one or the other; there is a continuum ranging from one extreme to the other, with most people somewhere around the middle, and only relatively few extreme cases at either end. For our purposes we shall regard this continuum as split into three roughly equal thirds, with introverts at the one end, extraverts at the other and ambiverts in the middle.

This is not the place to enter into details about the theory of extraversion, but we can briefly state the main points of that theory. Note first of all that this dimension of personality is strongly based on *genetic determinants*: thus for instance identical twins, even when brought up separately, are much more alike in respect to this variable than are fraternal twins. Note secondly that there is a physiological basis for this personality dimension; the cortical arousal system of the introvert is much more highly geared than that of the extravert, so that the introvert's cortex is normally in a higher state of arousal (Eysenck, 1967). Cortical arousal is subjectively felt as the difference between the drowsy state in which many of us are at the end of a hard day's work, lounging in an easy-chair and watching a boring programme on television (low arousal), and the mental state which we show in the middle of an important examination (high arousal). While each individual's state of arousal depends in part on circumstances, there is also a habitual level characteristic of a person, and this habitual level is significantly higher in introverts than in extraverts, with ambiverts in between.

This may seem to be the wrong way about. It is the extravert who is active, impulsive and uninhibited in his behaviour, yet he is said to have a low level of arousal! The answer is simply that the main function of the cortex is to *inhibit* the independent activity of the lower centres of the brain, and act as a kind of watchdog, to keep our behaviour in check. The more active the cortex, the more inhibited the behaviour. Alcohol furnishes us with a good analogue. Drinking alcohol reduces the arousal level of the cortex, thus decreasing the effectiveness of the watchdog, and allowing extraverted, uninhibited behaviour to take place. There is a great deal of direct physiological and indirect psychological evidence for the theory thus presented, and we may use it to make certain predictions in the behavioural and social field.

Thus, for instance, the extravert gets bored much more easily and requires some form of sensation-seeking and risk-taking behaviour in order to bring his cortical arousal up to a reasonable level. Another consequence is that the introvert assimilates social mores and customs more readily than do extraverts: it has been found over and over again that extraverts show more antisocial and even criminal behaviour than do introverts (Eysenck, 1977). Taking together all these considerations, and the very large literature of experimental work on which they are based, we arrive at the following predictions:

(1) Extraverts will have intercourse *earlier* than introverts.
(2) Extraverts will have intercourse *more frequently* than introverts.
(3) Extraverts will have intercourse with *more different partners.*
(4) Extraverts will have intercourse in *more* different positions than introverts.
(5) Extraverts will indulge in more *varied* sexual behaviour outside intercourse.
(6) Extraverts will indulge in *longer precoital love play* than introverts.

How do the facts stack up against these predictions?

There are three main studies which have investigated this question.

The first of these was done on German students by H. Giese and A. Schmidt (1968), two German sexologists whose book on sexuality in students has never been translated. They reported their results in terms of percentages for males and females separately subdividing each group into extraverts, ambiverts and introverts. These percentages are interesting, and on the whole tend to bear out the hypotheses outlined above.

Let us start with petting behaviour. Taking the males first we find that 78 per cent of the extraverts, 72 per cent of the ambiverts and only 57 per cent of the introverts took part in petting behaviour. For the women the percentages were 76 per cent, 71 per cent and 62 per cent. For both sexes therefore there is a constant decline in petting behaviour from the extraverted through the ambiverted to the introverted group.

Next let us look at actual intercourse at the age of nineteen: 45 per cent of the extraverts, 31 per cent of the ambiverts, 15 per cent of the introverts had had intercourse in the male group; 29 per cent, 20 per cent and 12 per cent respectively in the female group. Here again, then, there is a regular fall from the extraverts to the ambiverts and the introverts, as predicted. We may next look at the median frequency of coitus per month, using only the answers from sexually active students. For the men the frequency is 5.5 for extraverts, 3.7 for ambiverts and 3.0 for introverts. For the women, the figures are 7.5, 4.5 and 3.1. Again we see that the more extraverted a person is, the more sexually active he will be.

Let us next look at the number of coital partners in the last twelve months, using unmarried students only. Taking those who had four or more coital partners in the last twelve months the percentages for men are 25 per cent for the extraverts, 12 per cent for the ambiverts, and 7 per cent for the introverts. For the females the percentages are 17 per cent, 6 per cent and 4 per cent respectively. Again the figures bear out our hypothesis.

Next we may take a look at some variations in sexual behaviour. Taking cunnilingus first, we find the percentages in the male group are 64 per cent for the extraverts, 62 per cent for the ambiverts and 52 per cent for the introverts. For the females the percentages are 69 per cent, 69 per cent and 58 per cent. (Again we are of course only dealing with students who are sexually active.) For fellatio, the percentages for the men are 69 per cent, 60 per cent and 53 per cent; for the women they are 61 per cent, 59 per cent and 53 per cent. Some of the students had intercourse in more than three different coital positions; the percentage figures for the men are 26 per cent for extraverts, 16 per cent for the ambiverts, and 10 per cent for the introverts; for the women, the figures are 13 per cent, 18 per cent and 12 per cent. (It will be noted that for this last item the differences between the women are not as clearly in agreement with the hypothesis as are the figures for the men. This is probably due to the fact that what goes on in a sexual relationship depends more on the man than on the woman; the man leads and the woman follows. This would tend to throw out the figures for the women to some extent.)

One further item in this study is of interest, namely the experience of orgasm. Among the women, introverts who *nearly always had orgasms* constituted only 17 per cent of all the subjects; for extraverts and ambiverts the figure was almost double, with no difference between these two groups. These figures then strongly support the hypothesis stated.

The second study was undertaken by Professor M. Zuckerman and his colleagues in the USA, who studied heterosexual activities in two different populations, and correlated the number of these activities, separately for men and women, with a sensation-seeking scale, parts of which correlate quite highly with extraversion. Zuckerman also asked questions about the number of heterosexual partners each individual had had. Our hypothesis would predict that all the correlations would be positive, and this was indeed found. Taking the subscale which comes the closest to a measure of extraversion, he found, both for men and women, that the extraverts in each case had more heterosexual experiences and also a greater number of heterosexual partners. This work then gives support to our hypotheses, as does that of Giese and Schmidt.

A third research study (Eysenck, 1976) used a lengthy questionnaire of sexual behaviour and attitudes, administered to thousands of men and women, both students and non-academic adults. Statistical analysis showed that groups of questions were answered in a similar manner by respondents, and the nature of the questions made it possible to label these groupings in a meaningful manner. There were eleven of these groups, and they will be labelled in the following paragraphs to indicate the nature of each of these groups, or factors; we will also quote a few of the items going to make up each factor, so that the reader may have some idea of just what is meant by the title given in each case. (The questions as quoted are paraphrased from the original, in order not to make the length of this chapter inordinate. Sometimes the original question is worded in one direction, so that the 'no' answer would be in agreement with the title of the factor; thus one item in the questionnaire read 'it is better not to have sex until married'; this item came into the factor with the minus sign, that is to say that permissive people would say 'no' to this item.)

The first grouping or factor was called 'permissiveness'. Items in this set were: it wouldn't bother me if the person I married was not a virgin; the 'pill' should be universally available; pornographic writing should be freely published; prostitution should be legally permitted; abortion should be the concern of no one but the woman concerned; there are not too many immoral plays on TV; sexual permissiveness does not threaten to undermine civilization. Respondents scoring high on this factor tended to have had intercourse early in life.

The second factor was labelled 'satisfaction' and some of the major items in it are: I am satisfied with my sex life; I have not been deprived sexually; sex contact has never been a problem for me; my love-life has not been disappointing; my partner satisfies all my physical needs.

The third factor was called 'neurotic sex', and contained some of these items: it is a problem for me to control my sex feelings; sexual feelings are unpleasant; I have felt guilt about sex experiences; I am afraid of what I might do sexually; sex disturbs me more than it should; conscience bothers me too much; I worry a lot about sex.

Factor four was called 'impersonal sex', and contained items like these: 'impersonal sex' is highly satisfactory; we should do away with marriage entirely, faithfulness is nearly as silly as celibacy; I would enjoy watching my partner having intercourse with someone else; I would vote for a law permitting polygamy; group sex appeals at me; I would prefer a new sex partner every night; it would not disturb me if my partner had sex with someone else.

Factor five was labelled 'pornography', and contained some of these items: I like to look at sexy pictures; if I had a chance to see people making love, I would take it; I would accept an invitation to see a 'blue film'; the naked body is a pleasing sight.

Factor six was one of 'shyness', characterized by some of these items: I have never had many dates; I have had strong sex feelings but can't express them; I feel nervous with the opposite sex; I find it hard to talk with the opposite sex; I am embarrassed to talk about sex; I am afraid of sexual relationships.

Factor seven was labelled 'prudishness' and contained these items: I don't like to be kissed; I don't enjoy petting; seeing a nude person doesn't interest me; sex jokes disgust me; I can't stand being touched.

Factor eight was called 'sexual disgust' and contained items like these: there are some things which I wouldn't do with anyone; I do some things only to please my sex partner; the opposite sex's genitals are aesthetically unpleasing; some forms of love-making are disgusting.

Factor nine was called 'sexual excitement' and contained items like these: it doesn't take much to get me excited sexually; the strength of my sexual desires is great; if I love the person I could do anything with them; I think about sex nearly every day; sex is my greatest pleasure; conditions don't have to be right for me to get excited sexually.

Factor ten is one of 'physical sex' characterized by these items: few things are more important than sex; being good in bed is terribly important in my sex partner; sex is the most important part of marriage; physical attraction is very important; when I am sexually excited I can think of nothing but satisfaction; I have had more than one sex affair at a time.

The last and eleventh factor is called 'aggressive sex', and contains these items: sometimes I have felt like humiliating my sex partner; sometimes I feel like biting or scratching my sex partner during intercourse; I have felt hostile to my sex partner; I make lots of vocal noises during intercourse.

These are the major factors that emerge from the statistical analysis, and of course they make quite good sense in psychological terms. These various factors of course are not independent of each other, and some are quite highly correlated with each other. We can therefore go on to analyse the relations between these factors themselves, and when this is done we find that all the observed relationships can be interpreted in terms of two major factors, as indicated in Figure 4. The first of these we have called *libido* or sexual desire: it is made up of the factors of impersonal sex, pornography, permissiveness, aggressive sex, sexual excitement and physical sex, with prudishness, sexual disgust and sexual shyness at the opposite or negative end. The other factor is closely similar to that of 'satisfaction' already noted, but has at its negative end factors of neurotic sex, sexual shyness, sexual disgust and prudishness. What is interesting and noteworthy is that these two factors are quite independent; in other words, a person's satisfaction with his sexual life is in no way related to the amount of libido or sexual desire which he shows. It is equally easy to be satisfied or dissatisfied with one's sex life whether one attributes a great deal of importance to physical sex or whether one does not. This is an important general finding which came out again and again in each of the analyses we conducted on the different types of populations studied.

Before turning to a discussion of the relationship between sexual attitudes and behaviours, in terms of these factors and in terms of the original items of the questionnaire, and personality, it may be

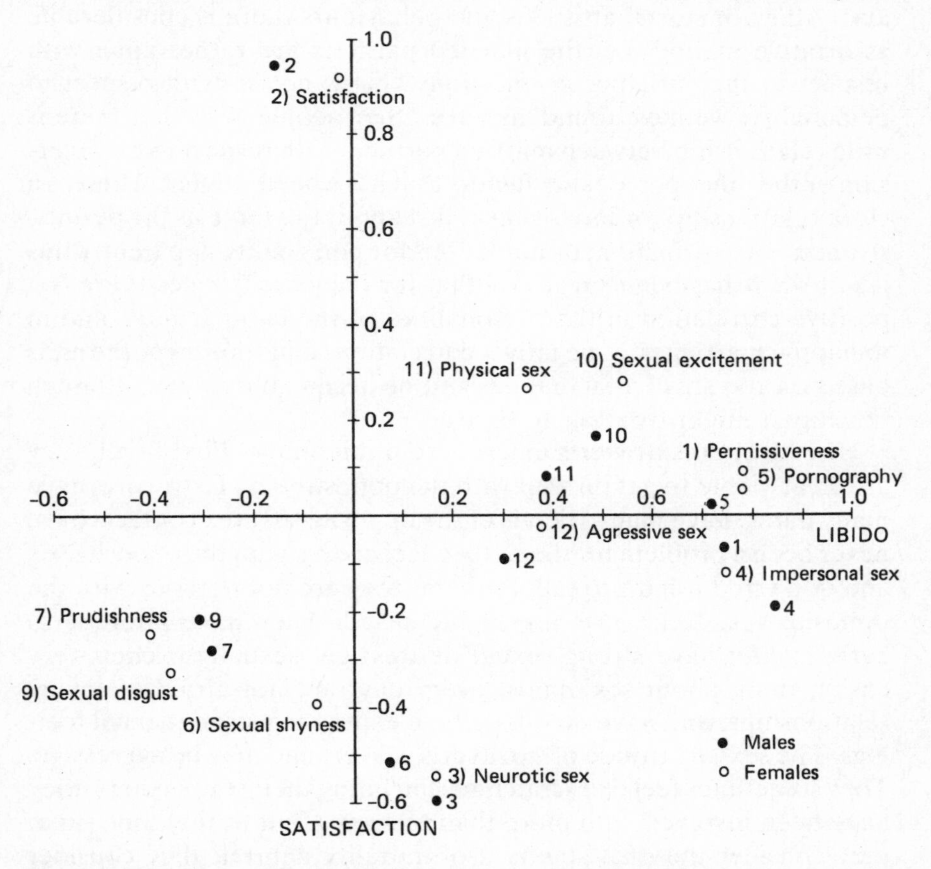


Figure 4 Diagram showing two major features of sexual attitudes and behaviour

interesting to have a look at the amount of assortative mating that is present, i.e. the relationship between married partners on these various factors. On permissiveness the relationship is pretty close, i.e. permissive men are usually married to permissive women; it is still strong, although somewhat weaker, on satisfaction, impersonal sex, physical sex, aggressive sex and libido or sexual desire. It is still positive but quite low for neurotic sex, sexual shyness, prudishness, sexual disgust, with pornography being in between these very low factors and the higher ones. In terms of our two major factors we may say that where one partner in the marriage is satisfied, there is a strong tendency for the other to be satisfied too, and where one partner has a strong libido, the other is likely to have a strong libido also. Thus for sexual attitudes and behaviours there is considerable assortative mating, i.e. the married partners are rather alike with respect to the variables in question. This is not so with respect to personality; we have found, as have other people also, that there is little relationship between married partners with respect to extraversion or the other personality factors that have been studied. There is a close relationship for intelligence, just about the same as for permissiveness, or satisfaction, or libido; but for personality apparently this is not so. It has been suggested that for happy marriages there is a positive correlation in the personalities of the two partners, and in unhappy marriages a negative correlation, but this hypothesis is based on too small a factual basis to be acceptable as yet, although possibly it might turn out to be true.

How then do extraverts emerge from this study? First of all, they are clearly able to get on well with the opposite sex. Extraverts have many dates; have many friends of the opposite sex; sex contacts have never been a problem for them; they feel at ease with the opposite sex and don't find it hard to talk to them; they are not nervous with the opposite sex. Extraverts are highly sexed. They have intercourse early in life; have strong sexual desires; get sexually excited very easily; think about sex almost every day; are not afraid of sexual relationships; and have no difficulty in expressing strong sexual feelings. The sexual attitude of extraverts is overt and may be aggressive. They sometimes feel like scratching and biting their sex partners, they have been involved with more than one sex affair at the same time; they consider the dual standard of morality natural; they consider absolute faithfulness in marriage silly and would take part in an orgy if invited; hedonistic to the last, they believe in taking their pleasures where they find them. Their sexual development has clearly been healthy and acceptable to them; they have discussed sex with their parents; they are not embarrassed to talk about sex; their religious beliefs are not against sex; they don't mind people touching them; and on the whole they are satisfied with their sex lives. In terms of our Figure 4 extraverts are high on libido, and show somewhat more satisfaction; in other words they are rather permissive, easily excited sexually, believe in physical sex, impersonal sex and aggressive sex. Introverts of course are at the other end of the continuum in the low libido part. They may show greater satisfaction at older age levels; extraverted behaviour is more appropriate to youth.

We can now see why extraverts may be predicted to prefer women with large breasts, introverts women with small breasts. Extraverts, having a low degree of cortical arousal, seek out experiences which strongly stimulate them and raise their arousal level to a satisfactory degree; hence they prefer women with large breasts. Introverts, on the other hand, already have a high degree of cortical arousal; they take care not to be over-stimulated, and hence prefer women with small breasts, i.e. women less likely to produce this over-stimulation which is an ever-present danger in people with high cortical arousal levels. This hypothesis is clearly superior to the Freudian, because not only does it make the right prediction, but also it is based on a large body of factual evidence derived from laboratory research.

Both the extraverted and the introverted modes of sexual adjustment are viable; the degree of satisfaction experienced by extraverts and introverts depends on whether or not they are high or low on the next personality trait to be considered, which is neuroticism or emotionality. These terms are used interchangeably by psychologists to refer to people whose emotions are strong and easily elicited; these emotions also tend to persist over a long period of time and to die away only slowly. The term 'neuroticism' does not mean that these people are psychiatrically abnormal, it merely means that under strong environmental stress they are more liable to develop neurotic disorders, so that their neuroticism is a kind of predisposition that may under certain circumstances blow up into a full neurosis or neurotic breakdown. Neuroticism is quite independent of extraversion/introversion; in other words extraverts can be highly emotional or very stable, and introverts too can be highly emotional or stable – or indeed of course anything in between! Neuroticism too is a continuous variable, with most people being somewhere in between the extremes.

Neuroticism, like extraversion, is to a considerable extent a personality trait which is inherited; here too studies with identical and fraternal twins have demonstrated the importance that hereditary predispositions play in the causation of this trait. Knowing, as we do, a good deal about the effects which strong emotions have on a person's life, and knowing also something about the sexual difficulties of actual neurotics we may make a number of predictions about the relationship between neuroticism and sexual attitudes and behaviours. We would predict that high scorers on this factor would suffer more frequently than low scorers from various sexual disorders such as frigidity, premature ejaculation, etc.; we would also predict that worries, guilt feelings, etc. would be much more frequent in this group. When we turn to the actual figures, they very much substantiate these expectations. High N scorers, as opposed to low N scorers were found to complain much more frequently of impotence and premature ejaculation in the males, and frigidity and lack of orgasm frequency in the females. As regards the attitude questionnaire, high neuroticism males and females show evidence of considerable abnormality and disturbance. They find thoughts about sex disturbing, they worry a lot about sex, feel nervous with the opposite sex, have felt guilty about sex experiences and cannot discuss sexual matters with their spouses. Yet they are highly sexed. They confess to strong sexual desires, declare that sometimes sexual feelings overpower them, they have sometimes been afraid of what they might do sexually, can think of nothing but satisfaction when excited, and consider sex far and away their greatest pleasure. Physical attraction is extremely important to them, sex thoughts almost drive them crazy, yet thinking about sex makes them very nervous. They get excited sexually very easily, believe in taking pleasures where they find them and consider few things more important than sex. However, there is also considerable dissatisfaction with their love-life. Conscience bothers them too much; they are not satisfied with their sex life; something is lacking in their sex life, their love-life has been disappointing; they have had some bad sexual experiences; parents' influence has inhibited them sexually and they have been deprived sexually. There is an aura of abnormality about their desires. They have sometimes felt hostile to their sex partners; are excited by the thought of an illicit relationship; have sometimes felt like humiliating their sex partner; sometimes have problems in controlling their feelings; have been bothered by perverted thoughts; males prefer a sex partner several years older; usually feel aggressive about their sex partner; and consider that the need for birth control upsets lovemaking because it makes everything so cold-blooded and planned.

In terms of our Figure 4, high neuroticism scorers would come in the lower left corner, i.e. the third quadrant, when introverted, and in the lower right-hand corner when extraverted. The main relationship between neuroticism and the sex factor is with the satisfaction dimension; they are clearly very low on this. This agrees very well with the evidence from clinical studies of neurotic patients; these tend mostly to be introverted as well and show all the complaints characteristic of the third quadrant at the lower left-hand side of our diagram.

Many psychologists and psychiatrists consider neurosis as being based on a conflict, and our own findings seem to support this. High N scorers seem to show a conflict between their strong desires and equally strong inhibitions; the inhibitions make it impossible for them to act out their strong desires, and where they do act out their desires they experience guilt feelings and hence a lack of satisfaction as a result of their activities. Neurotics usually are in what is sometimes called a double-bind or a kind of Catch 22 situation; psychologists usually prefer to call this an approach-avoidance conflict. A person is attracted by a certain course of action but also repelled because of the dangers he fears; thus in the worst kind of state he is unable to act at all and remains in a state of doubt, uncertainty and conflict. This is precisely what seems to be happening to our high neuroticism scorers.

We may say that low and medium neuroticism scorers have two acceptable ways of reaching a satisfactory adjustment. If they are introverted they go into the top left-hand quadrant, i.e. the low-libido/high-satisfaction quadrant; if they are extraverted, they go into the top right-hand quadrant, i.e. the high-libido/high-satisfaction one. High neuroticism subjects have little hope of achieving a satisfactory adjustment, and this lack of sexual adjustment will only act to inflame their neurotic fears and emotions even more. Time fortunately has been found to be a great healer in this as in many other things as well; there is very frequently a spontaneous remission of neurotic fears in the sexual as in all other fields, and such people may reach a satisfactory outcome after a few years of torment. This is just as well; the evidence of psychiatric, psychoanalytic or other help in this state does not suggest that the outcome of intervention is very hopeful, or any better than spontaneous remission. (Behavioural programmes of intervention are much more successful, fortunately, and are now becoming more widely available.)

We must now turn to the third of our personality factors. This one may be called 'toughmindedness'; people with high scores on this particular factor often show male as opposed to female characteristics, and in extreme cases may show psychopathic, hostile and even sadistic behaviour. Because of this association with psychopathic, and in very extreme cases psychotic behaviour this factor has been called the P factor, and we shall refer to it in those terms later on (Eysenck & Eysenck, 1976). Men tend to have much higher scores on this P factor than do women; so do psychotics, psychopaths, prisoners and people guilty of antisocial behaviour in general, and also children and adolescents who present what psychiatrists call behaviour disorders. High P scorers are also very strongly determined in their behaviour by genetic factors, and this is probably mediated by male hormones. We shall take up this point very shortly; here let us merely note that the answers given to the questionnaire by high P scorers, as opposed to low P scorers, are almost identical to the answers given by males as opposed to females. In other words high P males and females answer in the masculine direction, low P males and females in the feminine direction. This makes an actual summary of the behaviours of the high P scorers slightly redundant in view of what was said in the second chapter, but we will give at least a brief rundown on the items which characterize them. First of all, then, we note that male high P scorers are clearly opposed to current morality and customs. They wish to do away with marriage; they favour polygamy; they believe it is all right to seduce a person old enough to know what they are doing; they consider premarital sex all right. High scorers have a realistic, not an idealistic, view of sex. They believe that romantic love is an illusion; they don't think it disgusting to see animals having sex; they believe in taking pleasures where they can find them; they believe that tenderness in sex is not important, and that faithfulness in marriage is silly; they would not be disturbed if their sex partner had sex with someone else. High scorers are very permissive. They believe that pornography should be freely available; they don't object to four-letter swear words being used in mixed company; they are not disturbed by seeing necking in public; they don't think sex orgies are disgusting; they consider sex play among children to be harmless; they do not believe that the opposite sex will respect you more if you are not too familiar with them; they do not believe that men are more selfish in their love-making than women – although they do believe that most men are sex mad! All in all, high P scorers emerge as advocates of impersonal, permissive sexual practices, the abandonment of social rules and laws concerning marriage and other aspects of sexual behaviour, and an 'all's fair in love and war' attitude; one might be tempted to call this the Don Juan Syndrome. It is interesting to note the absence of items signifying satisfaction; if anything there is some indication of nervousness and even guilt. In terms of our diagram (Figure 4) high P scorers seem to be anchored in the lower right quadrant, i.e. having high libido but being prevented from enjoying satisfaction by the somewhat pathological nature of their attitudes, behaviours and personality. While in some ways they resemble the happy extravert, this pathological component destroys the satisfaction the extravert derives from his very permissive and explicit sexual behaviour and makes the life of the high P scorer more of a fruitless chase from woman to woman after an ever-receding satisfaction that he can never reach.

We must now turn to the possible biological causes of individual differences in sexual attitudes and behaviours, and also the question of heritability – the extent to which these characteristics are transmitted genetically. Only one study has been found in the literature to deal with the genetic question, the study undertaken by the English biologist B. Chilton (1972) and using only a small number of subjects. This study found significant evidence of heritability for age at first masturbation, age at first orgasm, age at first passive genital stimulation, age at first active stimulation, and slight evidence of heritability for age at first sexual intercourse in males but not in females. Chilton summarized the results as follows:

> The sexual drive is not a uniform one – just as the need and appetite for food varies from one individual to another, so does sexual drive and capacity . . . the results from this pilot study suggest that genetic factors play a part in determining this variation, that the age at which an individual begins development and exploring his sexuality is not just a function of environmental experiences but is also, in part, an expression of his genotype.

Eysenck's (1976) study was carried out on a much larger group, including 153 male twins and 339 female twins. On this sample also, strong evidence for the importance of genetic factors in determining sexual adjustment was obtained. Thus the heritability of the libido factor for instance was 67 per cent, and the others were in the same neighbourhood. The topic of heritability is a very complex one and there would be little point in going into too much detail here; in so far as these data are compatible with those of Chilton, they lead us to the same conclusion.

This concludes our discussion of the findings relating to personality and sexual attitudes. In view of the paucity of researches in this area it will not be surprising that the total amount of knowledge is relatively small, and that replications of many of the points made are urgently needed before we can come to any definitive conclusion. What is not in doubt, we think, is the fact that sexual attitudes and behaviours are strongly determined by genetic factors, that they are mediated by physiological and hormonal structures and secretions, and that they are closely related to personality variables of the kind here discussed. We are beginning to acquire an understanding of the causes of individual differences in sexual attitudes and behaviours, and we can see that these are fairly systematic. It was possible to formulate predictions about the relationship likely to be found on the basis of what was known about the personality dimension involved, and these predictions have been verified for the most part. Further work is of course urgently required to put these findings on a more secure basis, and to extend them in many directions; it is never safe to rely too much on single studies, done in one country by one investigator. Such replications as have been done have nearly always corroborated previous findings; that is encouraging. Whether our findings only hold true in the Western world or whether they apply universally in other cultures as well cannot, of course, be predicted with any degree of certainty. If it is correct that biological causes play a large part in the causation of individual differences in this field, then we would expect our findings to be replicable in other cultures as well. This would be another interesting field of study.

It may be useful to consider just in outline some of the possible social consequences of the findings reported in this chapter. What is most striking of course is the great diversity of attitudes and practices. Some girls of twenty have not even been kissed, others have indulged in intercourse in many different positions, and in a variety of sexual 'activities' with many different partners. Some of our subjects believe in the importance and continued value of virginity, others dismiss virginity with contempt. Some approve of orgies, of pornography, of blue films, while others regard all this with disgust and contempt. There is not one question out of the 160 or so which we used in our inventory on which there is unanimity or anything approaching it; on most there is the utmost variety and confusion. This clearly poses a social problem: how can we have one set of rules, or mores, or laws, to accommodate a plethora of divergent attitudes and opinions? It is obvious that laws, by their very nature, cannot take into account human diversity – what is allowed (or prohibited) to one person is allowed (or prohibited) to all others, leaving no leeway to allow for the fact that all human beings are essentially different. The only rational answer here would seem to be a lessening of legal concern with matters of individual conduct: legislation should be kept to an absolute minimum, protecting the rights of babies, minors and others who cannot take care of themselves, but not interfering with the conduct of 'consenting adults'. Such an answer is easy, but it also raises complex and difficult problems, some of these have been considered in Eysenck's book *Psychology is about People*, and we will not go into details again here.

Even more important than the legal consequences of the realization of human individuality and sexual behaviour might be the psychological one. We tend to think of ourselves as in general very much alike. Some are a little brighter, others a little duller; some are a little braver, others a little more fearful; some are a little more serious, others are full of fun. But essentially all these differences are slight, and probably due to upbringing or to events in a person's life; under the skin all are very much the same, Judy O'Grady or the Colonel's Lady. This easy and comforting illusion is often shattered, however, when we read in the papers or experience in our own lives the impact which the huge differences in personality, intellect and behaviour can have in the relations between different people. Newton, a psychopathic mass murderer, the sexuopathic 'Walter' who wrote *My Secret Life*, Shelley, Leonardo da Vinci, Buddha – these and many others are so far removed from the mean (along several different dimensions) that to consider them in terms of just a little more or a little less ceases to have any meaning. The truth seems to be that human beings are innately diverse in many different ways – so diverse that it is difficult even to begin to realize just how large these differences are, or how impossible it is to argue from one's own behaviour or reaction to those of another person – unless that other person happens to have a similar IQ, degree of extraversion, score on P and N, education and cultural background generally.

This truth is sad because it takes away from our common humanity; if you have an IQ of 80 you will never appreciate Schubert's 'Trout' quintet, understand canonical algorisms or take delight in a Barlach sculpture. Many people have by now accepted the great differences created by innate intellectual factors, although many others refuse to consider the evidence, for fear of what they might find. But it is in the broader field of personality that the idea has not even begun to sink in that people are inescapably different, innately diversified, and unimaginably unlike each other. Introverts and extraverts are like chalk and cheese; to group their behaviours and reactions together by some process of averaging is as absurd as to average chalk and cheese. But because these facts are in some ways sad does not mean that we can refuse to pay any attention to them, or that we can pretend things are not as in fact they are. No sexual rules, no laws, no ideals, will ever cover introvert and extravert, neurotic and stable; one man's meat truly is another man's poison. This realization is the beginning of sanity.

## References

CHILTON, B., 'Psychosexual development in twins', *Journal of Biosocial Science*, 1972, **4**, 277–86.

EYSENCK, H.J., *The Biological Basis of Personality*. Springfield: C.C. Thomas, 1967.

EYSENCK, H.J., *Psychology is about People*. London: Allen Lane, 1972.

EYSENCK, H.J., *Sex and Personality*. London: Open Books, 1976.

EYSENCK H.J., *Crime and Personality*. London: Routledge & Kegan Paul, 1977.

EYSENCK, H.J., & EYSENCK, S.B.G., *Psychoticism as a Dimension of Personality*. London: Hodder & Stoughton, 1976.

GIESE, H. & SCHMIDT, A., *Studenten Sexualität*. Hamburg: Rowohlt, 1968.

HIRSCHBERG, N., 'Individual differences in sexual judgement: A multivariate approach' in M. Fishbein (ed.), *Progress in Social Psychology*. New Jersey: Erlbaum, 1979.

SCODEL, A., 'Heterosexual somatic preference and fantasy dependency', *Journal of Consulting Psychology*, 1957, **21**, 371–9.

# 4 Fantasy and excitement

'Sex,' says therapist Helen Kaplan, 'is composed of friction and fantasy.' In other words, both physical and mental stimulation are necessary for adequate arousal and functioning. But while the kind of physical stimulation required is fairly well known and fairly standard, the mental component is more interesting because it is very idiosyncratic. In lower animals it is mostly comprised of direct physical sensations such as smells and visual configurations, but human beings have such highly developed representational processes that internal images such as memories and hopes, pooled and refined over time, are at least equally powerful as sources of sexual excitement. In fact, fantasies are often better as a source of arousal than direct sensations because they are private and do not arouse self-consciousness. Also, being tailor-made according to individual specification they can be more ideal than reality; the people involved are always desirable and always cooperative. In this chapter we consider the role that sexual fantasies play in our love-lives, and the origins of individual differences in sexual preference. Why is one man turned on by stealing ladies' underwear and another by imagining himself being whipped by a lady in high-heeled boots? Why does one woman require a long period of tender foreplay before being sexually aroused while another likes to be taken brutally and lustfully by a powerful and impatient man? Why do some people choose a heterosexual love object, others a homosexual one, while still others are interested only in children? These are the kinds of questions that we will discuss, although it has to be admitted at the outset that completely satisfactory answers are not yet available.

First, what are the most frequent sexual fantasies and the characteristics of the people who have them? There is no doubt that people vary enormously in the extent to which they think about sex. Some people are capable of sustaining reasonably satisfactory intercourse while thinking about the household chores or what has to be done at the office the next day. Other people are so preoccupied with sex that the most remote associations are capable of sparking off elaborate trains of fantasy. The content of people's fantasies is equally varied. Until recently, remarkably little information has been available about the sexual fantasy patterns of normal men and women. Most of our impressions of what people fantasized about came from second-hand reports from the psychiatrist's couch, usually from neurotic if not psychotic patients, or from erotic anthologies geared to maximum titillation value. Attempts at more scientific data collection often suffer from distortions due to sample bias. The Hite Report, for example, was based on answers to a survey questionnaire obtained from a large number of women in many different parts of the US. Unfortunately, the findings are of limited value because the questionnaire was distributed mainly through feminist sources such as *MS Magazine* and the return rate was only 3 per cent. We therefore have to be very cautious in evaluating some of the main conclusions, e.g. that male insensitivity is the prime cause of female sexual difficulty and that masturbation is generally a more satisfying sexual outlet for women than sex with a man. The political bias in Hite's sample is probably also responsible for what seems an excessively high frequency of reports of lesbian behaviour and fantasies.

A rather more useful survey of fantasy patterns in American women was reported in 1974 by Barbara Hariton and Jerome Singer of the City University, New York, although this time the women were all married and mostly middle-class and Jewish. Around two-thirds of these women reported having sexual fantasies 'at least some of the time' during intercourse with their husbands and more than one-third had fantasies 'very often' during love-making. Four main kinds of women were distinguished on the basis of their fantasies:

(1) Women who had many varied fantasies with a high frequency of occurrence.
(2) Women who had hardly any fantasies at all.
(3) Women who fantasized repeatedly about other lovers, other places and other times.
(4) Women who specialized in fantasies of forced compliance such as being dominated, raped, seduced, humiliated or abducted as white slaves.

The first kind of woman (with many varied fantasies) appeared to be very active and extravert in personality. Such women had a high degree of interest in sex and a nonconformist, exploratory approach towards it. Although they were likely to have had extramarital affairs there was no indication that their fantasies were motivated by marital unhappiness. Rather they seemed to reflect a need for novelty and stimulation. Apart from extramarital sex, these women were experienced generally in sexual matters, and were also more likely to participate in non-sexual creative activities such as pottery, painting and music. The second group of women (the low fantasizers) were the opposite to the first in nearly all respects. They engaged in little activity of any kind, whether sexual or non-sexual, and were traditionally feminine in personality, being 'conciliatory, unassuming, nurturant and affiliative'. The third group (fantasies of other lovers) shared some of the characteristics of the high fantasizers, being active, independent, impulsive and playful, but tended to be relatively dissatisfied with the sexual side of their marriage. The fourth group (fantasies of forced compliance) were more like the traditional, feminine non-fantasizer in personality. Their marriage relationships were generally fairly good, though they tended to be passive in love-making, allowing their husbands to take the lead. They regarded their fantasies as very erotic and as contributing to their enjoyment of sex.

This study suggests that sexual fantasies, rather than being rare, pathological manifestations, are actually fairly common in women during sexual intercourse. Although they were sometimes invoked to add novelty and excitement to an act (or partner) that had become slightly mundane, and in that sense could be viewed as symptomatic of unrest, most of the women seemed to regard them as a positive factor in their love life. Also, the indications were that a high rate of sexual fantasy was associated not only with a high libido but with a general creativity and lust for life. Thus the mere fact that a person has sexual fantasies does not mean that they have difficulties or deficiencies, though the precise content of these fantasies may, as we shall see, have diagnostic significance.

A survey of the fantasy patterns of normal women and men has recently been conducted in the London area by Wilson (1978). A questionnaire containing a wide variety of fantasy themes gathered from the clinical and survey literature and from pilot studies was distributed to people in the street in various areas chosen to represent different social classes and they were invited to return it anonymously using a stamped, addressed envelope that was provided with it. Replies were received from ninety people, being about one-third of the people who accepted the questionnaires, with an equal number coming from men and women. A factor analysis was conducted on these questionnaires to find out how the different fantasies clustered together. In other words, fantasies that tended to be endorsed by the same individual were classified into the same group. In this way, four major categories of sexual fantasy were obtained and these were labelled exploratory, intimate, impersonal and sadomasochistic. These four factors, and some of the items that defined them, are shown in the simplified form of the research questionnaire printed below. The reader may now like to entertain him or herself by filling out this questionnaire, after which a rough scoring system will be provided together with some comments about the meaning of the factors. Try to be as honest with yourself as possible, remembering that a wide variety of fantasies, many of them seemingly quite kinky, are reported by perfectly healthy, normal men and women.

## Fantasy Questionnaire

How often do you fantasize about each of these themes?
(Put a ring round the appropriate number)

| *Fantasy Factor 1* | *Never* | *Seldom* | *Some-times* | *Often* |
|---|---|---|---|---|
| (1) Participating in an orgy | 0 | 1 | 2 | 3 |
| (2) Homosexual activity | 0 | 1 | 2 | 3 |
| (3) Mate-swapping | 0 | 1 | 2 | 3 |
| (4) Being promiscuous | 0 | 1 | 2 | 3 |
| (5) Being much sought after by the opposite sex | 0 | 1 | 2 | 3 |
| (6) Sex with two other people | 0 | 1 | 2 | 3 |
| (7) Being seduced as an 'innocent' | 0 | 1 | 2 | 3 |
| (8) Sex with someone of different race | 0 | 1 | 2 | 3 |

Total Score on Fantasy Factor 1
(Add up the ringed numbers)

*Fantasy Factor 2*

| | Never | Seldom | Some-times | Often |
|---|---|---|---|---|
| (1) Making love out of doors in a romantic setting (e.g. field of flowers, beach at night) | 0 | 1 | 2 | 3 |
| (2) Having intercourse with a loved partner | 0 | 1 | 2 | 3 |
| (3) Intercourse with someone you know but have not had sex with | 0 | 1 | 2 | 3 |
| (4) Giving oral sex | 0 | 1 | 2 | 3 |
| (5) Making love elsewhere than in the bedroom (e.g. kitchen, bathroom) | 0 | 1 | 2 | 3 |
| (6) Having your clothes taken off | 0 | 1 | 2 | 3 |
| (7) Being masturbated to orgasm by a partner | 0 | 1 | 2 | 3 |
| (8) Kissing passionately | 0 | 1 | 2 | 3 |
| Total Score on Fantasy Factor 2 | | | | |

*Fantasy Factor 3*

| | Never | Seldom | Some-times | Often |
|---|---|---|---|---|
| (1) Watching others have sex | 0 | 1 | 2 | 3 |
| (2) Intercourse with an anonymous stranger | 0 | 1 | 2 | 3 |
| (3) Being excited by rubber or leather | 0 | 1 | 2 | 3 |
| (4) Looking at obscene pictures or films | 0 | 1 | 2 | 3 |
| (5) Using objects for stimulation (e.g. vibrators, candles) | 0 | 1 | 2 | 3 |
| (6) Sex with someone much older | 0 | 1 | 2 | 3 |
| (7) Being excited by silk or fur | 0 | 1 | 2 | 3 |
| (8) Wearing clothes of the opposite sex | 0 | 1 | 2 | 3 |
| Total Score on Fantasy Factor 3 | | | | |

*Fantasy Factor 4*

| | Never | Seldom | Some-times | Often |
|---|---|---|---|---|
| (1) Whipping or spanking someone | 0 | 1 | 2 | 3 |
| (2) Being whipped or spanked | 0 | 1 | 2 | 3 |
| (3) Tying someone up | 0 | 1 | 2 | 3 |
| (4) Being tied up | 0 | 1 | 2 | 3 |
| (5) Exposing yourself provocatively | 0 | 1 | 2 | 3 |
| (6) Teasing a partner to distraction | 0 | 1 | 2 | 3 |
| (7) Forcing someone to do something | 0 | 1 | 2 | 3 |
| (8) Being forced to do something | 0 | 1 | 2 | 3 |

Total Score on Fantasy Factor 4 ☐

*Scoring your fantasies*

Notice that the fantasies in the questionnaire are grouped into four sections. These correspond to the four main types of fantasy – exploratory, intimate, impersonal and sadomasochistic. For each type, add up the numbers that you have put circles around. This will give you four scores somewhere in the range of 0–24. The following notes will give you some indication of what these scores mean.

### Fantasy Factor 1: Exploratory

If you have scored more than 12 on this category you have strong urges towards excitement and variety in your sex life. High scores are characteristic of people with high libido (sex drive) and are much more typical of men than women: 4–12 puts you in the average range (4–8 for women and 6–12 for men), and less than 4 indicates that you prefer a stable, unexciting existence. Since most of us translate our fantasies into action at some time or another there is a good chance that if you have a high score you will have engaged in extramarital or premarital sex.

### Fantasy Factor 2: Intimate

A score of more than 15 puts you in the high range here. This means that you seek and enjoy deep involvement with a limited number of sex partners (perhaps only one). In all probability you have a steady partner with whom you are satisfied and in love. Men and women do not differ very much in average scores on this category, which are around 5–15. Less than this and you are probably not given to intimate sexual behaviour within the context of deep personal relationships. Either you are uninterested in sex or you adopt a very casual, playful attitude towards it.

### Fantasy Factor 3: Impersonal

Scores of more than 10 may be regarded as high on this factor. This indicates an interest in fetish objects, clothes, films and other indirect representations of sex with relatively little value on the personality and feelings of the partner. This tendency is much more common in men, and when women do develop such interests they are often secondary to those of their partner, being cultivated in order to please him. The result is that they tend to be associated with high sex drive in men but with intimacy and satisfaction in women. Average scores are about 3–8 in men and 1–4 in women.

### Fantasy Factor 4: Sadomasochistic

The interpretation of this category is fairly straightforward. High scorers (say more than 8) associate the giving and receiving of pain with sexual excitement. Most of them are quite content to keep it in the realm of fantasy and do not extend it to their actual behaviour in the bedroom, though they might play little games of bondage, slavery or spanking in which mild and well-controlled pain is inflicted for purposes of titillation. This interest is again more common in men than women and (contrary to some people's opinion) the predilections for sadism and masochism tend to go together in the same person. Average scores here are around 2–6 for men and 0–4 for women. Low scores in both men and women tend to go with reports of a satisfying love-life – although we cannot tell yet whether this connection comes about because such people are concerned about making a good impression when they fill in the questionnaire.*

These comments on how to interpret your questionnaire scores tell some of the main findings of Wilson's survey. Firstly, all the different fantasies tend to go together in the sense that having a high score on one factor raises the chances that you will score high on the others. In technical terms this means that there is a *general factor* in the domain of sexual fantasy. Evidence from this study as well as that of Hariton and Singer suggests that this general factor reflects an underlying disposition that we

* *Note:* This simplified form of the research questionnaire was prepared for the *She* magazine serialization of *The Secrets of Sexual Fantasy* and is reproduced here by kind permission of the Editor.

could call 'level of libido'. The importance of this factor in sexual behaviour and attitudes is laid out in Chapter 3 of this book, and it is gratifying to find it confirmed here in the field of fantasies. Also in Chapter 3, evidence for a genetic basis to libido is presented, its probable involvement with the male hormone testosterone, and its impetus towards aggressive and exploratory sexual behaviour. In Wilson's study, fairly direct evidence of a connection between sexual fantasy and libido was obtained by asking respondents a number of key questions about their sex lives. Of these, the most central questions were: 'Overall, how would you rate your sex drive? (very low; lower than average; average; higher than average; very high). How many orgasms do you have in an average week? And how many different people have you had intercourse with?' Although none of these questions taken by themselves are perfect measures of libido each views it from a different angle to build up a good overall picture of sex drive. Anyway, high scores on each of the four fantasy factors were associated with the sex drive ratings, orgasm frequency and experience of different partners, supporting the idea that a high libido is manifested in high levels of fantasy as well as activity. This connection was stronger for women than for men (perhaps because women are more variable in libido) but it emerged fairly reliably for men as well.

Before moving on to the other findings of this survey, there are other studies which support this connection between sexual activity and fantasy. J. Brown and D. Hart of the University of Utah found that sexually experienced women reported twice as much fantasy as virgins and that the highest rates of sex fantasy occurred between the ages of twenty-one and thirty-five (corresponding to the peak of sexual activity and incidentally the most favourable child-bearing period in a woman's life). L. Giambra and C. Martin, studying 277 men in the Baltimore area, found the amount of sex fantasy to be related to the number of different partners they had had, their frequency of intercourse during the first year or two of marriage and, in older men, the number of sexual events they could recall between the ages of twenty and forty. In this study, the amount of sexual fantasy reported declined steadily from the age of twenty onwards, so that men aged sixty to seventy were reporting only half the amount of fantasy as the twenty to thirty year olds. Clearly, age has a very powerful influence on libido. As men get older, it drops off, you might say. Women, on the other hand, seem to build up to a peak with increasing experience until at least their early thirties before a similar decline sets in.

Some people, including most psychoanalysts, have supposed that sexual fantasies are engaged in as a substitute for actually performing a given act. The survey findings show that the reverse is far more likely to be the case. In the original questionnaire respondents were asked to state the frequency with which they thought about each theme on each of three occasions separately (in the daytime, during intercourse or masturbation, and in dreams while asleep). They were also asked whether they had actually done that thing, if so how often, and whether they would like to do it in the future. There was a high correspondence in the answers to each of these questions. Thus, if a person fantasized about orgies in the daytime, he was also more likely to have fantasies about orgies at other times, to wish to participate in an orgy and actually to have attended orgies in the past. Fantasies, then, are positively connected to the actual behaviour either through memories or desires and there is no evidence that they act as substitutes for behaviour. If anything, dreams seemed to comprise the odd man out, but this might have been due to the fact that most people had great difficulty in recalling their dreams and attaching frequency scores to the different themes.

The scoring instructions for the above questionnaire also indicate that large sex differences were found in the survey. In fact, men reported more fantasies of all kinds than women. This was especially true of the exploratory, impersonal and sadomasochistic factors; on the intimate factor there was only a marginal difference in 'favour' of men. This overall picture is supported by analysis of answers to a final question on the research questionnaire which asked respondents to pick out the single theme from the complete list that they personally found most exciting of all. The most popular choice for both men and women was 'intercourse with a loved partner'. About one-quarter of both men and women chose this as their number one fantasy (which is bound to be a disappointment to the readers of *Forum*), but thereafter the sex differences were quite striking. Women were often greatly excited by 'making love out of doors in a romantic setting', 'kissing passionately' and 'receiving oral sex' (all items from the intimate factor) while the men more often chose promiscuity, seduction, homosexuality, orgies, whipping and spanking, giving oral sex, and having sex with someone of different race (mostly exploratory themes). These differences are consistent with some of the differences between men and women in temperament and sexual behaviour that are discussed in Chapter 2. Men generally show a greater interest in sexual adventure, are more active in initiating sexual behaviour, and are more given to kinky, impersonal activities. The argument that men are just more willing to admit to such anti-social tendencies is not very convincing considering that the questionnaire was filled in anonymously and that women were equally willing to cooperate by returning it. If women were relatively shy about revealing details of their sex lives and fantasies then this should extend to a reluctance to participate in the research in the first place. No such tendency was observed. It is also difficult to see how social pressures could be entirely responsible for some of the less obvious differences such as that seen between active and passive preferences. The questionnaire was constructed so that many of the fantasy items appeared in active and passive form, e.g. 'forcing someone to have sex', 'being forced to have sex'; 'giving oral sex', 'receiving oral sex'. When scores were derived for these active and passive categories separately the results in Figure 5 were obtained. Whereas men have slightly more active than passive fantasies, the women are very much more given to passive than active themes. A hormonal basis to this difference seems very likely in view of the evidence presented in Chapter 2.

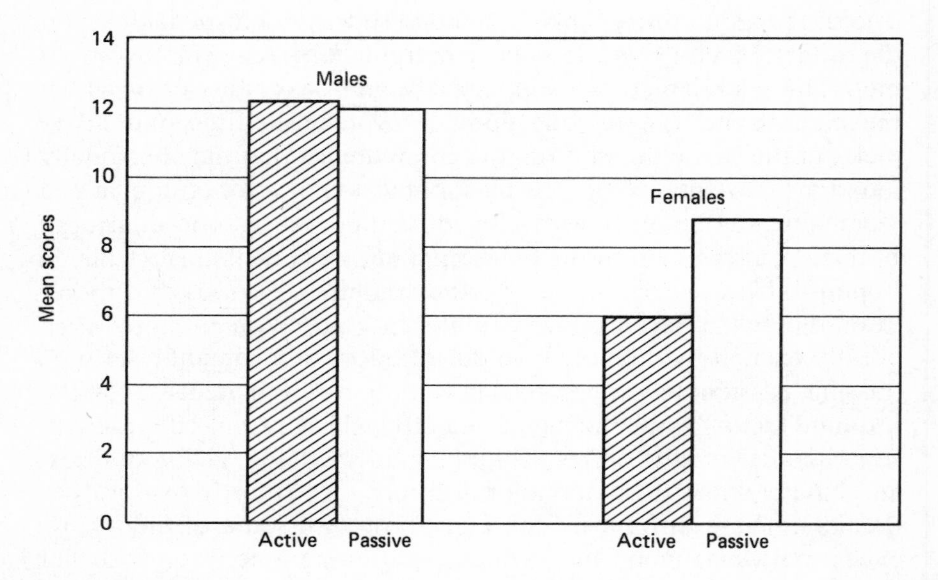


Figure 5 Comparison of men and women on active and passive fantasy scores

Incidentally, it is noteworthy that factor analysis did not naturally produce a dimension of activity versus passivity, even though the questionnaire was partly designed with this idea in mind. In a book called *The Fantasy Factor*, psychiatrist Peter Dally had proposed a factor of sadism versus masochism as the major principle of organization in the field. Everyone, he thought, would tend towards one or the other of these poles and their basically sadistic (dominant) or masochistic (submissive) orientation would permeate all their dealings with the world and the people in it, apart from its obvious manifestation in bedrooms and brothels. Our statistical analysis, however, has revealed a very powerful sadomasochism factor that is unipolar rather than bipolar. Sadism and masochism do not seem to be opposites; instead they appear together in the same person, or else not at all. Thus people who fantasize about whipping and spanking someone are usually the same people who fantasize about being whipped and spanked. People who think about hurting their partner also think about being hurt, and so on. This may seem counter-intuitive to some, but it is a very clear finding in our survey. What is more, the positive correlation extends to actual behaviour as well as fantasies. Responses to the 'have done in reality' column in our questionnaire show that people who whip and spank also get whipped and spanked, etc. Confirmation also comes from a study by Andreas Spengler (1977) of 245 male members of German sadomasochistic clubs. Only a minority were orientated in an exclusively sadistic or masochistic direction; most of the men in the sample alternated between these two roles. Therefore, it seems that while it is possible to score fantasies so as to differentiate active and passive preferences, this distinction is normally overridden by the more powerful factor of sadomasochism versus non-sadomasochism.

Another key question that went with Wilson's questionnaire concerned the extent to which respondents were satisfied with their sex life. Since the replies to this question were reasonably independent of the libido factor (in accord with the findings of Eysenck reported in Chapter 3) it is possible to arrange the fantasies within a two-dimensional diagram according to the extent to which they are associated with each factor. This has been done in Figure 6. As already noted, nearly all of the fantasies go with a high libido, especially in women. (The only fantasy that shows any real association with low libido is the incest fantasy in men, and the reason for this is not obvious.) As regards the satisfaction dimension, there is an interesting difference between men and women. With women, most of the fantasies go with reports of a satisfying sex life, whereas the fantasies of men are associated with feelings of dissatisfaction. This is a new finding, and again one that is not easily explained in terms of sex-role learning. Probably the best explanation is in terms of supply and demand. To a large extent, sexual pleasure is a commodity that is demanded by men and supplied (on condition) by women. If we accept that men have on average a greater lust for sexual adventure than women (because of their greater saturation with testosterone or whatever reason) then they are bound to have greater difficulty finding female partners with (or upon) whom to fulfil their desires. The result will be an excess of males with unfulfilled fantasies who therefore complain about unsatisfactory sex lives. By corollary, the few unusual women who are full of male-type lust, and who are likely to be labelled nymphomaniacs (by moralists posing as psychiatrists), will have little difficulty finding sexual diversion among the vast untapped pool of male lechery. Therefore they will not go unsatisfied for long. The validity of this argument is supported by the finding both in this study and in Eysenck's work that men score consistently higher on libido than women but women report more satisfaction with their sex lives. Another explanation, perhaps supplementary to the first, is that female fantasies are stimulated by, and to some extent dependent upon, an intimate sexual relationship with a man. Whereas the sex drive of the male is a steady imperative, women may have the capacity to turn off and become sexually quiescent for a long time if they are without a partner. This kind of variability in the female sex drive according to current biochemical and environmental conditions has frequently been postulated by keen observers – for example, it is widely supposed that women make better nuns than men do priests. Whatever the reason, it is clear that fantasy plays a different role in the lives of men and women respectively, and no amount of feminist propaganda or legislation is likely to alter this position.

Other major differences between the fantasies of men and women emerged clearly in a study by Andrew Barclay of Michigan State University. He had large samples of college men and women write out their favourite fantasies in full narrative form and subjected these to a content analysis. The fantasies of men were found to have a

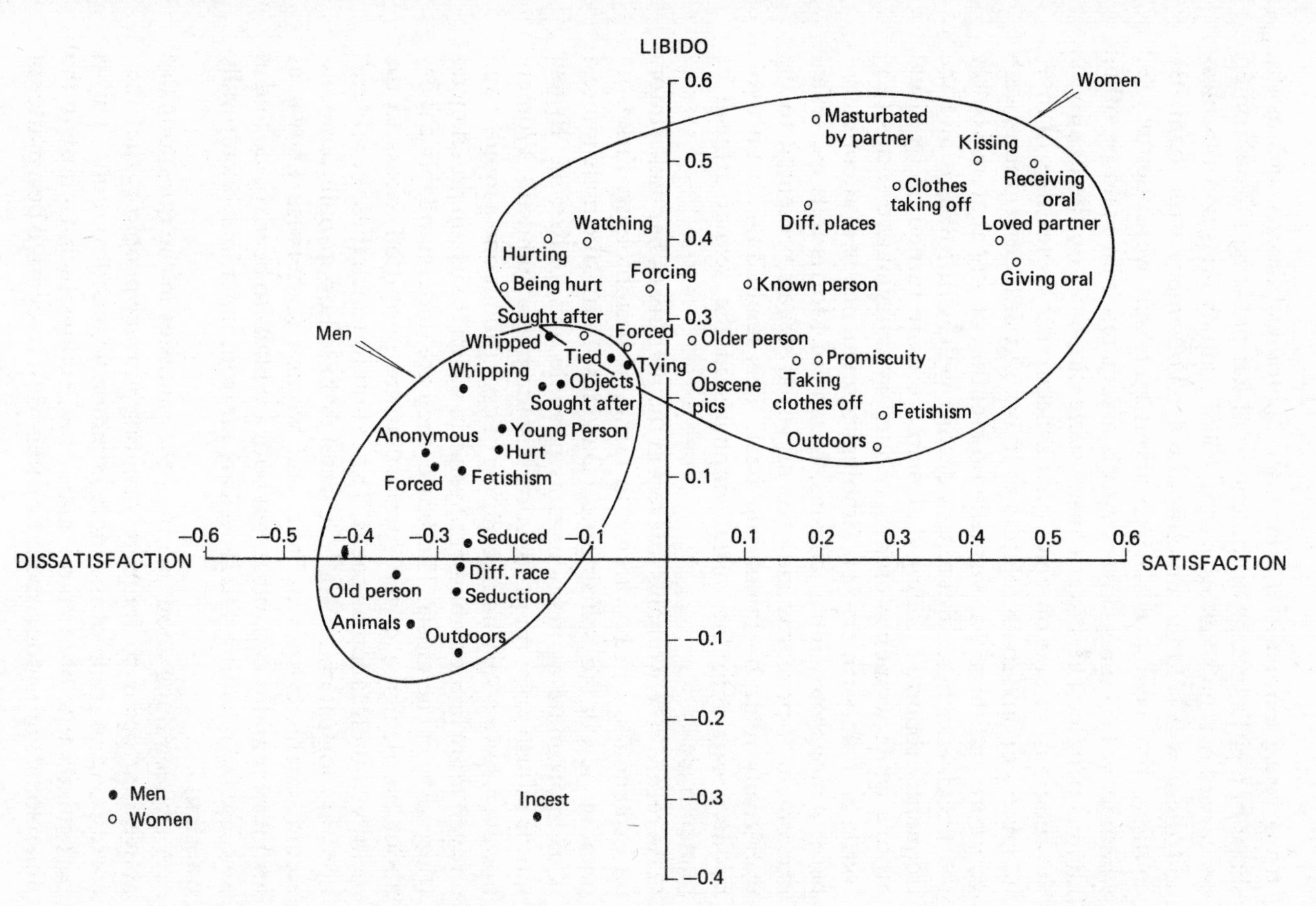


Figure 6 Fantasies during intercourse and masturbation related to libido and satisfaction

strong visual emphasis and included anatomical details such as the shape of a girl's breasts or the colour of her pubic hair. The women concerned in men's fantasies were usually anonymous if not faceless and there was seldom any emotional involvement with them. By contrast, the women fantasized about men that were identifiable, whether as husbands, lovers, work associates, film stars or other famous people. There was considerable emphasis on the quality of the relationship and on emotional aspects such as feelings of love, happiness or anxiety in relation to it, but physical descriptions were very rare and there was virtually no mention of any anatomy below the neckline. These differences accord well with folklore and the frequently reported finding that men are more turned on by visual erotica while women prefer more literary, imaginative forms (e.g. Byrne & Lamberth, 1971). Ethological evidence is also consistent here. Among our simian cousins, Desmond Morris tells us, sexual excitement is primarily initiated by visual signals presented to the ever-ready male by females in heat. This could suggest an evolutionary origin to the visual emphasis in the sexual arousal of human males.

As regards the woman's interest in the identity of her male suitors an explanation can be offered in terms of sociobiology. From the point of view of the 'selfish gene' (Dawkins, 1976), the male interest is to impregnate as many eggs as possible and, unlike the British motor industry, sperm production is seldom at a standstill. Women, however, have a very limited supply of eggs (about one a month) and an even more limited number of years in which to sustain pregnancies (thirty-five at the most). Therefore, they are understandably choosy about the pedigree of the sperm that are permitted access to the vicinity of their fallopian tubes. The extent to which these considerations are logical and socially learned or based on in-built temperamental characteristics of men and women (otherwise known as instincts) remains debatable, but both are likely to be involved and in any case the resulting differences are far from superficial or culturally transient.

A striking thing about many of the fantasies in the questionnaire above that occur so frequently among normal people is that they correspond to some of the more common sexual deviations. This is particularly true of the more male predilections such as those in the impersonal and sadomasochistic categories. It seems to be a matter of degree or emphasis whether people are content to hold the fantasy in their head, perhaps calling upon it sometimes to assist orgasm in masturbation or arousal in heterosexual intercourse, or whether there is a need to act it out in some way. And when a fantasy is acted out there are again degrees of deviation ranging from bedroom role-playing with a lover or spouse, through elaborate rituals involving prostitutes and paraphernalia, to outright criminal behaviour such as that of rapists, rippers and pederasts. Some of the more common sexual deviations (or 'variations' as they are increasingly coming to be called) are as follows:

| *Deviation* | *Basis of Arousal* |
|---|---|
| Fetishism | Non-human objects, e.g. shoes, stockings, leather. |
| Partialism | Particular aspects of the body such as ankles or knees. |
| Transvestism | Dressing in clothes of the opposite sex. |
| Exhibitionism | Exposure of the genitals to an unwilling viewer. |
| Voyeurism | Peeping at other people undressing or having sex. |
| Incest | Sexual relationship with a close family member, e.g. daughter, sister. |
| Rape | Sexual assault on an unwilling adult. |
| Paedophilia | Sexual contact with children. |
| Sadism | Inflicting pain on another person. |
| Masochism | Having pain inflicted upon oneself. |
| Urolagnia | Urinating on another person or being urinated upon. |
| Coprophilia | Defecation or faeces. |
| Frotteurism | Rubbing the genitals on other people in a crowd. |
| Necrophilia | Intercourse with dead people. |
| Bestiality | Intercourse with animals; masturbating animals. |

If there is one thing on which the psychoanalysts and behavioural psychologists agree it is the importance of sexual fantasy in the origins of sexual deviation. Freud's earliest theory of neurosis attributed most of our problems to the experience of seduction in early childhood, usually by a parent, nurse or some other adult in a position of care. Memories of this early traumatic incident were thought to underlie a great variety of neurotic symptoms from phobias to frigidity. Unfortunately, Freud's investigations failed to turn up any proof that his patients had in fact been seduced in infancy so eventually he modified his theory to say that *fantasies* of such seduction are responsible for difficulties in adulthood. Most modern psychologists do not take this idea very seriously; nevertheless, Freud was probably right in drawing attention to the importance of sexual fantasy in the mediation of sexual behaviour.

One of the most promising modern theories of sexual deviation is that of Ralph McGuire and his colleagues in Glasgow. They suggest that at some time during childhood or puberty the individual has an experience which is both emotionally arousing and sexual in connotation. Since this is usually the first memorable sexual event experienced by the individual it will often seem somewhat immature or indirect from the adult perspective. Anyway, this experience is used by the individual as an aid to masturbation and the pleasure obtained in this way 'reinforces' the fantasy as a sexual stimulus. Very likely the fantasy that is used during masturbation evolves in certain ways to accommodate other significant experiences from the past or present. If it becomes sufficiently powerful and exclusive as a determinant of sexual arousal it is likely at some point to be translated into action and if this action is very unorthodox or unacceptable we will label it deviant.

Take exhibitionists or 'flashers' as an example. These are men who feel a compulsion to expose their genitals to unwilling females in public places. Usually their sexual excitement depends upon a reaction of shock and disgust on the part of the lady victim; if she responds with amusement or derision they are usually disappointed and retreat sheepishly. There are around 2000 convictions for 'indecent exposure' in England each year, most of them involving men with a history of similar offences. No women are convicted of any parallel offence, and although men would be unlikely to complain to the authorities if a strange woman was to lift her skirt in a park or railway carriage, very few seem motivated to do so. McGuire's explanation of a typical case of self-exposure is along the following lines. A pubescent boy is urinating behind a tree when he is surprised by a passing lady who reacts with surprise and embarrassment. Although the incident is not necessarily experienced as either sexual and pleasant at the time, it comes into his mind when he is subsequently masturbating, possibly because the two events share common associations with guilt and genital protrusion. The pleasure of orgasm reinforces the excitement potential of the fantasy and increases the likelihood that it will be used again on the next occasion of masturbation. And so on, through a cycle of masturbation, fantasy and orgasm, a scenario which is some modification of the original incident acquires exclusive control of the boy's sexual arousal. While some such individuals find it possible to contain the idea within their fantasies, others apparently have a need to 'top up the batteries' with a real-life run every two or three weeks.

If we accept this explanation so far, there are some interesting implications to consider. First, it may help to explain why masturbation has been declared taboo in a majority of cultures (Ford & Beach, 1951). Europeans in the Victorian era, for example, attributed all kinds of physical, psychological and moral degeneration to the practice. Now we see there is a sense in which they may have been right; there are certain dangers in 'self-abuse' if socially unacceptable stimuli for arousal are being stamped in as a result of it. (This, is not to say of course, that any attempt to police the practice will be effective.) Secondly, the theory may help to explain why sexual deviation is so much more common in men than women. Men masturbate more than women and are therefore more likely to build up impersonal and unloving fantasies.

Predictions about the sort of man who is most vulnerable to sexual deviation can also be made on the basis of this theory. Men who are shy and socially withdrawn would be especially susceptible because, lacking the social skills with which to obtain normal heterosexual experience, they would have to depend longer on fantasy and masturbation for their sexual satisfaction. There is empirical evidence that rubber fetishists as a group tend to be rather shy and prudish (Gosselin, 1979) and a strong clinical impression that the same applies to voyeurs and paedophiles. It has also been found that sexual deviates of many different kinds continue masturbation into adulthood more than normals (Goldstein *et al*., 1971). Thus it seems that there is some truth to the stereotype picture of the 'pervert' as a socially 'inadequate' person. However, the importance of the personality factor as a causative influence is yet to be fully assessed; it is possible that the prior existence of the deviation is responsible for the social difficulties that are observed rather than the other way around.

We can also ask what effects pornography might be expected to have in the light of this theory. The answer is interesting because it seems to reconcile the two opposing arguments that pornography (a) precipitates sexual deviation and (b) gives immunity against the likelihood of deviation occurring. According to the present theory, early and continuous exposure to a wide variety of explicit sexual stimuli would lessen the chance that any one incident in early puberty would stand out as having striking significance when wet dreams and masturbation begin. Rather the fantasies and memories adopted would vary around a number heterosexual themes and thus lead naturally to an interest in girls as sex objects. On the other hand, if a child is protected from all sources of sexual stimulation until the age when his hormones will magnify the sexual excitement with which he is programmed to respond, then 'accidental' occurrences will take on special salience. Such events may include being surprised by a lady while urinating behind a bush or seeing a photograph of a nude woman wielding a whip. In such cases, can we say that the pornographic picture was responsible for the deviation, or the closeted upbringing? Both may be necessary, and since it is virtually impossible to ensure that a boy will never encounter deviant stimuli it might be wise to saturate the environment with 'normal' heterosexual sources of arousal.

The final implication of the McGuire theory of sexual deviation concerns the most appropriate method of treatment. If the deviant sex object has attained its strength through the reinforcement of masturbatory fantasies, then it follows that the best way to weaken it and replace it with something more acceptable is through a process of *fantasy retraining*. Several therapists have claimed success with this kind of approach. For example, J. Marquis, in California, treated fourteen patients by instructing them to masturbate using their favourite fantasy almost until orgasm, at which point they switched to another fantasy that had previously been chosen as more desirable. After doing this a few times they were told to start moving the desirable fantasy backwards in time towards the beginning of masturbation. In this way, the desirable fantasy eventually gained in excitement potential while the deviant fantasy became progressively unnecessary. Apparently, Marquis had succeeded in breaking the link between the deviant sex object and sexual arousal. At the same time, he had given his patients a more satisfactory basis for excitement. It is too soon to say how good this method for treating sexual deviation really is, but if the early indications of effectiveness are confirmed it is bound to be a very useful innovation. It can also be taken as support for the McGuire theory of the origins of sexual fixations and compulsions.

Fantasy incubation is not the only basis of sexual deviation. Genetic factors are bound to be involved, if only mediated through personality differences in susceptibility to various kinds of conditioning. There is one fascinating case report of a rubber fetishism having developed independently in a pair of identical twins (Gorman, 1964). One twin could recall an initial pleasurable experience at the age of five when he was laid on a rubber sheet by his mother after taking a bath. Rubbing his body against the rubber produced an exciting sensation which he sought to repeat frequently thereafter. The other twin reported a similar formative incident at the age of six and the development of his fetish followed a similar course. Neither knew of the other's interest in rubber until they compared notes at the age of ten. The fetish persisted into adulthood with both twins reporting similar fantasies and practices. While one had sought psychiatric advice on the prompting of his wife, neither had any real interest in giving up their fetish; they regarded it as something 'natural' in their make-up. In the classic twin studies of Kallmann one pair of identical twins who were transvestites was found as well as many who were concordant on homosexuality. Subsequently, however, a number of identical twins have been found that were not concordant on homosexuality (i.e. one was homosexual and the other heterosexual) so genetics cannot be solely responsible for this variation. At the moment it is difficult to assess the extent to which genetic factors are involved in sexual proclivities. A more comprehensive twin study of this question currently under way at the Institute of Psychiatry should provide us with a much better idea of the relative importance of genetic and environmental factors in determining the arousal value of the items given in the fantasy questionnaire above. 'It's the way I'm made' may turn out to be a much better explanation of kinky tendencies than the recent environmentalist Zeitgeist has led us to believe.

Apart from genetics, there are other biological factors likely to be involved in sexual preferences. Animal research and clinical studies of children born of mothers treated with hormones (see Chapter 2) have shown that adult sexual behaviour can be influenced by biochemical factors during embryonic development, particularly in the latter third of pregnancy. Sometimes the body and sex organs are simultaneously affected, but this is not necessarily always the case. The brain being the most delicate and finely tuned of all our organs can have its function modified without gross anatomical effects.

Subtle brain injuries occurring during or after birth may also have an effect on sexual behaviour. Lesions in the temporal lobe have been found to be associated with fetish-like behaviour (Epstein, 1961) and it may turn out that other sex deviations with compulsive characteristics, e.g. many cases of transvestism, exhibitionism and habitual rape, are also due to minor brain injuries. The parallels with epilepsy are quite appealing – these practices often occur cyclically (e.g. regularly every month or so) and they may be experienced as a compulsion or occur during a state of dissociation like sleep-walking.

Straightforward conditioning processes, without the McGuire fantasy build-up, are also likely to be involved in sexual deviation. In the final chapter we describe an experiment by S. Rachman in which 'fetishes' were induced in normal males by showing them boot pictures shortly before pictures of nude women. This is evidence for the positive conditioning of new sexual stimuli. More easily demonstrated is the negative kind of conditioning which in extreme form is manifested in phobias. Some sex deviates appear to gravitate towards unorthodox sexual outlets such as children or impersonal objects because these are seen as less threatening than adults of the opposite sex. Such individuals may have had a very unpleasant experience or series of experiences with the opposite sex leading to the impression that they are not very approachable. Or, as the psychoanalysts suggest, the relationship with the opposite sex parent might have been such as to put them off heterosexuality. In this connection it has often been noted that homosexual men have domineering mothers and weak or absent fathers; though it is not possible to assume simple cause and effect here, some homosexual men may have acquired a generalized image of women as rather fearsome creatures who are not to be trifled with.

This does not mean that we can easily predict a person's sex orientation from a knowledge of the personality of their parents. In all kinds of conditioning the precise timing is important as well as the stimuli that are available to be conditioned. When the Rachman experiment was repeated with the boot pictures coming after the nudes instead of before, no fetish-like connection between them could be achieved. This was an important check that Pavlovian conditioning was involved for it is a major principle of such conditioning that the neutral stimulus should precede the arousing stimulus, preferably by a very short period of time. A recent experiment by

Kantorowitz (1978) has shown that a stimulus occurring just *before* orgasm will be enhanced in arousal power, while the same stimulus occurring just *after* orgasm will have diminished power to excite us in the future. In this experiment pictures of nude women were shown to men either in the tumescence phase of masturbation or the detumescence phase (after orgasm) and the extent to which these same pictures were capable of arousing them was later tested. This may explain why people who use pornography as an aid to masturbation usually report that they put it quickly out of their sight after orgasm; no doubt they are afraid that it will lose its usefulness if it becomes associated with satisfaction rather than excitement. Also, women often complain that their husbands turn over and face away from them immediately after intercourse. Rather than feeling slighted they should consider the possibility that he is doing them a favour by preventing dearousal from becoming conditioned to the sight of their features or nude body. Be that as it may, the simple availability of a stimulus (or fantasy image for that matter) does not predetermine the kind of conditioning that will take place – time relations are critical.

Also critical is the nature of the stimulus. There is a distinct limit on the range of articles that lend themselves to the development of a fetish interest. Usually they are parts of the body, e.g. feet, or hair of a particular length, some article of clothing (shoes or underwear), or some material (fur, silk, leather or rubber). Nobody in our experience has reported a lawn-mower fetish or a dining-room table fetish. It is not surprising that clothing is so often associated with sexual arousal since sexual activity is usually preceded by its removal. What is more, our early sexual encounters usually involve a partner who remains at least partly clothed throughout the performance. The special attraction of leather and rubber is probably due to the fact that they resemble the skin in texture more than most materials. There are also certain sadomasochistic connotations to them in that they are often used in devices of restraint and flagellation. Fur and silk are the opposite in most respects, being soft and feminine both in touch and association. Also, it may be no accident that these materials will produce static electricity when rubbed with suitable other materials.

It is impossible to leave the topic of sexual preferences without mentioning the concept of imprinting. This term was adopted by ethologists to describe the way in which baby ducklings will follow and seek protection from the first moving object they see that remotely resembles their mother. Similar inflexible devotion is seen when the human infant attaches itself to a particular toy or blanket without which it will have difficulty in getting to sleep. This type of learning occurs only at critical periods of development and not always in early infancy. It happens quite suddenly at a particular moment in time and thereafter rewards and punishments have little effect upon it. The acquisition of language, food fads, musical taste and many other preferences involves some of the characteristics of imprinting and there is increasing consensus among clinicians and researchers that imprinting processes are involved in the origins of sexual deviations such as fetishism, transvestism and sadomasochism. The eminent sex researcher J. Money believes that sexual object choice occurs as a result of imprinting at an early age. This, he says, 'would explain why an adolescent or adult, safely past the critical period, can be forced or induced into an aberrant sexual experience without becoming a chronic practitioner of that experience'. Of course genetic and constitutional theories (e.g. prenatal hormone influences) would also explain why adult experiences do not have much impact on sex orientation. In fact, the imprinting theory is difficult to distinguish either from the constitutional theories or the McGuire fantasy reinforcement theory. Nevertheless, the animal models provided by ethologists studying imprinting processes are unmistakably relevant to the origins of sexual deviation.

The last approach to the understanding of sexual fantasy, arousal and deviation is equally fraught with theoretical difficulties but equally difficult to ignore. This is the approach which emphasizes the symbolic meaning of stimuli and behaviour. Often sexual excitement is dependent on a very specific sequence of events in which particular characters behave and say things in carefully prescribed order. For example, Gagnon (1977) describes the case of a man who was in most respects highly conventional and successful in his profession but who felt a need to visit a prostitute about once a month to act out a fantasy. The ritual was the same each time. He took off all his clothes and had a sheet pinned around him like a nappy. She wore a nursemaid's uniform and sat demurely next to him, pretending to be in the park. They engaged in child-nurse talk in which she instructed him to be a good little boy, not to have bad thoughts and not to talk to strangers. After a while she said 'I'm going to have to go away and you must not talk to anyone while I'm gone. You must be a very good little boy.' He promised that he would, but about fifteen minutes later she returned in an erotic costume (short black dress, garters, sexy make-up, etc.). Sitting beside him again, she tried to engage him in 'dirty' conversation and get him to touch her. After appropriate dithering refusals on his part, she took his hand and put it on her breast while he sat there highly aroused. She then left and returned a little while later as the nursemaid. He denied any wrongdoing but she wormed a confession out of him and then punished him physically. After a tearful reconciliation in which he promised never to do it again, he got dressed, paid her and returned to his very conventional life.

What are we to make of this little dramatic sequence? Simple conditioning or imprinting do not seem to provide an adequate explanation. It seems to require interpretation in terms of the different meanings that women have for this man and his need to follow sexual pleasure with expiation. He appears to have two concepts of women, one is motherly and provides a combination of nurturance and discipline. The other is sinful and erotic, providing pleasure and arousal. Perhaps the sequence above satisfies a need in him to reconcile these two important facets of women. Does he need to feel sexually desirable on the one hand and yet loved for his virtue on the other? Does the masochistic component in the ritual enable him to enjoy sex with a reduced burden of guilt because he is being punished at the same time? It is difficult to even guess at the dynamics involved, let alone verify them scientifically, yet analysis at this metaphorical level seems inescapable. The man is not mad, for at other times his behaviour is sensible and orderly. Anyway serial fantasies of this kind, or 'scripts' as they are sometimes called, are reported by quite a high proportion of people. It is important to try to understand these sequences because they are almost certainly prototypic of the rituals acted out by most vicious sex criminals such as Jack the Ripper, the Boston Strangler and Charles Manson. Hardly a year goes by without some community being terrorized by a compulsive sex maniac. In recent years in England there was the Cambridge Rapist, who donned a black leather hood to rape girls at the point of a knife, and, still at large at the time of writing, the Yorkshire Ripper, who once a month or so picks up a prostitute only to leave her brutally slashed body on some waste ground. Quite clearly, sexual gratification is not the only motivation involved in these rituals. In fact, it may be quite unimportant or even non-existent. Attitudes toward women, the need to dominate or be dominated, to aggress or be punished, are more often central to such fantasies and practices. In this sense, the sex killers are probably more similar to kleptomaniacs and pyromaniacs (people with compulsions to steal or start fires) than they are to the more harmless sex deviates. Attitudes to sex are also often involved; many of these individuals seem to have a high libido but regard sex as 'dirty' and unacceptable, and their ghastly crimes seem to be some kind of function of this conflict.

Psychiatrist Robert Stoller has produced a theory of sexual excitement and deviation which purports to explain why so many of our fantasies are sadomasochistic and why sex is so often linked to aggression in our mythology. He suggests that sexual arousal depends upon a certain amount of hostility towards the object of our lust, and that sexual satisfaction is in some sense equivalent to the feeling of revenge. At some time in early childhood, he supposes, we have been wronged by a parent or other person in dominant relation to us. As a consequence we build up a fantasy story which repeats many of the events and circumstances surrounding the original, formative incident, but with the ending rewritten so that we emerge triumphant. Thus do we reverse the injustice that was done to us in infancy every time the fantasy is rehearsed. Presumably the moment of triumph in this scenario coincides with orgasm. This theory, he says, accounts for many phenomena associated with sexual behaviour such as the ambivalence we very often feel towards our sex partners, the greater ease with which we are excited by novel partners, the popularity of sadomasochistic foreplay and the atrocities committed by sex maniacs.

It is an interesting idea, but again difficult if not impossible to verify. Also, there are other possible explanations of the link between sex and aggression. Ethologists tell us that the pattern of courtship in other animals frequently begins with a kind of fight between the partners in which the female is eventually subdued by the greater strength and speed of the male and then submits to love-making as an act of appeasement. Such a pattern is often observed in human lovers or married couples, and many people claim that their love-making is never better than when making up after a violent row. Since this instinctual pattern of male aggression in sexual approach is not acceptable to our civilized society, it is perhaps not surprising that it emerges in the form of fantasies of sadism, rape, humiliation, etc. and, in some cases, acts of this kind.

In trying to understand the origins of sexual excitement and deviation we are grappling with a complex and seemingly intransigent problem. Yet it is a socially important problem, and exactly the sort that psychology should be concerned with. Therefore it is a pity that more inroads have not been made into this territory. At least we are now in a position to appreciate the components that must go to make up a comprehensive and adequate theory. It will need to take account of genetic and other biological factors which determine differences between men and women as well as variations in temperament and sex orientation within each sex. It will also need to take account of various different kinds of learning, from the very primitive, inflexible (and usually emotional) kinds like imprinting and Pavlovian conditioning to the higher cognitive and symbolic learning processes that are a product of our advanced intelligence and civilization.

With the recent increase in permissiveness in society we have been able to undertake new research into these intimate areas which has revealed a hitherto undreamed of variety of fantasies and behaviour in people who are normal in the sense that they have not sought treatment or run afoul of the law. Such a high proportion of people, especially males, admit some special preference, predilection, or proclivity that would have been thought of as kinky if not downright filthy and immoral from a conventional perspective, that the very word 'normal' needs careful respecification. If normal means free of pathology then most of us are fairly normal. But if it means having no special 'turn-ons' that are statistically uncommon, then all of us are probably a little bit perverted. The greatest mistake that we can make in this area, and one that is still being made by legislators, is to assume that everybody else in the world is exactly like us, or that if they are not they ought to be.

## References


BARCLAY, A.M., 'Sexual fantasies in men and women', *Medical Aspects of Sexuality*, 1973, **7**, 205–16.

BROWN, J.J. & HART, D.H., 'Correlates of females' sexual fantasies', *Perceptual and Motor Skills*, 1977, **45**, 819–25.

BYRNE, D. & LAMBERTH, J., 'The effect of erotic stimuli on sex arousal, evaluative responses and subsequent behaviour', in *Technical Report of the Commission on Obscenity and Pornography, Vol. III.* Washington DC: US Government Printing Office, 1971.

DALLY, P., *The Fantasy Factor*. London: Weidenfeld and Nicolson, 1975.

DAWKINS, R., *The Selfish Game.* Oxford: Oxford University Press, 1976.

EPSTEIN, A.W., 'Relationship of fetishism and transvestism to brain and particularly to temporal lobe dysfunction', *Journal of Nervous and Mental Diseases*, 1961, **133**, 247–53.

FORD, C.S. & BEACH, F.A., *Patterns of Sexual Behaviour.* New York: Harper and Row, 1951.

GAGNON, J., *Human Sexualities.* Glenview, Ill.: Scott-Foresman, 1977.

GIAMBRA, L.M. & MARTIN, C.E., 'Sexual daydreams and quantitative aspects of sexual activity: some relations for males across adulthood', *Archives of Sexual Behaviour*, 1977, **6**, 497–505.

GOLDSTEIN, M.J., KANT, H.S., JUDD, L.L., RICE, C.J. & GREEN, R., 'Exposure to pornography and sexual behaviour in deviant and normal groups', in *Technical Report of the Commission on Obscenity and Pornography, Vol. VII.* Washington DC: US Government Printing Office, 1971.

GORMAN, G.F., 'Fetishism occurring in identical twins', *British Journal of Psychiatry*, 1964, **110**, 255–6.

GOSSELIN, C., 'Personality attributes of the average rubber fetishist', in M. Cook and G.D. Wilson (eds), *Love and Attraction: An International Conference*. London: Pergamon, 1979.

HARITON, E.B. & SINGER, J.L., 'Women's fantasies during sexual intercourse: normative and theoretical implications', *Journal of Consulting and Clinical Psychology*, 1974, **42**, 313–22.

HITE, S., *The Hite Report.* New York: Macmillan, 1976.

KANTOROWITZ, D.A., 'Personality and conditioning of tumescence and detumescence', *Behaviour Research and Therapy*, 1978, in press.

KAPLAN, H.S., 'No-nonsense therapy for six sexual malfunctions', *Psychology Today*, 1974, **8**, 77–86 (US Edition).

McGUIRE, R.J., CARLISLE, J.M. & YOUNG, B.G., 'Sexual deviations as conditioned behaviour: a hypothesis', *Behaviour Research and Therapy*, 1965, **2**, 185–90.

MARQUIS, J.N., 'Orgasmic reconditioning: changing sexual object choice through controlling masturbation fantasies', *Journal of Behaviour Therapy and Experimental Psychiatry*, 1970, **1**, 263–71.

SPENGLER, A., 'Manifest sadomasochism in males: results of an empirical study', *Archives of Sexual Behaviour*, 1977, **6**, 441–56.

STOLLER, R.J., 'Sexual excitement', *Archives of General Psychiatry*, 1976, **33**, 899–909.

WILSON, G.D., *The Secrets of Sexual Fantasy.* London: Dent, 1978.

# 5 Courtship and love

The study of human attraction and love may not have breached the last taboo but it certainly came after the study of sexual behaviour. This was partly because the subject was seen as too complex and esoteric to be amenable to scientific study and partly because people feared that a scientific analysis of their most intense and treasured experiences might in some way detract from their humanity and value. When Senator William Proxmire heard that the National Science Foundation in America had made a substantial grant for research into love he hit out as follows: 'Two hundred million Americans want to leave some things a mystery, and right at the top of those things we don't want to know is why a man falls in love with a woman and vice versa.' While it may be true that many people have misgivings about the invasion of science into delicate, emotional matters, the Senator is patently wrong in suggesting that we are not curious about them. The content of films, women's magazines, Sunday papers and bookstands attests to our insatiable interest in what transpires when boy meets girl. But the question remains as to whether science can contribute to the understanding of this area in which poetic insights and folk wisdom have accumulated over the ages. In this chapter we look at some of the recent research into attraction and courtship behaviour in the hope of demonstrating that although we do not yet fully understand these phenomena, some of the mysteries of love at least are amenable to scientific investigation.

One of the reasons some people think that love and attraction cannot be studied scientifically is that patterns of behaviour change with time and culture. In our own culture, for example, there has been a marked trend towards sexual permissiveness in courtship years with many more young people engaging in premarital intercourse than there were twenty years ago. This trend can be seen in Figure 7 which is drawn from averaging all the data that have been collected in surveys around the American college campuses from 1938 to the present day. A steep increase in the rates began in the 1960s after they had been fairly level throughout the 40s and 50s. This 'sexual revolution', as it has been called, has continued at about the same rate into the 1970s and shows no sign of tailing off. Note that the increase in incidence has been slightly greater for women than for men. Many researchers attribute this to the influence of women's liberation and a decline in the double standard of sexual morality, but it could also be due to the fact that the women's figure has more room for movement (improvement?), having started from a lower baseline.

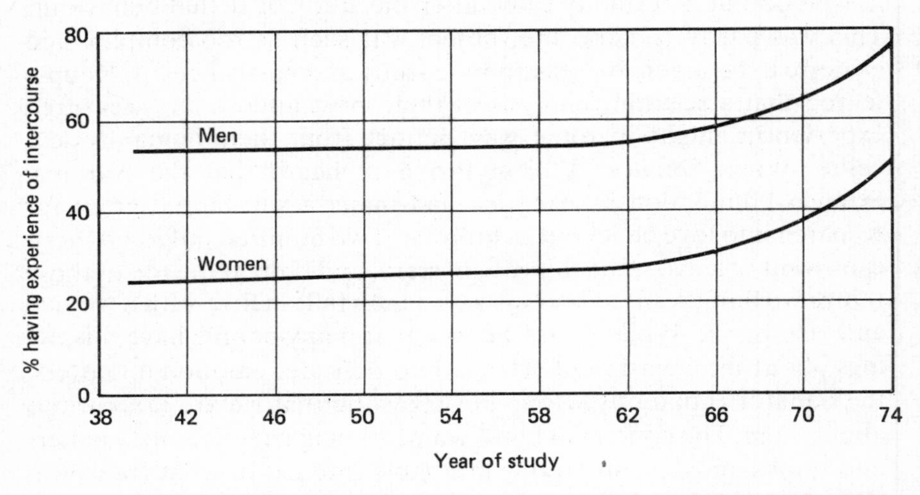


Figure 7 Incidence of premarital sex among US college men and women from 1938 to 1974 (based on data of Hopkins, 1977)

That the double standard in sexual morality is still alive (if not necessarily well) is seen in a study by K. King and colleagues at the University of Georgia. They asked a large sample of students whether they thought it was immoral for men and women to have intercourse with many different partners. The women were more conservative than the men in their standards of sexual morality, and both sexes expected women to be better behaved than men. Whereas 20 per cent of men thought that male promiscuity was immoral, nearly 30 per cent of women thought that male promiscuity was immoral; and whereas 30 per cent of men thought female promiscuity was immoral, over 40 per cent of women thought that female promiscuity was immoral. These figures, gathered in 1975, show that a double standard of behaviour remains (at least in this southern US student population), and it is agreed upon by men and women. The feminist suggestion that the double standard of sexual morality was imposed by men is, and always was, nonsense.

There are various other ways in which traditional courtship patterns have persisted despite the general shift in permissiveness over the last decade or two. It is still usually the man who makes the pace in suggesting intercourse and the woman who exerts control over its occurrence and timing. Many women require certain assurances before engaging in intercourse, for example, that the man 'truly loves' them, or that there is some prospect of marriage. This is especially the case if the woman is a virgin. In a study of 231 dating couples in the Boston area, A. Peplau and colleagues found that the characteristics of the woman were better predictors of whether or not a couple would engage in intercourse than the characteristics of the man. For example, 27 per cent of Catholic women abstained from intercourse altogether, compared to 16 per cent of Jewish women and a mere 2 per cent of Protestants, but there was no connection between the man's religion and sexual abstinence in the couple. The women's sexual experience was also more important than that of the man. If she was sexually experienced intercourse took place within an average of two months, regardless of the man's experience. If the woman was a virgin the average was eight months, depending on whether the man was experienced (mean of six months) or not (mean of twelve months). It appears that men have a fairly constant interest in sex and willingness to start intercourse and it is women that exert control over when and where it will take place. Therefore, although there are variations in courtship over time and culture, the consistencies are sufficient to make scientific studies worthwhile.

Some observers of modern courtship believe that differences in the behaviour of men and women, including the so-called double standard, will soon disappear completely. In our view this is most unlikely because their basis is very fundamental and to some extent biological (see Chapter 2). Throughout nearly all human societies, modern and historical, monogamy has been an ideal that women have been expected to adhere to more than men. Thus, among the ancient

Greeks it was usual for a husband to have sexual relations with prostitutes, foreign women and slaves, while the female was expected to be a virgin before marriage and loyal to her husband afterwards (Bardis, 1979). A man was permitted to have concubines so long as he could afford them; jealousy on the part of the legitimate wife was to a large extent avoided because her rank remained higher than that of the concubine and her children were also of higher social status. In fact, the position of the Greek concubine was not unlike the position of a mistress in modern Western society. This pattern of polygyny (one man being associated with several women) is by far the most prevalent among human societies, as well as in other primates such as apes and baboons. What normally happens is that the males compete with each other for a high position in the dominance hierarchy, or social class position as it is called in human society. The dominant males then control several women each while the lower order males wait their turn or even miss out completely.

An explanation for this chauvinistic custom in terms of sociobiology has been given in the previous chapter. Women produce a limited supply of eggs in their lifetime and it is important (as far as evolution is concerned) that they be fertilized by the most impressive males. In human society this means men who have distinguished themselves not just in strength but also in intellectual pursuits such as art, science or business. By breeding with men of quality, women are improving the human race for the future.

We are not so much applauding this process of genetic improvement as saying that this is how we came to evolve into the extraordinary animals, well geared to survival, that we are today. From one moral viewpoint it is very unfair that less successful men should enjoy sexual favours from fewer women or possibly none at all; this is probably one reason why religious and other moralists preach universal monogamy – one man for one woman. The ideal is a good one, but it is still important to recognize the source of the natural strains against such a system. No doubt it is an intuitive understanding that polygyny is to some extent a 'natural' order that has led the majority of people to retain some kind of double standard of expectation concerning the sexual behaviour of men and women. Even morality has to pay some homage to human nature.

This leads us to the question of what men and women are looking for in each other. A rather oversimplified, yet useful, way of summarizing the answer is to say that men are looking for physically attractive women, while women are looking for socially dominant men. Of course both sexes seek both attributes to some extent, as well as being interested in others like kindness, generosity, sense of humour and so on, but this is the outstanding difference in their orientations.

Take the well-known fact that women tend to marry a man who is a few years older than themselves. Many people think this is due to earlier maturation in girls than boys. It is true that girls are capable of reproducing on average about two years earlier than boys, but this maturational difference is totally irrelevant ten years later when they are typically thinking about getting married. The real reason for the age discrepancy in dating and mating is that the woman's prime value, her beauty, peaks in her late teens or early twenties, whereas the man's prime value, his social and economic power, usually continues to increase well into his thirties at least. If men and women established their mateships when they were each at prime, the most typical relationship would be between a man of around forty and a girl of around twenty. This sometimes happens (e.g. the recent wedding of Princess Caroline of Monaco and Philippe Junot), but more often the age gap is less than this because other factors are also valued by each sex and because we communicate more easily with people of our own generation (see the discussion on the similarity principle in mating in the next chapter).

There are other ways of establishing that looks count more for women. R. Centers of the University of California, Los Angeles, had students rate the importance of various attributes for men and women respectively. Both male and female students agreed that physical attractiveness, erotic ability and affectional ability (lovingness) were prime female attributes whereas achievement, leadership and occupational ability were relatively more important for men. All of these characteristics were regarded as desirable for both men and women to possess but they were picked out as particularly desirable in one sex more than the other. Other researchers have considered the extent to which popularity as measured by frequency of dating is connected with a person's physical attractiveness. For girls there is a very strong connection between attractiveness and dating popularity, but for boys the association is very slight (Berscheid *et al.*, 1971).

Further confirmation of the importance of looks in women but not in men comes from studies directed at the question of whether attractive people have happier lives. In the case of men, there is no connection between looks and happiness. For women, there is an interesting reversal with age. Good looking women are happier when young, but older women whose youthful photographs are rated as attractive are less happy than women who were plain when young. Presumably this is because some beautiful girls derive so much satisfaction from their sex appeal when young that once their looks begin to fade their life takes a noticeable turn for the worse, leaving them unhappy, resentful, or perhaps even suicidal (as in the case of some ageing film stars). Girls who are plain when young develop other sources of satisfaction which are more lasting and therefore they do not suffer such a decline in middle age (Wilson and Nias, 1976).

So far we have talked about physical attractiveness in women without specifying what comprises it. The simplest way of characterizing a physically attractive woman is to describe her as decisively not-male. This might seem fatuous, but what it really means is that physical attraction is based on the differences between the sexes. The points of maximum difference between men's and women's bodies are most attractive and arousing, and the more exaggerated are these differences, within reason, the more sexually attractive they will be. Part of the idea of beauty treatment and make-up is to emphasize ways in which a woman's face is different from that of a man (fuller lips, narrower eyebrows, softer complexion, absence of facial hair). Large breasts are usually seen as attractive unless they are so big as to become floppy and droopy. The narrow waist and relatively broad hips of a woman are also major sexual stimuli because they distinguish her from men. Most of these signals have a biological basis but others are socially conditioned: long hair and long fingernails are seen as sexy in women even though, without cutting, those of a man would grow just as long.

Beauty contests provide a good pointer as to what men look for in women. Averaging 'Miss World' winners over the years yields an English-speaking model, aged twenty-one years, 5 ft 8 in. in height, blonde with brown eyes and measuring 35-24-35. Some of these specifications are more invariant or telling than others. For example, the age and measurements do not vary a great deal from year to year but language and colouring do.

Another model for female sexual attractiveness is the 'playmate' that appears in men's magazines such as *Playboy* and *Penthouse*. Typical vital statistics for this kind of girl are 37-24-35, i.e. slightly larger breasts than Miss World, but waist and hips about the same. Their average height is somewhat less than Miss World because they do not depend upon making an impression on a remote stage.

Models appearing in women's magazines like *Vogue* are usually not so strikingly attractive to men. They tend to be narrower throughout, but especially at the breasts and waist, so that the hour-glass effect is somewhat reduced. An extreme example was Twiggy, with a 31-24-33 figure. The average British woman (37-28-39) is larger all over, particularly at the waist and hips. Such comparisons confirm that the sexual attractiveness of women is enhanced by large breasts and hips set against a narrow waist, i.e. exaggeration of the way in which the average female form diverges from that of the male.

While Miss World and the 'playmates' represent the norm for female attractiveness, there are variations in preference according to personality and other factors. A. Mathews and colleagues (1972) showed men a set of pictures of women culled from various sources ranging from soft pornography to women's fashion magazines. Some of the women in the pictures were fully clothed, some completely naked and others partially dressed in bikinis or underwear. Introverts preferred their women more fully dressed and thinner than extraverts. It seems that introverts feel overwhelmed by nude and well-developed women and are more at ease with thin and thoughtful girls. Homosexual men also preferred 'non-threatening' women – those which the majority described as sexless, unavailable, prim and antiseptic. Manual workers liked conventionally well-dressed women rather than those who were 'trendy'. When the question was reframed so that the men were asked which women they would favour as long-term mates, their preferences shifted towards elegant, well-dressed women, with sexy and provocative poses being valued less. Other studies of the way in which personality differences are reflected in sexual preferences and behaviour are described in Chapter 3.

As we have said, women are less concerned about the physical appeal of men, being more interested in factors such as intelligence and accomplishment which make for social dominance. Nevertheless, some studies of the way that men's bodies are viewed by women have been carried out just to keep the record straight. What these studies show is that the muscular 'Atlas' physique, with big chest, shoulders and biceps, is not generally a turn-on to women. Only about 1 per cent of American women reported sexual arousal in looking at men of this kind (Smith, 1975). The majority of women prefer men of modest proportions, clothed rather than naked (which might explain why male nude shows and magazines attract more interest from male homosexuals than from women) and they usually deny any interest in the size of a man's penis. Oddly, it is the sight of a man's bottom that women find most appealing (Beck, 1978). Small, firm bottoms, preferably clothed in tight trousers or jeans, are particularly popular with women. In one survey, conducted by a New York newspaper, no less than 39 per cent of women cited small buttocks as the feature they found most exciting in men. Other admired attributes included tallness, slimness (especially a flat stomach) and various expressions in the eyes.

These female preferences can also be explained in terms of characteristic physical differences between men and women. When viewed from behind, at least, a compact bottom is one of the best ways of identifying a man as distinct from a woman. Perhaps it is also taken as an outward sign of the narrow pelvic outlet that we suggested was importantly related to sexual behaviour (see Chapter 2). It is at this point of the skeleton that men and women are most clearly distinguished and for reasons that are vital to reproduction. Why bulging muscles are not regarded as attractive by many women is more of a mystery. Perhaps if the man's chest bulges too much it takes on a rounded look that incorporates female (breast-type) signals rather than the flatness which is more typical of a man. Alternatively, it could be a result of social learning: women may think that musclemen are thick-headed narcissists who are unlikely to be very successful in relation to the criteria that are important for establishing dominance in sophisticated human society. The preference for seeing men dressed rather than naked might be partly due to the fact that social status is difficult to ascertain without the cues provided by clothing.

Tallness is generally attractive in men, but its role is complex. A cardinal rule in dating and mating is that the man be taller than the woman, so *relative* height is just as important as absolute height. Probably a man appeals most to a woman when he is an optimal degree taller than her (say 5 or 6 in.); a much greater discrepancy and she is likely to feel that her own looks are not enhanced or that they appear ridiculous together. Absolute height is also important, though its effect is probably mediated by social status. A connection between perceived height and status was demonstrated in a study by Wilson (1968). A man was introduced to different groups of students as either a student, demonstrator, lecturer, senior lecturer or professor, after which they were asked to estimate his height. As he climbed the status ladder, he gained 2½ in. in perceived height. A survey by the *Wall Street Journal* revealed that male university graduates over 6 ft 2 in. had salaries 12½ per cent higher than those of men under 6 ft. It is also interesting that nearly every American president elected since at least 1900 has been taller than his rival. (The only notable exception is Jimmy Carter, who of course looks a bit like a Kennedy.) Male height, then, is probably attractive to women because it is associated with social status.

No account of physical attractiveness is complete without mentioning the face. Despite the assertion that 'you don't look at the mantelpiece when you're stoking the fire', this region is very salient. Unfortunately, little is known about what constitutes a pretty face short of the fact that symmetry and an absence of blemishes are desirable. This point was rather ingeniously demonstrated by Sir Francis Galton in the last century, using the technique of composite portraiture which he pioneered. A large number of faces are superimposed onto a photographic plate by fractional exposures to produce a single, average face. Features common to most of the faces are retained, while blemishes and peculiarities are eliminated. 'The result is a very striking face, thoroughly ideal and artistic, and singularly beautiful,' (Galton, 1883). A beautiful face, then, is produced by an absence of extremes. The nose is not too long or too short, the eyes not too close together or too far apart, and so on. Add to this a smooth, unblemished complexion (a sign of good health) and we have a face that will probably be judged beautiful. Contrast the kind of physique that is created through averaging, e.g. the vital statistics of the average British woman. Bodies have to be exceptional, but apparently faces are better not.

Of course, the averaging of faces was done for men and women separately, so we have two average faces – one male and one female. Since the opposite sex is attractive because it is different, slight exaggeration of the points of difference probably enhances attractiveness. We noted that make-up is used to highlight female differences; no doubt a woman who is naturally very feminine in her facial features (large eyes, narrow eyebrows, soft complexion) would also tend towards prettiness. Likewise, a man with a rugged, masculine face (strong jaw, bushy eyebrows, leathery skin) is more likely to be described as handsome. Still, the degree of difference between the sexes has evolutionary limits set upon it and great divergences cease to be attractive.

Some people think research on attractiveness is pointless because beauty is so much 'in the eye of the beholder'. In fact, when a well-designed rating scale is used to assess attractiveness a great deal of consensus among different observers is found. Particularly when facial photographs are used as stimuli, near perfect correlations are obtained, regardless of the age, sex or occupation of the rater. When more information about the ratees is introduced, as in beauty contests when the girls walk about in costume and have to answer questions, reliability drops somewhat because the judges attend to different characteristics. When people are asked to rate their own attractiveness there is an even greater amount of cue confusion, leaving a low though still significant correlation with the ratings of other people.

To some extent, our judgments of physical attractiveness are influenced by cultural standards of beauty, the most commonly cited examples of cultural variation being the Arab preference for plump women, and a liking for 'pendulous' breasts in certain primitive tribes. Exceptional cases should not, however, blind us to the existence of valid generalizations; they are better viewed simply as extremes of the variation which is always present, whether between cultures or within them. Reasons for these variations may often be found in other characteristics with which the attribute is associated. In our culture we value a suntan partly because it shows that we have been on a skiing or tropical holiday and therefore it imparts prestige. In other cultures, plumpness may be valued because it is a sign of sumptuous living (and therefore wealth), or maternity. Drooping breasts suggest age, which is the main basis of status in some primitive cultures, and so on. Women successful in the 'Miss World' competition or selected to adorn the pages of *Playboy* magazine probably represent the human male norm for desirability. Other things being equal they would be desirable to most men in any culture.

Physical attractiveness is of prime importance in determining the first impression a couple have of each other upon meeting. It is on the basis of this first impression that they decide to date each other. Other factors such as intelligence and personality become progressively important as the relationship continues and will determine its duration, but these factors only come into play after the initial screening based on physical attractiveness. An amusing demonstration of the priority of physical cues, particularly when men are judging women, was seen in a study of driver response to hitchhikers by C. Morgan and associates at the University of Washington, Seattle. Male drivers were more likely to stop for a female hitchhiker when her bust had been padded so as to accentuate the size of her breasts. Apparently the male vigilance for desirable female physiques operates from a distance of many yards so as to alter the chances of social contact occurring.

In practice, potential partners may be screened out as unsuitable either because they are too plain or because they are too attractive. This is because we get to know our own level of attractiveness and avoid trying to fly too high for fear of rebuff. Berscheid and associates (1971) tested this by having male and female subjects choose people they would like to meet as dating partners from a selection of photographs of the opposite sex. Girls in particular tended to be realistic in that they chose to meet partners of a similar level of attractiveness as themselves. Couples who are actually dating are also found to be similar in attractiveness. I. Silverman (1971) had his students observe courting couples in bars and theatre lobbies, male students rating the woman for attractiveness and female students rating the man in each couple. Most of the couples (85 per cent) were within one point of each other on a five-point scale of attractiveness, and those that were further removed were relatively unlikely to be engaging in physical intimacies such as holding hands or kissing, implying either that they were not involved or that their relationship was faltering.

Apart from the physical attractiveness of a person, the next thing that impresses us about them is whether or not they seem to like us. Since people are usually too polite to tell us directly what they really think of us this has to be judged from various non-verbal cues in the early stages of meeting. If a person attends to us, looks into our eyes, frequently smiles and finds excuses to touch us affectionately, we judge that they are interested in us. If they yawn, frown, look at the ceiling, stare coldly or move away from us, we might accurately estimate that they don't like us or do not wish to pursue an intimate relationship.

Some non-verbal cues are more subtle and may operate unconsciously. E. Hess (1965) showed men two photographs of the same girl, identical in every respect except that in one her pupils had been touched up so as to enlarge them. Most men chose the one with the larger pupils as more attractive, even though they were frequently unable to spot the difference between the two photographs. It is known that our pupils dilate when we are aroused and interested in what we are looking at. Apparently this may be transmitted as a sexual signal without our awareness. Perhaps this would explain why people look sexier at night – their pupils expand because the light is dim – but across the candlelit table this is interpreted as romantic interest by the partner.

In general, we like people who express liking for us – that is, providing they do not come across as insincere or ingratiating. Aronson and Linder (1965) compared the effects of being consistently nice to people, consistently nasty, and changing from one to the other. Subjects conversed with a confederate who then made remarks about them which they 'accidentally' overheard. Later they related their liking for the confederate, supposedly on the basis of their conversations with him. Not surprisingly, they liked a confederate who had made uniformly complimentary remarks about them and disliked those whose comments were entirely derogatory. But best of all they liked those whose comments had progressed from unfavourable to favourable during the course of the experiment. Apparently, the best way to win new friends and lovers is to start by showing dislike (without being too insulting) and then show progressive interest and approval.

There are various interpretations of this 'gain phenomenon', as it has been called. One is that early disdain makes it less likely that later warmth will be perceived as habitual or ingratiating. Another explanation is in terms of self-esteem. Experimental studies show that people who have a low opinion of themselves are less demanding in their expectations of other people, including opposite sex partners. Thus it has been found that women whose self-esteem has been lowered experimentally are more attracted to a particular man than women whose self-esteem has been raised, and men who are low in self-esteem are less likely to attempt to date a physically attractive woman than men who are high in self-esteem. If being rude or indifferent to somebody on first acquaintance lowers their self-esteem even temporarily, they might be more vulnerable to whatever charm we later conjure.

Experiments have been carried out to see if men and women who play hard to get are perceived as more desirable. E. Walster and associates (1973) had computer dates telephone a girl with whom they had supposedly been matched in order to arrange a meeting. Actually, it was always the same girl on the end of the telephone – a confederate of the experimenter. For half the men she was very available, being delighted to receive their call and grateful to be asked out; for the others she accepted a coffee date with some reluctance because she had many other dates and was not sure she wanted to get involved with anyone new. After this conversation, the man's impression of his date was assessed. Results of this and similar experiments failed to support the 'hard to get' hypothesis. The girls seemed to be equally desirable under the two conditions of attainability.

The researchers then revised their hypothesis. Perhaps the most desirable date is one who is apparently very keen on you (i.e. easy for *you* to get) but hard for everyone else. To test this 'selective difficulty' hypothesis they used another computer date design. One girl appeared *generally easy to get*, making it clear that she was keen to date anybody the computer assigned. Another girl made it clear that she was *generally hard to get*, i.e. not particularly eager to date any of the men assigned to her. A third girl was *selective*, i.e. apparently eager to date the subject but not interested in any of his rivals. This time the hypothesis was vindicated: the selective girl was decisively preferred above either of the other girls.

A question that has recently come to engage the ingenuity of social psychologists is that of the conditions under which a couple will say they are 'in love'. Most of us at some time in our lives experience an emotional upheaval that we describe as falling in love. This is perhaps the most dramatic and mysterious experience ever to befall us, and we have an insatiable curiosity about it. It may produce great euphoria or the deepest hurt, which makes it unique among our emotions. The preoccupation of Western society with love is evident in poetry, drama, novels and other forms of art and entertainment. But despite the assertions of some anthropologists, the phenomenon is neither of recent origin nor restricted to our culture. Although not always thought of as a necessary prelude to marriage, romantic and passionate love has appeared at all times and places.

Dion and Dion (1979) asked people whether they had ever been in love, and if so, how often, how intensely and for how long. Other questions dealt with the quality of their experiences, whether their love was requited and how they regarded the partner. They found that people who were 'internally controlled' (i.e. who viewed events as being largely under their own control, rather than seeing themselves as victims of external forces like 'fate') were less likely to have been in love. Furthermore, when they did fall in love they experienced it as less mysterious and volatile than 'externally controlled' people, and were less idealistic in their conception of it.

In another study, the Dions found that people low in self-esteem experienced romantic love less often than people high in self-esteem, but when they did fall in love their experience was usually more intense, less controllable and less often reciprocated. They interpreted this as meaning that people with low self-esteem are less adept in interpersonal relationships and thus less successful in persuading other people to fall in love with them. As a result, their love is more likely to be unreciprocated and the cause of emotional turmoil. Another finding in this series of studies was that people who are less defensive and more willing to disclose intimate details about themselves were more likely to experience romantic love. Highly defensive individuals, who were more guarded emotionally, were more cynical about love and less likely to experience it.

In these studies women were more apt to say they had been in love than men, and more likely to say they were in love at the time of study. They described their love experiences as more intense, euphoric and rewarding in general, and expressed greater liking, trust and admiration for their romantic partners than did men. On the other hand, they claimed to have experienced more unrequited love than men.

Taking these patterns together, Dion and Dion arrived at a 'dependency model' for understanding the relationships between personality and susceptibility to romantic love. They note that low self-esteem and female gender, which are associated with love proneness, both reflect an openness or need for being dependent on others. People of low self-esteem often seek to confirm their worthiness by cultivating relationships with others, and there is considerable evidence that women exhibit greater emotional dependency than men, especially towards members of the opposite sex. Internal control and defensiveness, which inhibit romantic attachments, are characterized by aversion toward emotional dependence and intimacy. Clearly, when one partner in a developing relationship begins to feel and express romantic love, the reaction of the other will depend to a large extent on his or her personality. The love-prone dependent types are likely to reciprocate, while the more independent others will probably feel 'crowded' and beat an emotional if not physical retreat.

Claims of being in love have also been tied in with a person's total life situation. Sociologist E. Duvall (1973) had more than 3000 adolescents complete a questionnaire asking about whether they were currently in love, their social background and future plans. Teenagers claiming to be in love (25 per cent of the boys and 36 per cent of the girls) appeared to be actively repudiating their parents' values in certain ways. They tended to disparage the kind of marriage their parents had, but were planning to drop out of college in favour of early marriage themselves. Duvall concluded that adolescent love may reflect a teenager's search for identity. It is therefore more likely to occur in young people with low self-concepts who look to marriage as an escape from an unpromising life situation. Teenagers who find a satisfying sense of identity within their own families, and in their vocational aspirations, are 'less urgent about cutting loose from their parents and developing adolescent love affairs'.

The idea of love as a search for identity has been taken up by R. Centers (1975). He assessed the personality needs of a large number of engaged couples in order to find out how each individual's needs were rewarded by attachment to the other. There were strong connections for sex drive and need for affiliation in the couples, high scores in one partner going with high scores in the other. But more interesting was the finding that men with very masculine needs such as dominance and achievement tended to have fallen in love with women showing very feminine needs like affiliation and nurturance. Centers took this as confirmation of his theory that a feeling of sex identity is one of the main rewards that lovers may provide for each other, and just about as important as sexual gratification and companionship.

People use the word love in such different ways – for example citing emotions as far removed as joy and despair to indicate that the state exists – that many researchers have felt the need of a questionnaire for defining and measuring it. One of the most widely used of these instruments is that designed by Z. Rubin (1970) which approaches the problem of defining love by distinguishing it from liking. His questionnaire has two scales. The *liking* scale includes statements to the effect that the person concerned is admirable, respectable and similar to oneself; *loving* involves a need to be with the person, willingness to help them even at great sacrifice, and a desire to be intimately and exclusively absorbed. Rubin's scales were completed by 182 dating couples at the University of Michigan, first with respect to their current boy/girl friend, then with respect to a close friend of the same sex as themselves. A fair degree of separation was found between the loving and liking scales in the sense that endorsing one set of items did not necessarily imply endorsement of the others, though there was some overlap between the two.

To check the validity of his scales Rubin observed the amount of eye contact engaged in by couples as they waited in a room prior to an experiment. Couples who loved each other a lot according to their scores on the love scale were found to spend more time looking into each other's eyes than couples with low love scores, while liking scores were not so associated. Enjoyment of eye contact as an end in itself seems to be characteristic of loving rather than liking.

However, other attempts to find behavioural correlates of loving as distinct from liking have failed. The Dions, for example, studied love and liking scores in relation to various perceptual, memory and attention effects that have been supposed to indicate intimate involvement between people. One such experiment used the Ames distorted room, in which a person appears to get larger or smaller depending upon which way they walk across it. The prediction was that people in love would see less distortion of their partner in this situation than a stranger with whom they had no involvement. This occurred only for women, not men, and there was no evidence to show that it was linked specifically with love rather than liking or familiarity. Similar relationships were found with memory games such as sitting round a table, reading out words in cyclic order and then trying to reconstruct what other people had said. Again, women attended selectively to their partner rather than strangers (which was not the case with men), but liking scores were implicated just as strongly as love scores. These studies, then, suggest that men and women have different degrees of selective interest in their partners, but they do not provide any support for Rubin's distinction between love and liking, at least as reflected in the scales he has developed.

Canadian sociologist J.A. Lee (1976) has adopted a somewhat different approach to the measurement of love, classifying it into various different types. Analysis of a long questionnaire covering all the aspects of the person's relationship – how it began, how soon intimacy occurred, whether jealousy was strongly felt, the effects of separation, the nature and frequency of arguments, break-ups and reunions, and so forth – revealed three primary types of loving that were fairly independent of each other. These he called *Eros* (characterized by immediate physical attraction, sensuality, self-confidence, fascination with beauty, close intimacy and rapport with the partner), *Ludus* (love that is playful, hedonistic and free of commitment), and *Storge* (which is affectionate, companionate and devoid of passion). Three blends of these primaries were also identified: *Mania* (feverish, obsessive and jealous love), *Pragma* (practical, realistic and compatibility seeking), and *Agape* (altruistic, patient and dutiful).

Relationships among these types of love were represented geometrically as in the diagram below (Figure 8). The distance between any two types of love indicates the difference or degree of incompatibility between them. According to Lee, if the two parties to a relationship have widely disparate approaches to love, misunderstanding is inevitable. For example, a ludic lover may resent a storgic partner for trying to trap him into a relationship, while she accuses him of playing games just to get her body. Eros insists on rapid intimacy, while storge may be enhanced by postponing sex, and so on. Two storgic lovers would be expected to have the best chance of a lasting relationship, while two ludic lovers would have the least chance. However, the ludic lovers might have a lot more fun while it lasts – after all, this is what they seek. It is presumed that most people enjoy some variety of different kinds of loving but have a general preference for one above the others.

A self-scoring questionnaire for discovering your own preferred love style is given below. In fact, it can only be used to apply to one particular relationship at a time, and of course we experience different kinds of love at different times with different people. Nevertheless, the reader may find it interesting to classify his or her current

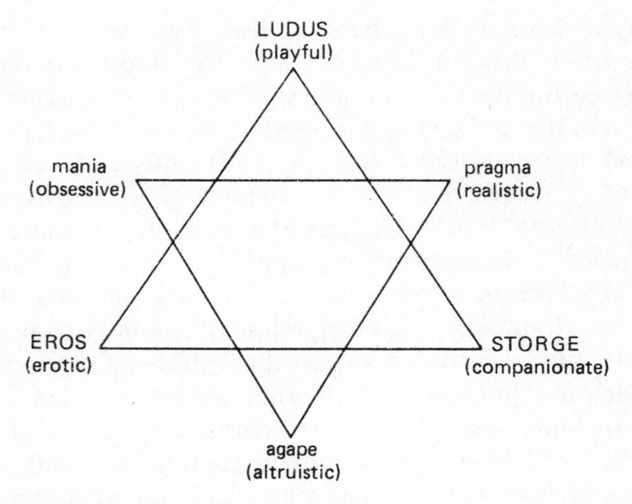


Figure 8 Lee's classification of different types of love

love relationship according to this system. Whether this relationship is an exceptional or usual one readers may decide for themselves. As with most tests of this kind, you will get the most out of it if you answer the questions honestly and do not discuss them with your partner until after you have finished.

## Lee's Lovestyle Questionnaire

Read each statement and choose the *one* answer which best completes the statement to describe the relationship. Next, look across at the columns on the right. You will notice one or more scores of x or 2x on the same horizontal line as the answer you have selected. Draw a circle around all the scores of x or 2x that correspond to your selected answer (that is, are on the same horizontal line). Select one and only one answer for each question, and try not to skip any question.

### *Twenty Questions About Your Love Relationship*

(1) At the time this relationship begins, I think of myself as having had:
- *a* a happier childhood than most people.
- *b* an average childhood. (no score)
- *c* an unhappier childhood than most people.

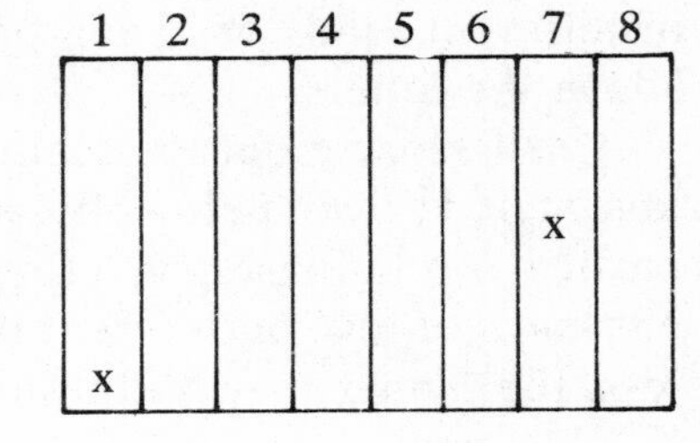

| | 1 | 2 | 3 | 4 | 5 | 6 | 7 | 8 |
|---|---|---|---|---|---|---|---|---|
| a | | | | | | | x | |
| b | | | | | | | | |
| c | x | | | | | | | |

| | 1 | 2 | 3 | 4 | 5 | 6 | 7 | 8 |
|---|---|---|---|---|---|---|---|---|
| (2) My feelings about my everyday life and work are: | | | | | | | | |
| *a* I am really enjoying life and I have some good, close friends. | | x | x | | | | x | x |
| *b* My life is about as good as anyone's. (no score) | | | | | | | | |
| *c* I feel something is missing, *or* I feel rather lonely. | x | | | | | | | |
| (3) The other person in this relationship begins it as: | | | | | | | | |
| *a* a complete stranger to me. | x | x | x | x | | | | |
| *b* someone I am already acquainted with. | | | | | x | | x | x |
| (4) I realize (perhaps using a little hindsight) that as this relationship begins: | | | | | | | | |
| *a* I am ready to enjoy any pleasant relationship that comes along, but I have no intention of 'getting serious' or 'settling down' with any one person. | | | x | x | | | | |
| *b* I am rather anxious to be in love with someone (though I may also be a little afraid of love). | x | | | | | | | |
| *c* The idea of being in love hasn't even occurred to me. I am just getting to know this person as a friend. | | | | | | | 2x | |
| *d* There is one type of 'looks' (physical appearance) that attracts me more than any other, and this person is 'my type'. | | 2x | | | | | | |
| *e* I am ready to 'settle down' with a partner who has a personality and background compatible with my own. | | | | | | 2x | | |
| *f* I am already committed to someone else but I am prepared to have a relationship with this person 'on the side'. | | | | | 2x | | | |
| *g* I feel that this person needs me (or needs my help). | | | | | | | | 2x |

| | 1 | 2 | 3 | 4 | 5 | 6 | 7 | 8 |
|---|---|---|---|---|---|---|---|---|
| (5) As I become involved with this person: | | | | | | | | |
| *a* I soon become preoccupied with happy, hopeful thoughts (dreams, fantasies) that this is the person I have been looking for. | | 2x | | | | | | |
| *b* I soon become preoccupied with anxious thoughts (concerns, worries) about the way the relationship will develop. | 2x | | | | | | | |
| *c* I soon begin to analyse carefully whether this person would make a suitable, compatible mate. | | | | | | 2x | | |
| *d* I go on with life more or less as usual, and don't give much thought to this relationship beyond the ordinary arrangements one needs to make. (no score) | | | | | | | | |
| (6) As we become more involved, I want to see this person: | | | | | | | | |
| *a* every day, if at all possible. | x | x | | | | | | |
| *b* fairly often, when it is convenient for both of us. | | | x | | | x | x | |
| *c* when it is convenient for me, without taking too much of my time. | | | | x | x | | | |
| *d* whenever my partner needs me. | | | | | | | | x |
| BY NOW YOU SHOULD BE FAIRLY INVOLVED WITH YOUR 'PARTNER' IN THIS RELATIONSHIP | | | | | | | | |
| (7) Now that we are 'involved' I feel that: | | | | | | | | |
| *a* I can only be truly in love with this one person, who is more important to me than any other. | x | x | | | | x | x | |
| *b* I like this person, but there are other people I could be (or am) involved with, who could be just as important. | | | 2x | 2x | | | | |
| *c* I must help this person who needs me, but there are other people who also need my love. | | | | | | | | x |

| | 1 | 2 | 3 | 4 | 5 | 6 | 7 | 8 |
|---|---|---|---|---|---|---|---|---|
| *d* I am already committed to someone else, and I will have to be careful not to let this new relationship hurt the other person to whom I am committed. | | | | | 2x | | | |
| (8) If my partner in this relationship I am assessing wishes to be involved with other 'lovers' too: | | | | | | | | |
| *a* I will do anything possible to prove that I can love my partner more than anyone else could, so that eventually my partner will love only me. | x | | | | | | | |
| *b* I will not compete for my partner's love: my partner will have to choose between me and anyone else. | | x | | | | x | | |
| *c* It's fine with me, because I intend to be involved with other 'lovers' too. | | | x | x | | | | |
| *d* It's fine with me, because I have a prior commitment to someone else anyway (for example, a spouse). | | | | | 2x | | | |
| *e* I'll go on loving my partner anyway. In fact, if it seems that some other lover would be of more good to my partner, then I will step aside. | | | | | | | | 2x |
| *f* I may not be happy but I won't ask my partner to make a choice. Time will tell, and eventually my partner will make a choice. | | | | | | | 2x | |
| (9) As my partner and I become more involved: | | | | | | | | |
| *a* I am the first to say 'I love you'. I want to show that I am really serious. | x | | | | | | | |
| *b* I have to warn my partner not to get too involved, because I am not ready to commit myself to anyone. I've given fair warning. | | | | 2x | | | | |

| | 1 | 2 | 3 | 4 | 5 | 6 | 7 | 8 |
|---|---|---|---|---|---|---|---|---|
| *c* I tell my partner that I really enjoy this relationship, but there are also other love relationships I want to enjoy. | | | x | | | | | |
| *d* I become more and more aware of the ways my partner's body really fits 'my type' (and/or the ways it does not fit). | | x | | | | | | |
| *e* I feel that only after we have come to know each other really well, will we be sure of our love and able to make a commitment. | | | | | | x | x | |
| *f* I am ready to help in any way I can, 'no strings attached'. | | | | | | | | x |
| *g* I remind my beloved that I am already committed to someone else. | | | | | 2x | | | |
| (10) I want to have sexual intercourse: | | | | | | | | |
| *a* very soon after we begin seeing each other – within the first few encounters or 'dates'. | | 2x | 2x | | | | | |
| *b* only after we have come to know each other well and feel some commitment to each other. | | | | | | x | 2x | |
| *c* when it is enjoyable, without interfering with my other love relationships. | | | | x | x | | | |
| *d* perhaps not at all, and certainly not early on. Sex is basically for the purpose of procreation. | | | | | | | | x |
| (11) Our sexual relationship: | | | | | | | | |
| *a* must be ecstatic and compatible almost from the start, or I am likely to decide we are not suited to each other. | | 2x | x | | | | | |
| *b* can be worked out as we go along. We can learn to have good sex even if we don't 'turn each other on'. | | | | | | 2x | x | |
| *c* may not work out, but I'll go on loving just as much (and perhaps 'hope for the best'). | x | | | | | | | x |

| | 1 | 2 | 3 | 4 | 5 | 6 | 7 | 8 |
|---|---|---|---|---|---|---|---|---|
| *d* should be enjoyable or 'fun' but not become serious or overly emotional. | | | | x | x | | | |
| (12) I express my feeling for my partner: | | | | | | | | |
| *a* as often and intensely as possible, even if my feelings are not reciprocated, in the hope that eventually I will persuade my partner to love me. | 2x | | | | | | | |
| *b* as openly and honestly as possible, but not more intensely than my partner's feelings are expressed to me. Our feelings should be just about mutual; I don't want to get 'ahead of' my partner. | | | x | | | | | |
| *c* as openly and intensely as I feel, without much consideration of whether my partner will reciprocate or feel the same way for me. | | x | | | | | | x |
| *d* in quiet, restrained, and sensible ways, as I would with a close friend. | | | | | | x | x | |
| *e* in polite, sophisticated ways which do not embarrass or over-commit either one of us. | | | | x | | | | |
| *f* freely, when in private with my partner, but only discreetly when observed by other who may not approve. | | | | | 2x | | | |
| (13) I will reveal my deepest thoughts so my partner: | | | | | | | | |
| *a* early in the relationship and often as it goes on, even when such honesty might hurt our relationship. I want my partner to know me really well. | x | x | | | | | | x |
| *b* only when necessary to prevent my partner from getting the wrong idea and becoming too involved. Most of the time I hope we can be pleasant without baring our souls. | | | 2x | | x | | | |

| | 1 | 2 | 3 | 4 | 5 | 6 | 7 | 8 |
|---|---|---|---|---|---|---|---|---|
| *c* gradually, over a long period of time, as we grow more accustomed and trusting with each other and feel committed. | | | | | | x | x | |
| *d* rarely or never. I expect my partner to respect my privacy. | | | | 2x | | | | |
| (14) If there is trouble ahead in our relationship it will: | | | | | | | | |
| *a* probably develop because my partner does not meet my rather demanding expectations. I will simply have to explain that a mistake has been made. | | x | x | | | x | | |
| *b* probably develop because my partner becomes too serious, involved, argumentative, or jealous, so that the relationship is no longer fun for us. | | | | x | x | | | |
| *c* probably prove to be a test of our real friendship and patience. If we are meant for each other, things will work out. | | | | | | | x | |
| *d* be my opportunity to show how I can go on loving my partner no matter what happens. No trouble will prove greater than my love. | x | | | | | | | x |
| (15) I will want to discuss our future plans together with my partner: | | | | | | | | |
| *a* early in the relationship, so that I can show my partner how serious I am, and, hopefully, obtain my partner's commitment to our future together. | x | | | | | | | |
| *b* as we become more committed to each other, to make sure we agree on such basic matters as money, children, etc. | | | | | | 2x | | |
| *c* very little. It will really be up to my partner to decide in the future how much I am needed or can be of help. | | | | | | | | x |

| | 1 | 2 | 3 | 4 | 5 | 6 | 7 | 8 |
|---|---|---|---|---|---|---|---|---|
| *d* very little, because life should be taken as it comes. As long as we really care about each other, the future will take care of itself. | | | | | | | x | |
| *e* very little or not at all, because our relationship does not have a 'future'. Each of us will eventually go our own way. | | | x | x | x | | | |
| (16) If our love is 'for real' it should last: | | | | | | | | |
| *a* forever (my lifetime). | x | x | | | | | | |
| *b* as long as I enjoy it. If our relationship ceases to be pleasant I will break off (even if my partner doesn't want to). | | | | 2x | x | | | |
| *c* as long as we both enjoy it. I expect that whoever loses interest first will let the other down gently so that each of us can find other relationships. | | | 2x | | | | | |
| *d* as long as we are compatible with each other and want to go on living together. | | | | | | 2x | | |
| *e* as long as we remain friends, even if we cease to be lovers. | | | | | | | x | |
| *f* as long as my partner needs me, whether I need my partner or not. | | | | | | | | 2x |
| (17) As our relationship develops, fights and arguments happen between us: | | | | | | | | |
| *a* quite often. My partner often says or does things that hurt me, or seems to take advantage of my love. | x | | | | | | | |
| *b* occasionally, because we may disagree, but I try to work things out rationally. | | | | | | x | | |
| *c* occasionally, but we are basically good friends, so fights and arguments are not likely to break us up. | | | | | | | x | |
| *d* rarely, because once we started to fight or argue a lot, it would be time for me to break off. | | | x | x | x | | | |

| | 1 | 2 | 3 | 4 | 5 | 6 | 7 | 8 |
|---|---|---|---|---|---|---|---|---|
| *e* rarely, because unless we are so close to each other in our bodies and minds that important disagreements do not arise, I would be convinced that this was not the beloved I seek and I would look again. | | x | | | | | | |
| *f* rarely, because I don't make any demands of my partner. I will suffer patiently and in silence if necessary. | | | | | | | | x |
| (18) The opinion of others, such as friends and parents, about our relationship: | | | | | | | | |
| *a* is not important to me. If I know my love is real I don't care what the whole world thinks. | x | x | | | | | | |
| *b* is important to me because my partner should be able to get along well with my friends and fit into my social life. | | | | | | x | x | |
| *c* is not important to me, because it is my duty to love, regardless of what others may think. | | | | | | | | x |
| *d* is important to me, if our relationship interferes with other obligations which have a prior claim on me. | | | | | x | | | |
| *e* is only important to the extent that these opinions make our relationship difficult or unpleasant, in which case it would be simpler to find another partner. | | | x | x | | | | |
| (19) If my partner should lose interest in me: | | | | | | | | |
| *a* I will hang on and keep trying. I'd never be the first to give up. | 2x | | | | | | | |
| *b* I will simply look elsewhere for a new partner. Anyway, it is more likely that I will lose interest first. | | | | x | | | | |
| *c* I will take this in my stride and look for someone new. | | | x | | | | | |

*d* I will try to remain friends, and perhaps later start in again, unless I've found someone new.
*e* I will talk things over with my partner to find out what's not working and if possible mend the problem. But if we are basically incompatible I will look again.
*f* I will feel that my duty is done, but if I am needed again later I'll always be available.

(20) If we ever do break up, 'getting over it' will take me:
*a* a long time. I would be really hurt.
*b* a long time, but I would try to understand and remain a friend.
*c* very little time. There are other fish in the sea.
*d* not so long, if I could find someone new who came close to meeting my expectations.
*e* very little time. I expect to be in and out of love a number of times.
*f* very little time, as I would still have the other person I am involved with (or married to).
*g* perhaps a little time, because I'm only human, but I will try to be unselfish and realize that my partner must be free to live his or her own life with no demands from me.
(Are you still answering *honestly*?)

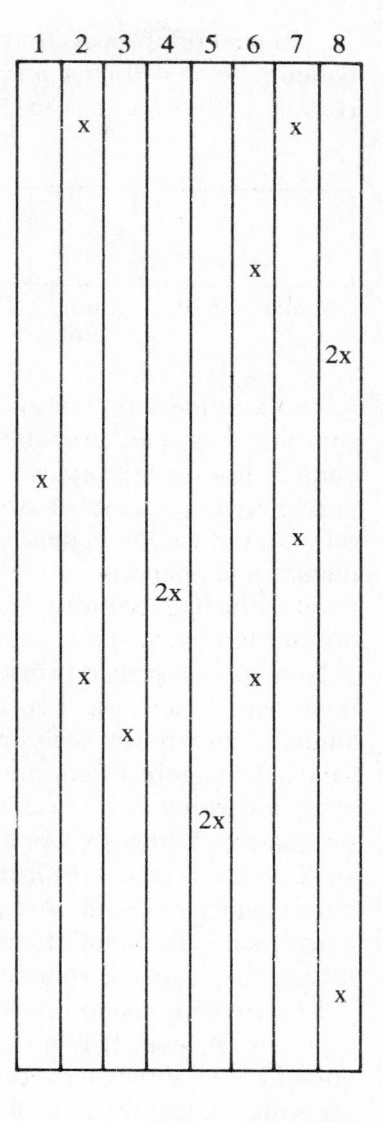

## *Scoring*

1. Go back to question 1. Looking only at column 1, count the number of scores (x or 2x) which you have circled in this column. Each 2x is counted as two x's, of course. Keep counting scores in column 1 until you have reached question 20, and then, in the box below for column 1, enter the total number of x's you have circled in column 1 for the whole test.

2. Repeat this process for the circled scores in each of the remaining columns. You will have a score for each box below, ranging from 0 (lowest possible score) to 22 (highest possible score).

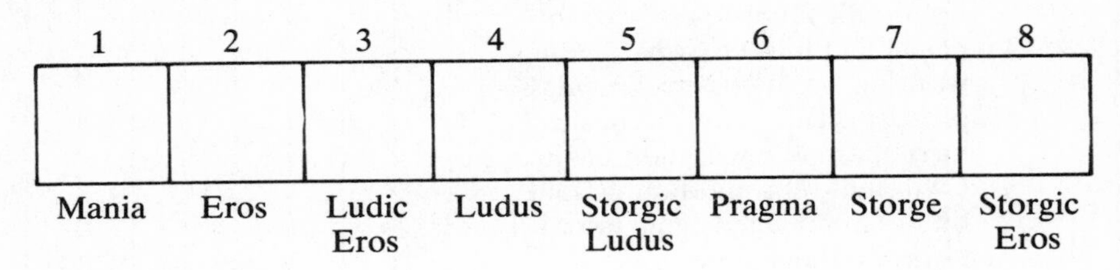


These eight scores will give you some idea of what type of relationship yours is, and probably also your preferred type of love. Of course, few people are so extreme that their love conforms to a perfect type (a score of twenty-two on one scale and zero on the others). In fact, the highest score observed by Lee was a nineteen on mania, and that was 'a very manic relationship indeed'. For most people, the highest score, indicating the type of love that is present, is around ten or eleven.

Note that no scale is provided for agape, the selfless, dutiful form of love. This is because Lee found it non-existent in the people he studied. Apparently such love is a theoretical ideal reserved for the saints. The nearest Lee found in reality was a mixture of storge and eros, consisting of intense, idealistic intimacy without physical preoccupation. Likewise, Lee finds that other mixtures of his primaries, such as ludic-eros are distinguishable from their compounds like mania which take on new characteristics beyond the sum of their constituents. For a full description of these various types of love and lovers, the reader is referred to Lee's book *Lovestyles*.

Lee's work is an impressive first shot at producing a comprehensive typology of love. It is possible to criticize the statistics he used to compile it (a somewhat primitive form of factor analysis) and there are some conceptional problems yet to be solved. Nevertheless, the main point he makes about the measurement of love – that we must first ask 'what kind' before 'how much' – is a valid and important one. There are many different kinds of love, some quite unconnected with others. In failing to take note of this point a great deal of the research effort to date has been wasted.

How do men and women differ with respect to their preferred

styles of love? T. Hatkoff and T. Lasswell (1979) gave a questionnaire like Lee's to 544 students and other volunteers in the south and west of the US. Women were more pragmatic and storgic than men. Presumably they have to be practical about affairs of the heart because they are so often economically dependent upon their husbands. On the other hand, they also scored higher than men on what might seem to be the opposite characteristic, mania. No doubt it is the dependence of women on men that causes them to be jealous and possessive – two of the main characteristics of mania. The men, of course, were more inclined to be erotic, in line with their sexual urgency and emphasis on physical attraction, and more ludic – they can afford to be more playful about sex and love because they do not run the risk of getting pregnant and becoming unmarried mothers.

This suggestion that women may be cooler in matters of the heart than men is supported by other findings. As we have noted, women are less influenced by physical appearance than men, and when social class lines are crossed they are less likely to marry down than men. W. Kephart (1967) found the percentage reporting that they were 'very easily attracted to the opposite sex' was nearly twice as high for males as females. It is also interesting that twice as many men reported having loved an older woman (61 per cent) as women reported having loved a younger man (30 per cent). What is more, the females who had been romantically involved with a younger man showed evidence of maladjustment on a personality inventory and relatively poor college grades, which was not the case with males who had been involved with older women. Lastly, the difference between men and women is seen in their answers to the question: 'If a boy (girl) had all the other qualities you desired, would you marry this person if you were not in love with him (her)?' Nearly two-thirds of boys said 'no', but less than one-third of girls did so. Apart from placing less value on physical attractiveness, women seem to regard love as less important in marital choice than men do.

What happens to a budding relationship if the parents of one or other of the parties express opposition or attempt to interfere with it in some way? R. Driscoll and associates (1972) found that dating and married couples who perceived a high degree of 'parental interference' produced higher scores on Rubin's love scale. Furthermore, a follow up some months later revealed that where parental interference had increased, so had the couple's mutual passion. Similarly,

Rubin found higher love scores in couples with different religions compared to couples who shared the same religion, although this finding applied only to couples who had been together for less than eighteen months. Thus it appears that under some circumstances obstacles which threaten a relationship can, at least temporarily, act to fertilize the blooming of romantic love within it. One way of explaining this paradoxical 'Romeo and Juliet effect' is in terms of a 'cognitive dissonance'. The 'logic' may go something like this: 'Everything is against us and yet we are still together, therefore we must be very much in love.' Social isolation might also heighten the experience of love in couples who do not have parental consent. As Duvall noted, young people who fall into conflict with their family for any reason will seek solidarity within an alternative social unit, in this case their courtship or marriage.

Perhaps some weaker relationships are actually disbanded in response to parental pressure, leaving only the deeper, more intense relationships to remain. This would also make for a correlation between parental opposition and love scores in the relationships which survive. Nevertheless, parents who seek to interfere with an 'unsuitable' love match should be warned that a reaction may occur if they are unsuccessful in breaking up the relationship.

Almost any form of arousal seems to be conducive to love. It does not seem to matter whether it is positive in nature (e.g. excitement or success arising out of amateur dramatics, mountain climbing or passing an examination) or unpleasant (e.g. danger, fear, pain), though it helps if the experience is shared. In a classic experiment, S. Schachter (1969) showed that people who had been rendered anxious in an experimental situation sought affiliation with others in a similar plight. Female students who were strangers to each other took part in an experiment supposedly on the physiological effects of electric shock. Half were told the shocks would be painful; the others were told they would only cause a tingling sensation. Before the experiment the women were asked whether they would prefer to wait alone or in a classroom with other subjects. Twice as many girls whose anxiety was aroused chose to wait with others in the same predicament.

This suggests that people seek human contact when feeling anxious. There is also evidence that anxiety increases sexual arousal. D. Dutton and A. Aron (1974) studied the behaviour of men on two types of bridge – a dangerous suspension bridge and an ordinary, safe bridge. The suspension bridge overlooked a 230-foot drop onto rocks below and swayed dangerously so that people had to walk across slowly, clasping onto a low hand-rail. Male traversers were approached by an attractive female interviewer who gave them a projective personality test called the Thematic Apperception Test. The sexual content of their answers was greater on the suspension bridge. Also, the interviewer gave the men her phone number saying she would be happy to give them further details about the study. Significantly more of the men on the suspension bridge attempted subsequent contact with her.

Apparently fear is conducive to attraction and love, which might explain the striking increase in romances during the war years, as well as the widespread belief that illicit love affairs are more rewarding than socially sanctioned ones.

The work of Schachter has led to a theory as to why emotional arousal is conducive to falling in love. It seems that the experience of any given emotion involves two separate stages. The first is an awareness of physiological arousal (e.g. quickened breath, a beating heart), and the second is the labelling of the arousal as a particular emotion, such as anger, fear or love. The rules for this labelling are learned from other people, both directly and through the mass media, and a person will experience love only if he concludes that love is an appropriate label for his feelings of arousal.

Support for this 'attribution theory', as it is called, comes from experiments in which subjects are injected with adrenalin (a drug which produces a general arousal reaction). The emotional experience that they describe is found to depend upon their cognitive appraisal of the situation, e.g. what effect they expect the drug to have and the way in which other people supposedly on the drug are seen to behave.

Sexual arousal would seem particularly well placed to be labelled (mislabelled?) as 'love', which might explain why both sexual gratification and frustration have been cited by different theorists as conducive to romantic love. What at first sight seems a direct contradiction is easily accounted for by attribution theory. A person who is aroused in the presence of an attractive partner either because sexual consummation is blocked or because gratification has been obtained may under appropriate circumstances classify his (her) emotion as love. S. Valins (1966) has shown that even the erroneous belief that a woman has excited a man can facilitate his attraction for her. Male college students were given false feedback concerning their heart rate as they looked at a series of *Playboy* pin-ups. For some of the slides the heartbeat was heard to quicken, while for others there was no reaction. When the men were subsequently asked to rate the girls in the pictures they markedly preferred the ones they thought had aroused them. This effect was found to persist even when they were interviewed again a month later in a totally different context.

The attribution theory is relevant to a great variety of experimental findings and intuitive observations about love. The facilitating effects of parental obstruction, forced separation, rejection, fear and excitement can all be accounted for. Even some deviations such as masochism can be partly comprehended in this light, as well as the revitalizing effects of lovers' tiffs. No other theory seems capable of explaining why the sensation we call love can incorporate elements of emotions as far apart as grief, jealousy, fear and joy, and why such a wide variety of arousing experiences have the capacity to fuel romantic passion.

## References

ARONSON, E. & LINDER, D., 'Gain and loss of esteem as determinants of interpersonal attractiveness', *Journal of Experimental Social Psychology*, 1965, **1**, 156–71.

BARDIS, P.D., 'The concept of love in Homer' in, M. Cook & G.D. Wilson (eds), *Love and Attraction: An International Conference.* Oxford: Pergamon, 1979.

BECK, S.B., 'Women's somatic preferences' in M. Cook & G.D. Wilson (eds), *Love and Attraction: An International Conference.* Oxford: Pergamon, 1978.

BERSCHEID, E., DION, K., WALSTER, E. & WALSTER, G.W., 'Physical attractiveness and dating choice: a test of the matching hypothesis', *Journal of Experimental Social Psychology*, 1971, **7**, 173–89.

CENTERS, R., 'The completion hypothesis and the compensatory dynamic in intersexual attraction and love', *Journal of Psychology*, 1972, **82**, 111-26.

CENTERS, R., *Sexual Attraction and Love: An Instrumental Theory.* Springfield, Illinois: C.C. Thomas, 1975.

DION, K.L. & DION, K.K., 'Personality and behavioural correlates of romantic love' in M. Cook & G.D. Wilson (eds), *Love and Attraction: An International Conference.* Oxford: Pergamon, 1979.

DRISCOLL, R., DAVIS, K.E. & LIPETZ, M.E., 'Parental interference and romantic love: the Romeo and Juliet effect', *Journal of Personality and Social Psychology*, 1972, **24**, 1–10.

DUTTON, D.G. & ARON, A.P. 'Some evidence for heightened sexual attraction under conditions of high anxiety', *Journal of Personality and Social Psychology*, 1974, **30**, 510–17.

DUVALL, E.M., 'Adolescent love as a reflection of teenagers' search for identity' in M.E. Lasswell and T.E. Lasswell (eds), *Love, Marriage, Family: A Developmental Approach*. Glenview, Illinois: Scott-Foresman, 1973.

GALTON, F., *Inquiries into Human Faculty and its Development*. London: Macmillan, 1883.

HATKOFF, T.S. & LASSWELL, T.E., 'Male-female similarities and differences in conceptualizing love' in M. Cook & G.D. Wilson (eds), *Love and Attraction: An International Conference*. Oxford: Pergamon, 1979.

HESS, E.H., 'Attitude and pupil size', *Scientific American*, 1965, **212**, 46–54.

HOPKINS, J.R., 'Sexual behaviour in adolescence', *Journal of Social Issues*, 1977, **33**, 67–85.

KEPHART, W.M., 'Some correlates of romantic love', *Journal of Marriage and the Family*, 1967, **29**, 470–8.

LEE, J.A., *Lovestyles*. London: Dent, 1976.

MORGAN, C.J., LOCKARD, J.S., FAHRENBRUCK, C.E. & SMITH, J.L., 'Hitchhiking: Social Signals at a distance, *Bulletin of the Psychonomic Society,* 1975, **5**, 459–61.

PEPLAU, L.A., RUBIN, Z. & HILL, C.T., 'Sexual intimacy in dating relationships', *Journal of Social Issues*, 1977, **33**, 86–109.

RUBIN, Z., 'Measurement of romantic love', *Journal of Personality and Social Psychology*, 1970, **16**, 265–73.

SCHACHTER, S., *The Psychology of Affiliation*. Stanford: Stanford University Press, 1969.

SILVERMAN, I., 'Physical attractiveness and courtship', *Sexual Behaviour*, September 1971, 22–5.

SMITH, H., 'What is sexiest about men?', *Cosmopolitan*, January 1975.

VALINS, S., 'Cognitive effects of false heart-rate feedback', *Journal of Personality of Social Psychology*, 1966, **4**, 400–8.

WALSTER, E., WALSTER, G.W., PILIAVIN, J. & SCHMIDT, L., ' "Playing hard to get": Understanding an elusive phenomenon', *Journal of Personality and Social Psychology*, 1973, **26**, 113–21.

WILSON, G.D. & NIAS, D.K.B., *Love's Mysteries*. London: Open Books, 1976.

WILSON, P.R., 'Perceptual distortion of height as a function of ascribed academic status', *Journal of Social Psychology*, 1968, **74**, 97–102.

# 6 For better or worse

Most of us get married at some time in our lives and at least half of us regret it quite bitterly. Some of the regretful ones remain trapped in misery for life; the more desperate (or resourceful) escape by getting separated or divorced. In Britain today there is about one divorce to every three marriages and the gap between 'input' and 'output' rates is closing. Some people get divorced and remarried several times in the hope of eventually getting it right. A few, like Richard Burton and Elizabeth Taylor, marry the same person more than once. Divorce is on the increase in our society, and so are some of the alternatives to conventional marriage such as communes and cohabitation, but marriage itself remains as popular as ever. Young people and recent divorcees alike are heading up the aisle to the altar like lemmings to the sea or sheep to the slaughter.

Why do so many people get married when they ought to know that, statistically at least, there is a good chance it will not work out? Most people, if asked, will give 'love' as their reason for getting married but, as we have seen, this catch-all justification bears analysis into a variety of more practical considerations. At one time it might have seemed that men got married for a regular supply of sex and women got married for economic security (given the likelihood that they would soon have children to support as well as themselves). Today these reasons are not sufficient; men have much greater scope for finding sex outside marriage and women have better opportunities to support themselves economically, particularly if they choose not to have children. Bernard Murstein (1976) asked a large sample of engaged couples in Connecticut what they expected to get out of marriage. 'Companionship with the spouse' was seen to be the prime value of marriage by both men and women, followed by 'healthy and happy children', 'a satisfactory sex life' and 'a home where one feels one belongs'. 'Economic security' came a poor fifth in this league of marital advantages and there were no differences between men and women in this, or in the value placed on sexual satisfaction. Apparently, the prime function of marriage today is to forestall loneliness by providing steady companions in the form of a spouse and children.

Apart from the individual needs which are served by marriage, the institution is powerfully sponsored by society, which of course has an interest in stabilizing people and seeing that their children are provided for by both parents. The result is that tremendous pressure is exerted upon boys and girls by church, state, parents and other agents of society, to get married almost from the time they are capable of reproduction. Girls in particular are sold a glorified, fairy-tale image of marriage which pushes them inexorably towards it, and this deception is a cruel one, for as we shall see, the marriage state is frequently more distressing to women than to men.

The next question is why we marry the particular person that we do. Here the main dispute over the years has been between those who say that 'opposites attract' and those who claim that 'like marries like' or 'birds of a feather flock together'. The former position is called *complementation* theory and it maintains that a person with one temperamental trait is best suited by a partnership with someone having the opposite characteristic. Thus a dominant person gets on with a submissive person, an extravert with an introvert, an anxious person with a stable person, and so on. *Similarity theory*, on the other hand, suggests that we gravitate towards people that we see as being like ourselves because we have more in common with them. Both positions have a ring of plausibility about them yet they seem to be directly contradictory. Therefore we must look to empirical studies to sort out which is correct or under which conditions each may be expected to apply. There are various ways of going about this.

The simplest method is to give personality tests to large samples of engaged or married couples and study the answers to see whether they have paired up on the basis of similarity or complementation. When this is done we find hardly any support for the complementation idea but a great deal of similarity between the partners, particularly as regards age, race, religion, social class, intelligence, political attitudes, physical attractiveness, hobbies and interests. The similarity effect is less striking with respect to personality traits but it remains a more important principle of attraction than complementation. Even the personality dimensions that would have been thought most likely to go according to the complementation principle, such as dominance and submission, show a pattern of likeness rather than opposites.

In a fairly typical study of this kind, D. Nias (1977) studied the intercorrelations between husbands and wives on various questionnaires concerning personality and interests. Below are shown some of the items on which the couples were most similar (the higher the correlation the more similar were the couple on that item; if complementation applied, the figures would be negative).

| | |
|---|---|
| *Personality:* | Have you had more trouble than most? (.25) |
| | Are there people who wish to harm you? (.26) |
| | Would you take drugs which may have strange or dangerous effects? (.21) |
| | Are you usually very unlucky? (.29) |
| | Do people tell you a lot of lies? (.19) |
| | Do you like going out a lot? (.20) |
| | Do you prefer to have few but special friends? (.19) |
| *Leisure:* | Going out for a drink (.34) |
| | Going to dances (.34) |
| *Television:* | Variety shows (.29) |
| | Pop music programmes (.37) |
| *Reading:* | Pop music magazines (.31) |
| | Romance magazines (.22) |
| *Sport:* | Watching favourite sport (.40) |
| | Watching with children (.47) |
| *Encouraging children:* | Music (.57) |
| | Part-time jobs (.51) |

There were quite a number of respects in which the couples showed no similarity at all (for example, cooking, reading, watching adventure films, sports ability while at school) but there were no instances in which the couple could be said to be opposite in temperament or inclination.

Of course it could be objected that in this kind of study the couples might have grown to be similar because they had been living together, even though they started out as opposites when they first met and fell in love, but there are ways of checking on this possibility. One widely used technique is called the 'computer dance'. Students are given a ticket for a dance on condition that they accept for the evening a partner who is chosen for them supposedly by computer. Various personality tests are given at the time the ticket is collected and after the dance the students are asked how much they were attracted to their partner and whether they intend to pursue the relationship. The first outstanding finding of these studies concerns the importance of physical attractiveness in determining first impressions. After a three-hour encounter on the dance floor the extent to which people were liked by their partner depended almost entirely on their looks. Other attributes such as intelligence and personality counted for very little at this stage. However, studies using this blind date approach with a longer period of enforced contact have shown that similar personality and attitudes do make for increased liking and once again there is no evidence for complementation as a factor in partner preferences.

There have also been a number of studies of the outcome of commercial computer dating and here again it is found that partnerships are more successful if based on similarity rather than supposed complementation. Indeed, the similarity principle is now so well established that most marriage bureaux and computer dating agencies incorporate it as one of their major matching criteria. A typical partner matching programme operates according to a hierarchical or 'hurdle' process by which matching criteria are taken in successive order of presumed importance until the number of partners is reduced to the required number, like so:

(1) *Gender:* Select partners of opposite sex.

(2) *Geographical proximity:* Select partners within tolerable distance, say twenty-mile radius.

(3) *Age:* Range from equal age to man fifteen years older than woman.

(4) *Height:* Range from equal height to man one foot taller.

(5) *Social attitudes/religion:* Not more than two points removed along a five point scale of liberalism versus conservatism.

(6) *Social class/intelligence/education:* Not more than two points removed along a five point scale.

(7) *Sex drive:* Not more than two points removed along a five point scale of libido.

(8) *Physical attractiveness:* Not more than two points removed along a five point scale based on rating of supplied photo.

(9) *Personality/interests:* Not more than two points removed along a five point scale of Outdoor/active/extravert versus Indoor/quiet/ introvert.

(10) *Smoking:* Concordance.

(11) *Drinking:* Concordance.

(12) *Attitude towards marriage:* Similarity on favourable/unfavourable dichotomy.

(13) *Attitude towards children:* Similarity on favourable/unfavourable.

(14) *Attitude towards extramarital sex:* Similarity on tolerant/intolerant.

In this programme, which is similar to the system used by one of London's largest computer matching companies, the computer first selects all people of the opposite sex as potential partners, thus eliminating 50 per cent of cards in the pool. (This is reasonable since their advertisements make clear that they do not cater for homosexual matchings.) The next most important piece of information is where the person lives, since few people are able to travel vast distances for courting. Next comes age. In general, we are attracted to people of similar age, though it is optimal if the man is slightly older than the woman. And so on, through height, social attitudes, social class, sex drive, physical attractiveness, personality and interests. At each stage a high proportion of prospective partners is eliminated on the basis of their dissimilarity. If by this stage there are still a lot of partners in the pool to choose from, then more are eliminated on the basis of specific habits and attitudes that are known or supposed to be important for compatibility, such as smoking, drinking, attitudes towards marriage, children and extramarital sex. In addition, people are allowed a certain number of absolute exclusions, by which is meant they are able to specify at the outset that they do not want to meet people of a particular race, religion, political persuasion or habit. These exclusions take priority over the hierarchical series shown above, which only comes into operation after these preferences (or prejudices as they may be called) have been satisfied. Finally, when enough criteria have been applied to leave only one or two prospective partners to be considered, further elimination is carried out on the basis of a detailed reading of the requirements of the parties concerned and the clients are shown full questionnaire responses and photographs of each other before agreeing to meet. This reduces the risk of embarrassment later on. Note that the outstanding feature of this matching procedure is the emphasis placed on similarity of various attributes. With the exception of gender, the couple are matched entirely on the basis of similarities; the principle of complementation does not enter into the programme at all.

Even attempts to detect more subtle principles of complementation have failed. Birtchnell (1979) thought that our sibling position in the family (i.e. whether we have brothers or sisters, older or younger) might influence our choice of mate. He was particularly interested in the idea that strong heterosexual relationships sometimes develop between siblings and that some people select marriage partners so as to replicate an early relationship with a sibling of the opposite sex. This idea, which was first put forward by psychoanalyst W. Toman, supposes that a man with an older sister, for example, would be inclined to pair off with a woman who has a younger brother. Theoretically, each would then bring to the marriage appropriate experience in relating to the opposite sex and the marriage would be happier. In a study of 2000 people, half reporting successful marriages and half unsuccessful, Birtchnell found no evidence for assortative mating according to the sibling positions of the individual and his/her spouse. Nor was there any difference between successful and unsuccessful marriages in this respect. In all his data only one positive finding appeared; among a subgroup of 27 per cent who expressed a special fondness for a particular sibling, there was a tendency for men especially fond of an older sister to be married to women who only had a younger brother. This was not, however, related to the success of their marriage. As Birtchnell says, this finding would be more noteworthy had it been supported by a similar association of women expressing fondness for younger brothers, marrying men with older sisters. Nor were there any positive findings with respect to men who were especially fond of younger sisters or women who were especially fond of older brothers. Sibling relationships may be important in the marital choice of a few particular individuals but the Toman theory does not have much efficacy as a universal law.

It seems, then, that complementation, if it applies at all, does so only in a few exceptional cases. Perhaps there is the occasional masochist who marries a sadist in order that they might satisfy reciprocal needs, or the odd young man who marries an older woman because he is seeking motherly security. But universal patterns of this kind are very difficult to find. For the most part, people seem to pair off with others who are similar to themselves.

The tendency for couples to pair off in terms of a similar level of physical attractiveness has been demonstrated in a number of ingenious experiments. For example, in one study, wedding photographs were cut in half so as to separate the husband and wife who were then individually rated for attractiveness. Such studies show that people tend to mate with somebody who is about equally good looking or plain, as the case may be. Where there is a striking discrepancy between the attractiveness of the two partners it can usually be accounted for in terms of a trade-off of some other highly valued commodity such as wealth, intelligence or social status. It is not uncommon for a man of exceptionally high social standing to marry a woman very much younger or more beautiful than himself. Most people would agree that Carlo Ponti is less beautiful than Sophia Loren, but their partnership is fairly stable because he contributes talent and accomplishment to it. Similarly, Charlie Chaplin was able, as a rich, talented and highly respected man, to marry women very much younger than himself. Occasionally we see reversals on this pattern when a well-known woman becomes associated with a relatively unknown man who is closer to his physical prime, e.g. Barbara Hutton and a certain English princess. Relationships of this kind could be described as depending upon a kind of complementation, though not complementation of personality.

There is one other sense in which complementation could be said to apply. Several traits show average differences between men and women. Height is a fairly obvious physical dimension of this kind, but there are also sex differences on some personality dimensions such as dominance versus submission. On average, women tend to be submissive and men dominant, even though there is considerable overlap between the two sexes. When this fact of male-female differences on the trait is combined with the fact that there is a positive correlation between partners, we are led to the model illustrated in Figure 9 below. This suggests that dominant men tend to marry women who are dominant in relation to their own sex but on the submissive side of their male partner. This pattern of optimal difference is repeated all the way down the dimension to the bottom where submissive men are marrying women slightly on the submissive side of themselves.

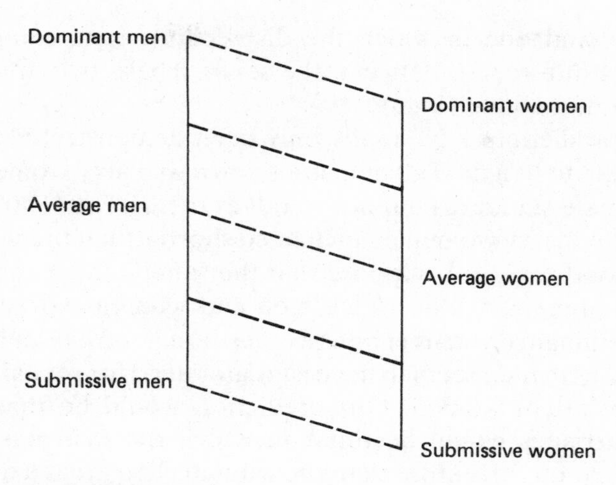


Figure 9 Expected partnerships

This model is appealing because it partly reconciles the similarity and complementation theories. On the one hand, it squares with the fact that people marry similar others rather than opposites as revealed by correlational analysis, and on the other it suggests that men like women who are on the traditionally feminine side of themselves and vice versa. The implication is that there are two types of unlikely and unstable relationship – one where the discrepancy on the variable is

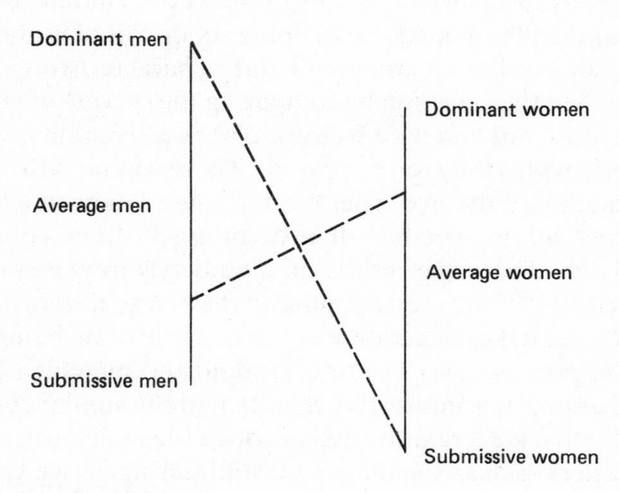


Figure 10 Unstable partnerships

too great, and one in which the discrepancy runs counter to the traditional differences between the sexes. These two arrangements are illustrated above (Figure 10).

These predictions have really only been demonstrated to operate with respect to height. Tall men are known to marry women who are tall by female standards but not so tall as themselves, and short men also tend to marry women an inch or so shorter than themselves. But there is good reason to suppose that the same pattern applies to all important dimensions on which men and women characteristically differ. Dominance versus submissiveness is a good example; another is libido, where men seem to have a greater need for sexual adventure and variety than women. Our prediction would be that the most stable marriages would be those in which the man has a slightly greater need for adventure than the woman. Too great a discrepancy would strain the relationship because the man would be chronically unsatisfied while a reverse discrepancy would be very threatening to the male ego and thus also fairly unstable. What seems to be needed at this point is a predictive study of mateships and marital success based explicitly on this elaborated similarity model. However plausible it seems, and despite the fact that the computer matching companies implicitly base their matching on such a concept (as illustrated by the programme given above), the evidence so far is mostly indirect.

If in most respects we marry a spouse who is similar to ourselves, are we making the right choice in doing so, or would we be better off marrying someone with complementary characteristics? K. Barton (1976) studied this question by comparing the success of marriages in which the husband and wife were similar in personality with that of marriages in which they were opposite. There was no difference in the overall stability of the two types of marriage as indicated by answers to questions about whether divorce or separation had ever been contemplated. There was, however, a tendency for wives to be more sexually satisfied if they were similar to their husbands in personality. (Husbands' sexual satisfaction was not dependent on being similar to the wife in personality.) Bearing in mind the matching hypothesis described above, it is interesting to note that the similar couples were more likely to have a relationship in which the male took a dominant role in matters such as spending and childrearing, as well as sex. One wonders if this male dominance in the bedroom could have been responsible for the sexual satisfaction in the wives. Many theorists (admittedly mostly male) have supposed that women need to be dominated in order to enjoy sex to the full. In any case, Barton's study provides some slight support for the idea that people are happier if they marry someone similar to themselves in personality.

The advantage of marrying someone similar in personality has recently been confirmed using the superior predictive approach. P. Bentler and D. Newcomb (1979) studied 162 couples who were just embarking on marriage, taking details of their background and having them fill out personality questionnaires. Four years later they recontacted them to find that, being Californians, about one-third of their marriages had already collapsed. Their interest was in comparing the characteristics of those couples whose marriages had survived with those of the couples whose marriages had been disbanded. Again, the clearest finding concerned the similarity in personality between the partners at the time of their marriage. Similar partners were significantly more likely to have stayed together. Certain other characteristics of the individuals also had some prognostic significance; for example, emotional instability in either partner was a bad sign, while bourgeois materialistic values on the part of the wife were a good sign (at least as regards the survival of the marriage). Whether or not the couple had lived together before getting married made no difference to the chances of the marriage lasting.

Divorce, of course, is far from being a perfect indicator of marital failure. After all, there is no guarantee that marriages which continue are happier than those that do not. To a large extent the likelihood of divorce depends on the strength of the social pressures operating against it – family pressures, legal and religious strictures, and so on. There is a striking difference between the divorce rate in Italy and that in California but few people are inclined to say that Italian marriages are happier. It is just that, as depicted in the film *Divorce Italian Style*, in Italy it is usually easier to kill your spouse in a fit of jealous rage and serve a nominal prison sentence than go through legal divorce proceedings. Many people think that film stars must lead very unhappy lives because their marriages are always breaking up. Perhaps their marriages break up for purposes of publicity, or because they are having such active extramarital sex lives and such a lot of fun that a few broken marriages is small price to pay. Therefore, while we may be able to examine factors that affect the chances of divorce, it is not always possible to say that divorce is a bad thing in terms of causing great unhappiness to the parties involved. Sometimes people are desperately unhappy because they have stayed together in a relationship that was a mistake from the outset and destructive to each individual.

The other way of assessing marital success is to ask the couple (or the two parted individuals) whether they regarded it as successful. This is what Birchnell did in his study of Toman's theory, but to a large extent he found that their judgments depended on whether the marriage had lasted or not, which brings us back to the same problems as using divorce as an index. And if couples are simply asked whether they are happy in their marriage, it is difficult to tell whether they are happy *because of* their marriage or whether the marriage is happy because it comprises two individuals who would be happy in most circumstances, married or not. This is a very real theoretical problem, because there is a striking tendency for happy individuals to make happy marriages. Despite these problems, researchers have developed questionnaires for assessing marital happiness. One of the best known of these is Locke's 'Marital Adjustment Test', a modified form of which follows. Scores for each answer have been entered on the questionnaire so that if you wish you can easily add up your own marital adjustment score. The scores given are for husbands; the wives' scores are the same except where a different score appears in brackets after that of the husband.

## Marital Happiness Questionnaire

All the questions can be answered by placing a check next to the appropriate answer. Please fill out all items. If you cannot give the exact answer to a question, answer the best you can. Give the answers that best fit your marriage at the present time.

(1) Have you ever wished you had not married?

*a* Frequently 2

*b* Occasionally 2

*c* Rarely 6

(2) If you had your life to live over again would you:

| | | |
|---|---|---|
| *a* | Marry the same person | 7 |
| *b* | Marry a different person | 1 |
| *c* | Not marry at all | 1 |

(3) Do husband and wife engage in outside activities together?

| | | |
|---|---|---|
| *a* | All of them | 5 |
| *b* | Some of them | 4 |
| *c* | Few of them | 2 |
| *d* | None of them | 2 |

(4) In leisure time, which do you prefer?

| | | |
|---|---|---|
| *a* | Both husband and wife to stay at home | 6 |
| *b* | Both to be on the go | 3 (4) |
| *c* | One to be on the go and other to stay home | 2 |

(5) Do you and your mate generally talk things over together?

| | | |
|---|---|---|
| *a* | Never | 2 |
| *b* | Now and then | 2 |
| *c* | Almost always | 4 |
| *d* | Always | 5 |

(6) How often do you kiss your mate?

| | | |
|---|---|---|
| *a* | Every day | 5 |
| *b* | Now and then | 3 |
| *c* | Almost never | 3 |

(7) Check any of the following items which you think have caused *serious* difficulties in your marriage.

Mate's attempt to control my spending money

Other difficulties over money

Religious differences

Different amusement interests

Lack of mutual friends
Constant bickering
Interference of in-laws
Lack of mutual affection (no longer in love)
Unsatisfying sex relations
Selfishness and lack of cooperation
Adultery
Desire to have children
Sterility of husband or wife
Venereal diseases
Mate paid attention to (became familiar with) another person
Desertion
Non support
Drunkenness
Gambling
Ill health
Mate sent to jail
Other reasons

| Scoring: | *Number checked* | *Score* |
|---|---|---|
| | 0 | 6 |
| | 1 | 6 |
| | 2 | 4 (5) |
| | 3 | 4 |
| | 4 | 2 (3) |
| | 5 | 2 (3) |
| | 6 | 2 |

(8) How many things satisfy you most about your marriage?

| | |
|---|---|
| *a* Nothing | 3 |
| *b* One thing | 3 |
| *c* Two things | 4 |
| *d* Three or more | 5 |

(9) When disagreements arise they generally result in:

*a* Husband giving in 2 (3)
*b* Wife giving in 3 (2)
*c* Neither giving in 2 (2)
*d* Agreement by mutual give and take 6 (6)

(10) What is the total number of times you left mate or mate left you because of conflict?

*a* No times 7
*b* One or more times 1

(11) How frequently do you and your mate get on each other's nerves around the house?

*a* Never 5
*b* Occasionally 5 (4)
*c* Frequently 3
*d* Almost always 3
*e* Always 3

(12) What are your feelings on sex relations between you and your mate?

*a* Very enjoyable 5
*b* Enjoyable 4 (5)
*c* Tolerable 2
*d* Disgusting 2
*e* Very disgusting 2

(13) What are your mate's feelings on sex relations with you?

*a* Very enjoyable 5
*b* Enjoyable 4 (3)
*c* Tolerable 3
*d* Disgusting 3
*e* Very disgusting 3

State approximate extent of agreement or disagreement between husband and wife on the items overleaf:

| *Check one column for each item below* | | *Always agree* | *Almost always agree* | *Occasionally disagree* | *Frequently disagree* | *Almost always disagree* | *Always disagree* |
|---|---|---|---|---|---|---|---|
| (14) | Handling family finances (Example: instalment buying) | 5 | 5 | 2 | 2 | 2 | 2 |
| (15) | Matters of recreation (Example: going to dances) | 5 (4) | 4 | 4 (3) | 3 | 3 | 3 |
| (16) | Demonstration of affection (Example: frequency of kissing) | 5 | 4 | 3 | 3 | 3 | 3 |
| (17) | Friends (Example: dislike of mate's friends) | 5 | 5 | 3 (2) | 2 | 2 | 2 |
| (18) | Intimate relations (Example: sex relations) | 5 | 5 (4) | 2 (3) | 2 (3) | 2 (3) | 2 (3) |
| (19) | Ways of dealing with in-laws | 5 | 5 | 2 (3) | 2 (3) | 2 (3) | 2 (3) |
| (20) | The amount of time that should be spent together | 5 (6) | 4 | 2 (3) | 2 | 2 | 2 |
| (21) | Conventionality (Example: right, good, or proper conduct) | 5 | 5 (4) | 2 | 2 | 2 | 2 |
| (22) | Aims, goals and things believed to be important in life | 6 | 4 | 2 | 2 | 2 | 2 |

(23) On the scale line below check the mark *which best describes the degree of happiness*, everything considered, of your marriage. The middle point, 'happy' represents the degree of happiness which most people get from marriage, and the scale gradually ranges on one side to those few who experience extreme joy in marriage and on the other to those few who are very unhappy in marriage.

| | Very unhappy | | | Happy | | | Perfectly happy |
|---|---|---|---|---|---|---|---|
| Scoring: | 0 | 1 | 3 | 7 | 10 | 13 | 18 |

If you answer all the questions and add up the scores for each item, you will come out with a total of between 48 and 138. Scores towards the top of this range indicate a high degree of marital compatibility and very low scores suggest there is considerable discontent in the marriage. The average score of a large sample of American husbands and wives was around 109 and the vast majority of people were within twenty points above and below this number (Kimmel & Van der Veen, 1974). Couples seeking marriage guidance typically score less than 80.

This overall score is to some extent a simplification since it was found that sexual compatibility and companionship did not always go together. Some couples get on very well together domestically but do not find each other sexually exciting or satisfying. A smaller number of others hit it off sexually but otherwise have nothing in common and do not enjoy each other's company. Nevertheless, the total score based on both these aspects is a good measure of the general health of the marriage. One item in the questionnaire is peculiar in that it differentiates men and women more than good and bad marriages. Most wives report that they 'rarely get on each other's nerves', while most husbands say they 'frequently get on each other's nerves'. It might be thought that this means marriage is a less desirable state for men than for women. But not so; although the differences are not very great, husbands tend to come out as slightly happier than wives on the questionnaire above (mean scores of 110 and 108).

The finding that husbands are more content with their marriages than wives has cropped up several times. In a very large study of 5000 married couples in California (Renne, 1970), 9 per cent of women reported that they had seriously considered separation or divorce quite recently, compared to only 6 per cent of the men. Similarly 46 per cent of husbands said they were 'very happy' in their marriage compared to only 42 per cent of wives. Probably this is because women have greater expectations concerning marriage and are more dependent upon the marital relationship for identity, companionship and sex. The average husband divides his time about equally between his wife on the one hand and his business contacts and office girls on the other. The wife is relatively isolated in the home and must make do with a cup of tea with a neighbour, a chat with the butcher, and the children after school. Also, women's lib notwithstanding, it is easier for a man to have affairs than a woman. For one thing, he has more excuses for being away from home. In any case, a man's job is usually just as important to him as his family. For a woman the marriage may be almost everything.

Whatever the reason, marriage is clearly no rose garden for the average woman. It may even be detrimental to her health. J. Bernard (1972) cites a great deal of demographic data to prove that married women have poorer mental and physical health than either single women or married men. Married women are more prone to 'nervous breakdown' and depressive illness than married men, and when it comes to an analysis of death rates it emerges that being married is about twice as good for men as it is for women in terms of its effects on survival. Perhaps we shall see the day when marriage certificates carry a Government Health Warning to women. Altogether the facts are sufficient to question the popular assumption that marriage is an institution designed by women for their own protection and benefit.

The first few years of marriage may be particularly stressful for a woman because the newly-wed stage is more 'transitional' for wives than for husbands. Frequently they have to move from some kind of career orientation to a new orientation of housewife or mother, with all the anxieties that are typically generated by any major change of life style. For the husband life carries on pretty much as before. According to W. Barry (1970) this would explain one of the most reliable generalizations to emerge from decades of marriage research, that various attributes of the husband and the way in which he is perceived by his wife are critical to marital success and happiness.

> Background factors generally considered to lead to a stable male identity, such as happiness of the husband's parents' marriage and the husband's close attachment to his father, are related to happiness in marriage. The higher the husband's socioeconomic status and educational level, the greater the marital happiness. The more stable and nonneurotic the husband portrays himself on personality inventories at the time of marriage and the more consistent he is in self-portrayal over the course of the marriage, the happier the marriage. The higher the wife rates him on emotional maturity as well as on fulfilling his role as husband in conformity to cultural expectation, the happier the marriage. The more the wife comes to resemble her husband on attitude and personality inventories over time, the happier the marriage.

Barry's idea is that husbands with stable self-identities can supply their wives with the security and emotional support that they need to tide them over the difficult years of transition to married and parental life. If the man fails to provide this strength and support his wife is likely to resent the sacrifice she is making for him or blame his inadequacy for her unhappiness. This is an appealing idea, but one cannot help thinking that if marital adjustment is more difficult for the wife than for the husband (as indeed it seems to be) then the personality characteristics of the wife herself should be at least equally important to the stability of the relationship.

An indication that the wife's ability to adjust to her changed role and life style is important to marital stability is found in a study of the personality predictors of divorce undertaken in California by T. Peskin and associates (see Horn, 1977). These researchers monitored the paths taken towards marriage and divorce by a group of people born around 1930. Subjects were interviewed every six months up until the age of seventeen to assess their personality and intellectual development, and they were interviewed again in 1960 and 1970 to see what had become of them at ages thirty and forty. There was little to distinguish men who were divorced from those who were still married; subjects in both groups were more warm, gregarious and popular than those who remained single. The single men were also less compliant and conventional and tended to be more independent. (Since these ratings of personality were taken during adolescence, they could not have been influenced by the marital status of the men.) With women the position was different. Single women were not distinguishable from the other groups, but divorced women were different from those who remained married. The married woman had been described in adolescence as more productive and intellectual than the divorced women, but at the same time they were relatively submissive and conventional. Girls who later divorced were rated as nonconformist, rebellious, negativistic and self-indulgent. Peskin interprets these results in terms of the particular importance of marriage for women. Unlike men, women effectively have to choose between 'personal growth' and 'relationship making'. The women who remain happily married are those who can absorb their individuality in the marriage relationship, becoming to some extent appendages to their husbands. These are of course the traditional, submissive women. Those who are more independent and assertive have difficulty in abandoning their own identity and are therefore strong candidates for divorce.

At this point we might recall the finding of Schlegel reported in Chapter 2 that women with atypical, masculine pelvic shapes, who tended to show assertive, masculine personality traits and sexual behaviour, also had more difficulty in holding down stable marriages. This seems consistent with findings of Peskin and others that women who fall naturally into the traditional female role of subservience to their husbands are less prone to divorce. Remember that we are making no value judgment about this. Divorce is usually a very unpleasant business, but that is not to say that it is necessarily more ghastly than the situation thus replaced.

Another finding emerging from Renne's large-scale American survey mentioned above was that couples currently raising children were more likely to be dissatisfied with their marriage than couples without children. (This might also seem counter-intuitive to many readers who have supposed that children normally bring happiness to their parents along with a feeling of accomplishment and purpose, yet the same finding is reliably reported elsewhere.) The *number* of children was not a significant factor – having one dependent child predicted marital unhappiness just a strongly as a whole tribe. While it is tempting to think of ways in which the arrival of children could have altered the relationship for the worse, perhaps interfering with the wife's career plans, education or recreation, this finding might be adequately explained by the relative ease with which childless couples can dissolve their marriage. In other words, couples who are unhappy with each other are more likely to 'make a go of it' if they have children than if they are free of responsibility. It is a fact that childless couples have a higher divorce rate. Here we have a good example of how divorce and marital unhappiness may be mutually exclusive alternatives rather than parallel indicators of marital failure. The tendency of poor and sick people to report greater marital unhappiness (also found in Renne's survey) may similarly be due to the fact that such people are more trapped in marriage than the healthy and wealthy who are better placed to dispose of an ailing marriage.

Difficulties in sorting out cause and effect also apply to the observation that children coming from broken homes run an increased risk of experiencing marital disruption themselves. This is often taken to imply that the development of such children has been impaired because they lacked a stable model in their parents. Possibly true, but it is also possible that they inherited certain character traits from their parents which are responsible for the unsettled lives of both their parents and themselves. A likely culprit is the personality variable of emotional instability (sometimes called neuroticism) which is known to be partly hereditary, being determined by the action of many different genes in concert. There is little doubt that people who are emotionally unstable tend to have more marital difficulties than stable people (Rogers *et al*., 1970). There remains some argument concerning which is the cause and which the effect, though there is more evidence to support the idea that unstable people make unstable marriages than the other way about. Note that this is one trait on which it is better to be different from your partner if you are highly unstable yourself. Marriages between two neurotics are not better than marriages between one neurotic and one stable person – if anything, the reverse is the case. And there is no evidence to support the 'contagion' theory which maintains that if one partner is neurotic the other will eventually be driven to emotional distraction as well. In Rogers' study, couples who had been together for a long time were no more similar in degree of neuroticism than couples married a short time.

Just how antithetical to marital peace and stability is mental disorder? Psychiatrist C. Blacker looked at the divorce rates among 8000 patients admitted to the Bethlem and Maudsley Hospitals in the years 1952–4 who had ever been married. Adding together those who were divorced, separated or cohabiting with someone other than their spouse, he found that the rates of marital breakdown were greatly varied for different patient groups. For patients diagnosed as psychotic (e.g. schizophrenic, paranoid and manic-depressive) the marital breakdown rate was 7 per cent. For neurotic disorders such as anxiety, hysteria and reactive depression the rate was 10 per cent. By far the highest incidence of broken marriages (23 per cent) was in the group of 'character disorders', including such conditions as psychopathy, alcoholism, drug addiction, delinquency and sexual deviation. Although these figures are given for men and women combined, the pattern was very similar for men and women separately. It is not difficult to see that conditions such as alcoholism and sexual deviation might make a person hard to live with, though it is possible that some of the symptoms could be exacerbated by an unhappy marriage. In the case of the neuroses particularly, the cause and effect could go either way. Neurotic people are often difficult to get on with, as suggested by the Rogers study above, but anxiety and depression also occur as reactions to the loss of a spouse.

While it is tempting to look at Blacker's results as showing divorce to be a kind of pathological manifestation, as indeed he does, it is only fair to the institution of divorce to look at comparable figures among people who might be presumed to be psychologically healthy and fulfilled. A suitable example would seem to be people distinguished in the arts and science who were studied by L. Hudson and B. Jacot using information contained in the 1969 British *Who's Who*. Certain groups showed very high rates. Social scientists, comprising mostly psychologists and anthropologists, topped the poll with a divorce rate of 23 per cent, which the keen reader will note is identical to that reported earlier for psychopaths, alcoholics, etc. After the social scientists came biological scientists with a rate of 12 per cent. Physical scientists were much less likely to be divorced, their rate being only 3 per cent. Artists and writers had a moderately low rate of 5 per cent, but they were an exceptional group in that about one-third of them had remained single or childless. These percentages cannot be directly compared with those of Blacker's mental patient groups because the average ages and exact eras were different. Likewise, it is difficult to compare these rates with general population norms because era and age and the time of study would have to be taken into account. Nevertheless, it is quite clear that divorce is not the preserve of people who are inadequate failures in life; there is a very substantial rate of divorce in eminent men of letters and science whose contribution to society is undenied.

How should we interpret the strikingly different rates of divorce for the different areas of specialization reported by Hudson and Jacot? Perhaps the easiest explanation is in terms of the Bohemianism of artists and social scientists relative to the more respectable (mundane?) physical scientists. But it is also interesting once again to view these results in relation to the Schlegel pelvis-shape findings. If we were to order the disciplines in terms of masculinity versus femininity we find again that the more 'masculine' men (physicists) are more likely to get married, stay married and have children than the more 'feminine' men (artists, writers and social scientists). As with the Bohemianism interpretation, it is consistent that the biological scientists fall in between the other groups. What a pity *Who's Who* doesn't provide statistics relating to pelvis shape! If this measure does turn out to be a reliable predictor of marital breakdown we may one day see marriage guidance counsellors as well as dentists equipped with X-ray machines.

While on the subject of tricky ways to predict divorce we might note a rather more practical approach adopted by J. Howard and R. Dawes of the University of Oregon. These researchers discovered that while the rate of sexual intercourse in married couples or the frequency of their arguments do not by themselves relate very much to marital happiness, the difference between them does very well. Nearly all couples who describe their marriage as 'happy' have intercourse more often than they have arguments, whereas nearly all couples who regard their marriage as 'unhappy' argue more than they have intercourse. Therefore, Howard and Dawes proposes the following simple formula:

Marital happiness = Rate of intercourse − Rate of argument

In their research, intercourse referred to 'genital union with or without orgasm' while an argument was defined as any occasion on which at least one party became uncooperative, including physical attack or departure, verbal attack or withdrawal, or emotional outbursts.

As its authors point out, this measure is so simple that anyone capable of counting and subtracting can use it. Readers might find it interesting to monitor their own relationship for an early signal of trouble in their marriage. Indeed, it has been found that couples with consistently negative scores are likely to separate or divorce within a short period of time. Of course, curing the problem on the basis of this early warning system might not be so easy. Correlations do not indicate cause and effect so we do not know what would happen if the rates of sex or argument were manipulated experimentally. Could we increase the marital happiness of a couple who argue a lot by encouraging them to have intercourse more often? It would be interesting to try. And what if we could persuade them to stop arguing? Would their rate of intercourse then increase spontaneously, or would we simply have substituted apathy for conflict?

Locke's questionnaire has been criticized for concentrating on discord rather than apathy in a marriage. D. Quinton and associates at the Institute of Psychiatry note that a marriage may be sick either because the couple are always quarrelling or because they are totally indifferent to each other and do not cooperate on any mutual activities. Therefore they developed an interview technique by which marriages were separately rated on discord and apathy. It is sometimes said that a marriage characterized by complete indifference is worse than one with strong elements of antagonism, since the latter at least implies some kind of relationship. That may be so, but when it comes to predicting divorce it appears that discord is the more important component. Over a quarter of the couples in Quinton's study who showed high levels of discord were separated or divorced within four years. Of eight couples rated as severely apathetic, none had divorced or separated during this follow-up period (though most of them remained apathetic). Thus, while indifference could hardly be described as an ideal state for a marriage, outright hostility more often leads to disbandment.

Another interesting indicator of marital adjustment was devised by D.G. Dean and associates at Iowa State University. These researchers reasoned that if a couple were fully communicating and sensitive to each other's wishes they would be able to make accurate guesses concerning the other's colour preferences for domestic articles such as cars, living-room walls and telephones. Each member of a pair was asked first to indicate his or her own preference by making selections on a colour chart and then to predict which colours the spouse would choose. The discrepancy between an individual's actual choice and the spouse's prediction of that choice was found to correlate quite well with scores on a Locke-type questionnaire. This technique, which is used as the basis of a popular television game show, could be useful as a disguised way of measuring marital happiness, and as with the previous method, readers may find it amusing to try for themselves.

The importance of communication in a marriage relationship was highlighted in a survey by R. Burke and colleagues at York University. In this study, 189 husband-wife pairs were asked how likely they were to disclose unpleasant and distressing feelings to their spouse. In general, wives were more likely to make such disclosures than husbands and those with happy marriages were more likely to discuss their problems than those with unhappy marriages. Husbands and wives gave similar reasons for disclosing problems to their spouses, prime among them being unburdening or 'cartharsis', the seeking of solutions, advice, clarification, new perspectives or ego-support and enhancement of interpersonal understanding. Wives who withheld personal information said they did so because they did not want to burden or worry their husband or because they felt he would be unresponsive to their problems. The more reticent husbands reported that they did not disclose worries to their wife because they preferred to compartmentalize work from home or because they thought she would lack knowledge necessary for appreciation of the problem. Of those respondents who were prepared to specify ways in which they would like their spouse to change, the wives wanted their husbands to be more responsive and receptive to their problems and husbands wished their wives would react to their problems less hysterically so as not to add further stress. These preferences as regards the ideal mode of communication, and particularly the differences between men and women, could well be at the root of a great deal of marital strain. We probably all need to share our inner feelings with somebody and it is certainly most convenient if we feel free to do so with the person we live and sleep with. An inability to communicate for whatever reason, intellectual or emotional, is bound to erode the happiness of a marriage in the long run.

Emotional support is one torm of help that may be supplied from one spouse to the other. In another paper, R. Burke and T. Weir (1977) have developed the idea that mutual helping is the main basis of a stable and happy relationship. They studied the amount and kinds of help rendered by husbands and wives to each other and some of the variables affecting it. There was little doubt that when a husband and wife helped each other a lot their relationship tended to be happier, and so did life in general. Wives were generally more active in initiating help than husbands. Not only were they more willing to express their own emotions but they were also more sensitive to emotional states of their husbands even when unspoken and they were more aware of their problems. This fits the stereotype of the wife as intuitive and supportive. Some of the factors associated with a decline in the amount of mutual helping were length of the marriage (although it was not clear whether this was because couples become progressively alienated with time or because modern marriages are characterized by better communication) and the introduction of children into the family unit (either because they compete for the energies and attention of the parents or hold unsatisfactory marriages together – recall the earlier discussion). When the wife was working there was also a decreased amount of helpful communication between the pair. It appeared that the wife's career added further responsibilities and problems to the sum total affecting the marriage, while at the same time making her less available to her husband. This interpretation fitted with the finding that the greater the life pressures on the marriage from whatever source the less likely the partners were to be satisfied with the help offered by the other. This area of husband-wife helping relationships is clearly one that would repay further study. It seems that one of the prime sources of satisfaction in marriage is the help that one receives from the spouse, either through direct activity or simple attention and understanding. If mutual helping ceases, then so will mutual affection and eventually the marriage will founder. (See Chapter 8 for a discussion of marital therapy based on the exchange-of-favour principle.)

Also critical to the prospects of a marriage is the manner in which the partners handle the disagreements which are bound to arise whenever two people live together for any length of time. Certain methods of dealing with disputes may be regarded as civilized and mature, while others are likely to be destructive to the relationship. D. Kipnis and colleagues (1976) have devised a questionnaire for studying the various ways in which husbands and wives react to disagreements and attempt to change each other's mind. This questionnaire is given below along with instructions on how to complete it. If you wish to try it out on yourself and your spouse cover up the average ratings for men and women given in the two columns down the right hand side as these would be bound to influence your responses.

## Marital Power Questionnaire

You will find below seventeen statements, each representing one way in which married people attempt to change their spouse's mind when disagreements arise.

Please use the nine-point scale ranging from 1 = never to 9 = very often – in marking how often within the last year or so you used each of these ways to change your husband's/wife's mind.

Never — Very Often

1 2 3 4 5 6 7 8 9

| | | Your rating | Average Men | Average Women |
|---|---|---|---|---|
| (1) | Write a letter explaining my reasons for wanting him/her to change. | — | 1.4 | 1.9 |
| (2) | Make my spouse realize that I know more about the matter – that I have expert knowledge. | — | 4.0 | 3.9 |
| (3) | Act cold and say very little to him/her. | — | 2.5 | 2.9 |
| (4) | Argue until my spouse changes his/her mind. | — | 4.3 | 4.2 |
| (5) | Show how much his/her stand hurts me (by crying, pouting, sulking). | — | 2.9 | 3.9 |
| (6) | Use rewards that make my spouse happy in exchange for agreement (e.g. be more loving, give gifts). | — | 2.7 | 2.3 |
| (7) | Make the other person miserable by doing things that he/she does not like (e.g. shouting insults). | — | 1.7 | 1.8 |
| (8) | Hold mutual talks in which both persons' points of view are objectively discussed without argument. | — | 6.8 | 7.2 |
| (9) | Get angry and demand that he/she give in. | — | 2.2 | 3.2 |
| (10) | Appeal to the person's love and affection for me. | — | 2.7 | 4.0 |
| (11) | Make my spouse realize that I have a legitimate right to demand that he/she agree with me. | — | 3.2 | 4.7 |
| (12) | Offer to compromise, in which I give up a little if he/she also gives up a little. | — | 5.7 | 5.8 |
| (13) | Present the facts as I see them and let my spouse decide. | — | 4.2 | 5.9 |
| (14) | Threaten to use physical force if spouse doesn't agree. | — | 1.0 | 1.0 |
| (15) | Give in on other issues so my spouse will agree. | — | 3.2 | 3.3 |
| (16) | Call in an outside party to help convince my spouse. | — | 1.5 | 1.3 |
| (17) | Give up quickly: there is very little I can do to change my spouse's mind once it is made up. | — | 2.6 | 2.5 |

The scores for men and women given with this questionnaire can only be taken as a rough guide to the replies of average men and women. They were based on the responses of a hundred Israeli men and women who had been married for at least one year (including forty couples) described in an unpublished report by Y. Rim of Technion-Israel Institute of Technology. The most commonly used means of influence according to these results are discussion without argument, offers of compromise and presentation of the facts leaving the spouse to decide. Threats of physical violence, calling in outside parties to help, writing letters to the spouse to persuade them to change and making the spouse miserable by shouting and insults were very seldom adopted as approaches to solving disagreements, at least according to the self-report of the people studied.

Women are apparently more likely to use emotions in order to get their own way, for example by appealing to their husband's love and affection, by crying, pouting or sulking, acting cold, or getting angry. Men are marginally more likely to manipulate their spouse with gifts and rewards, to claim greater expertise in the disputed matter and to argue until their spouse changes her mind. The two sexes are equally likely to give up without a fight. Rim noted a very interesting role-reversal based on the duration of the marriage. Wives tend to start off by being accommodating and dependent (e.g. having discussions, compromising and appealing to love) but become progressively authoritarian in their approach (e.g. demanding their rights). Men, on the other hand, become progressively accommodating and dependent through the duration of the marriage. Similarly, whereas young wives are more willing to 'give up' in the case of an argument than their husbands, men who have been married a long time are more likely to give up than their wives. Apparently there is some truth to the hen-pecked husband syndrome in the latter years of marriage.

There were also some personality differences in preferred means of influence. As assessed by the Eysenck Personality Inventory, extraverts were more likely to use accommodative methods like discussion and compromise than were introverts, and people high on the neuroticism scale were more likely than stable people to use emotional/dependency methods or simply to give up. These relationships are consistent with the picture of the extravert as sociable and talkative and the neurotic as emotional and fearful.

Exactly how these methods of conflict resolution bear on marital happiness and unhappiness has not yet been tested directly, although previous research (see Barry, 1970) suggests that happily married people more often use discussion to settle their differences, while unhappily married people use aggression or withdrawal. This sounds perfectly reasonable. Kipnis found that people who used authoritarian means of influence were more likely to perceive themselves as controlling the behaviour of their spouse. Such people were also likely to show little respect for the spouse that they influenced in this way and regarded themselves as more important and desirable people. This confirms the widespread awareness that you do not gain respect from another person by allowing yourself to be used as a doormat. Husbands and wives who adopt this attitude in order to appease their spouse and in the hope that they will be better liked and treated as a result are in most cases destined for progressive indignity and hurt.

One fairly common source of conflict in married couples is the desire for or occurrence of extramarital sex. Traditionally this has been one of the prime grounds for divorce, and although tolerance of such diversion is increasing it remains a major source of dissension between married couples. Few are so liberated that they can openly discuss their affairs with their spouse.

While there can be little doubt that extramarital sex is often connected with marital breakdown (either as a cause or effect), the relationship with marital happiness is more complicated. It is at least theoretically possible that some marriages survive and are happy *because* one or both parties are supplementing their satisfaction through affairs. One can envisage, for example, a marriage in which the couple are close companions with common interests, perhaps including mutual love of their children, but who seek and gain their sexual excitement outside of the marriage. Such an arrangement may be quite open, unspoken or unaware (in the sense that each spouse does not know about the other's extracurricular activity). S. Glass and T. Wright (1977) studied the relationship between marital satisfaction and extramarital sex in a large sample of men and women who had responded to a questionnaire in the magazine *Psychology Today*. There were 831 married respondents and 115 who were divorced (and not currently remarried). Although this sample could not be called representative of the whole US population (they tended, for example, to be highly educated and interested in psychology) some of the findings were nevertheless quite interesting. As expected, people with experience of extramarital sex were more likely to be divorced than those without such experience. However, extramarital sex was not uniformly connected with marital unhappiness among those currently married. Overall, people with extramarital experience were less happy with their marriage, but there was no difference where women in recent marriages were concerned, or men in longer standing marriages. In fact, men with extramarital experience were the only group whose marriages appeared to have improved over the years. All other groups showed a decline in happiness with duration of the marriage.

Taking the divorce and marital happiness data together, the Glass and Wright study seemed to suggest that if women are sexually discontented with their marriage they will opt out while fairly young or else not at all. Thus 35 per cent of women who had affairs in the first two years of marriage were divorced by that time. Extramarital sex in older women is usually also a symptom of marital unhappiness because women tend to engage in affairs for emotional rather than sexual reasons. Once beyond their late thirties, however, they are less likely to break up their marriage because they tend to be socially and economically dependent on it. While the occurrence of extramarital sex early in a man's marriage is also a sign of unhappiness with the relationship, it is not necessarily so in later years. Older men very often engage in affairs for purely sexual reasons while remaining quite happy with the companionship provided in their marriage.

There are also differences between men and women in terms of the age at which they first become adulterers. Most men start the practice fairly early if they are going to at all. Two-thirds of males with extramarital experience began their affairs in the first five years of marriage. One possible reason for this is the onset of parenthood, with the wife diverting her attention from the husband onto the business of childrearing. Women, on the other hand, show a surge of extramarital sex in their late thirties and early forties, perhaps partly as a result of loneliness due to the children growing up and leaving home. As Glass and Wright point out, some of these trends may be found to change with moves towards equality of the sexes, more premarital sex and open marriages, and higher frequencies of divorce and remarriage.

A form of extramarital sex which does not seem to be associated with either divorce or marital unhappiness is mate-swapping, usually called 'swinging' by participants. This is a response to the problem of sexual boredom in marriage which involves no deception between the spouses. Rather, it adds another shared leisuretime activity to the couple's repertoire, though admittedly they still have the problem of jealousy to contend with. Swinging is not very widespread. Estimates of the numbers involved are usually in the region of about 2 per cent of the population, but around 7 per cent say they would be willing to try it (more men than women of course) and the figures seem to be on the increase.

Swinging is generally considered deviant not only because it is unusual but also because it is disapproved by a high proportion of people. Aware of this, most swingers are very careful about revealing their activities to children, neighbours and business associates. Nevertheless, they themselves value their behaviour positively, and defend it on the grounds that it is less threatening to the nuclear family than most other forms of sexual diversion. In fact, swinging is usually conducted within a context of strict rules which are designed to avoid most of the possible ill effects. These include exclusion of single people (especially men), keeping the fun and games within the group rather than peeling off to separate bedrooms, and not contacting anyone's husband or wife independently between parties. Such ethics function to keep the non-marital relationships on a strictly sexual basis and to prevent progressive emotional involvement. In this respect they are fairly successful, for such evidence as is available indicates that the marital adjustment of swingers is, if anything, better than that of non-swinging controls (Spanier and Cole, 1975). Furthermore, nearly all studies of swingers show them to be well-educated, middle-class citizens, who are generally well-adjusted and who in all other respects uphold the cherished values of society. Most of them have traditional kinship relations, children, socially acceptable jobs and membership in community organizations. This is far from the picture presented by other forms of deviant behaviour like alcoholism and delinquency. Swinging is unique in having so many socially lauded elements – honesty, spending time together, mutual enjoyment, etc., and perhaps it is this very combination which makes it seem so threatening to traditional moralists. Not only do these couples engage in extramarital sex, they are brazenly unashamed of it.

The emergence of swinging as a new form of extramarital sexual behaviour underlines what is probably the clearest trend in modern marriage. Marriage is not going out of fashion at all, but it is no longer viewed as the sole outlet for sexual passion. The advent of effective contraception has given us the power to separate paternity from sex, allowing the latter to be treated more as a leisuretime activity. Thus sex is increasingly used for recreation rather than procreation. There is recognition of the difficulty of restricting sexual passion to one person and containing it within the context of a life-long bond, particularly as we are constantly titillated by models of permissiveness and pleasure on television and in other media. The result is increasing tolerance of sexual behaviour outside of marriage, both premarital and extramarital. Extramarital sex is no longer regarded as sufficient reason for divorce; other circumstances such as its duration, motivation and meaning to the individuals involved are taken into account before drastic domiciliary changes are deemed necessary. Swinging is another response to the recognition of this need for sexual exploration in many people. At the moment it is fairly impersonal, but the next stage may well be to allow deeper and rounder involvement with other persons.

Marriage also ceases to be seen as quite so irreversible. Easier divorce laws mean people are less inclined to view it as a life sentence. In fact, the vows might well be reworded, 'Till divorce or death us do part' as suggested by W.S. Gilbert in *The Grand Duke*. If a couple do get divorced, far from being 'once bitten, twice shy', they tend to remarry fairly quickly. And in doing so they have about as much chance of being happy and successful in their new marriage as other people have in undertaking marriage for the first time. Although the men do slightly better than the women after the age of thirty-five (Glenn & Weaver, 1977), both sexes do quite well in terms of remarried happiness. This would suggest that most people who get divorced are more disillusioned by their particular partner than by marriage as an institution.

But the truth is that neither the single nor the married state is ideal for many people. For most of us there are powerful positives and negatives associated with each condition. We want to get married because we are expected to by our parents and society, because most of our friends are married and we feel out of it, because we want stable companionship, deep commitment to another person, a family, and a general sense that we belong somewhere and are truly loved and needed by one person at least. At the same time, we want to be single (or get divorced) in order to feel free and mobile, to enjoy a variety of deep friendships and to pursue exciting sexual adventures. This is the great dilemma of our time, if not of all time. Both sets of needs are present in some degree in all of us; few people are so decisively motivated in one direction that they can be perfectly contented husbands or playboys, wives or career girls. Given this conflict, we are forced either to sacrifice or compromise, and with heroes and martyrs thin on the ground these days, more and more compromise is being seen. Traditional marriage is the casualty; its rigid boundaries have begun to crumble and we are witnessing a great diversity of lifestyles, many of them spanning the gulf between married and single life. Cohabitation, communes, swinging, open marriage, serial polygamy (repeated divorce and remarriage) all contain elements of both security and excitement. It will be interesting to see whether survey interviewers of the future bother to ask respondents about their formal marital status. Even by 1984, the answer to this question may tell very little.

## References

BARRY, W.A., 'Marriage research and conflict: An integrative review', *Psychological Bulletin*, 1970, **73**, 41–54.

BARTON, K., 'Personality similarity in spouses related to marriage roles', *Multivariate Experimental Clinical Research*, 1976, **2**, 107–11.

BENTLER, P.M. & NEWCOMB, D., 'A longitudinal study of marital success and failure' in M. Cook & G.E. Wilson (eds), *Love and Attraction: An International conference*. Oxford: Pergamon, 1979.

BERNARD, J., *The Future of Marriage*. New York: World Publishing Co., 1972.

BLACKER, C.P., 'Disruption of marriage: Some possibilities of prevention', *Lancet*, 1958, March 15, 578–81.

BIRTCHNELL, J., 'A test of Toman's Theory of mate selection', in M. Cook & G.D. Wilson (eds), *Love and Attraction: An International Conference*. Oxford: Pergamon, 1979.

BURKE, R.J. & WEIR, T., 'Husband-wife helping relationships: The "mental hygiene" function in marriage', *Psychological Reports*, 1977, **40**, 911–25.

BURKE, R.J., WEIR, T. & HARRISON, D., 'Disclosure of problems and tensions experienced by marital partners', *Psychological Reports*, 1976, **38**, 531–42.

DEAN, D.G., LUCAS, W.L. & COOPER G.L., 'Perceptions of colour preferences – a clue to marital prediction', *Journal of Psychology*, 1976, **93**, 243–4.

GLASS, S.P. & WRIGHT, T.L., 'The relationship of extramarital sex, length of marriage and sex differences on marital satisfaction and romanticism: Athanasiou's data reanalysed', *Journal of Marriage and the Family*, 1977, **39**, 691–703.

GLENN, N.D. & WEAVER, C.M., 'The marital happiness of remarried divorced persons', *Journal of Marriage and Family*, 1977, **39**, 331–7.

HORN, J., 'Personality and divorce', *Psychology Today*, 1977, **3**, 50–1.

HOWARD, J.W. & DAWES, R.M., 'Linear prediction of marital happiness', *Personality and Social Psychology Bulletin*, 1976, **2**, 478–80.

HUDSON, L. & JACOT, B., 'Marriage and fertility in academic life', *Nature*, 1971, **229**, 531–2.

KIMMEL, D. & VAN DER VEEN, F., 'Factors of marital adjustment in Locke's Marital Adjustment Test', *Journal of Marriage and the Family*, 1974, **36**, 57–63.

KIPNIS, D., CASTELL, P.J., GERGEN, M. & MANCH, D., 'Metamorphic effects of power', *Journal of Applied Psychology*, 1976, **61**, 127–35.

MURSTEIN, B.I., *Who Will Marry Whom?* New York: Springer, 1976.

NIAS, D.K.B., 'Husband-wife similarities', *Social Science*, 1977, **52**, 206–11.

QUINTON, D., RUTTER, M. & ROWLANDS, O., 'An evaluation of an interview assessment of marriage', *Psychological Medicine*, 1976, **6**, 577–86.

RENNE, K.S., 'Correlates of dissatisfaction in marriage', *Journal of Marriage and the Family*, 1970, **32**, 54–67.

ROGERS, R., YOUNG, H.H., COHEN, I.H. & DWORIN, J., 'Marital stability, mental health and marital satisfaction', *Journal of Consulting and Clinical Psychology*, 1970, **35**, 342–8.

SPANIER, G.B. & COLE, C.L., 'Mate-swapping: perceptions, value-orientations and participation in a midwestern community', *Archives of Sexual Behaviour*, 1975, **4**, 143–59.

# 7 The elusive orgasm

Orgasm is the ultimate pleasurable sensation. If there is any modern equivalent of the Holy Grail, surely it is the quest for the big 'O'. Psychologically, it is experienced as an intense, climactic thrill following a build-up of excitement centred in the genital area, and leading to an aftermath of perfect relaxation and contentment. Physiologically, it may be observed as a peak in heart rate of up to about 180 beats per minute (compared with the usual 60 to 80), a similarly doubled or even trebled respiration rate together with irregularity and gasping, and contractions of the anal sphincter. There are also contractions in other muscles, most notably the genitals themselves, but also the neck, arms, legs, back and buttocks. Blood pressure is raised, the skin becomes flushed, the face is contorted into an 'agonized' grimace and vocal noises are likely to be emitted, particularly by women.

There is great cross-cultural similarity in what people say during orgasm. English, French, Indian and Japanese women all babble about dying, call for Mother, or invoke the deity (Comfort, 1972). Men are more likely to growl unintelligibly or utter aggressive monosyllables like 'In, in, in'. Many women, and a few men, talk continuously in a sort of baby whisper or repeat four-letter words that are out of character. Some people yell loud enough to be heard several blocks away while others are dead silent or laugh or sob disconcertingly. There is in fact an enormous variety of non-speech sounds produced during orgasm. The American Indians classified them and compared them with bird-cries, warning that parrots and mynah birds pick them up very easily and are likely to repeat them on a later occasion to the embarrassment of the owner.

Is orgasm the same for men and women? The evidence gathered by Masters and Johnson and other laboratory researchers suggests that, physiologically speaking, male and female orgasms are remarkably similar. Even the rhythmic contractions in the penis and vagina are timed at the same interval – about one spasm per second. But what about the *experience* or orgasm? Perhaps this is different for men and women. Some people with a philosophical bent have argued that this question is impossible to answer, claiming that just as it is difficult to prove that the 'red' one person sees is not the 'green' experienced by another, there is no way of comparing people's subjective sensations of orgasm. We can at least investigate whether men and women describe the experience in similar terms. Ellen Vance and Nathaniel Wagner had students write brief accounts of how they feel when having an orgasm. After eliminating or replacing any wording that was an absolute give-away as to the sex of the writer, e.g. substituting 'partner' for 'husband', 'wife', 'boyfriend', etc. and 'genitals' for 'penis' or 'vagina', forty-eight descriptions of orgasm (half male and half female) were chosen on a random basis to form the *Sex of Orgasm Questionnaire* given below. The reader may now like to work through this questionnaire trying to identify which descriptions were written by men and which by women. Your ability to differentiate will then be compared with scores obtained by expert gynaecologists and psychologists.

## Sex of Orgasm Questionnaire

The following three groups of statements are replies by both men and women to a request to describe what an orgasm feels like. For each group please indicate in the blank spaces provided whether you think the statement was written by a male or female. Put an M for male and an F for female.

### *Group A*

(1) — A sudden feeling of lightheadedness followed by an intense feeling of relief and elation. A rush. Intense muscular spasms of the whole body. Sense of euphoria followed by deep peace and relaxation.

(2) — Feels like tension building up until you think it can't build up any more, then release. The orgasm is both the highest point of tension and the release almost at the same time. Also feeling contractions in the genitals. Tingling all over.

(3) — I often see spots in front of my eyes during orgasm. The feeling itself is so difficult to describe other than the most pleasurable of all sensory impressions. I suppose the words 'fluttering sensation' describe the physical feeling I get. All nerve endings sort of burst and quiver.

(4) — There is a great release of tensions that have built up in the prior stages of sexual activity. This release is extremely pleasurable and exciting. The feeling seems to be centred in the genital region. It is extremely intense and exhilarating. There is a loss of muscular control as the pleasure mounts and you almost cannot go on. You almost don't want to go on. This is followed by the climax and refractory states!

(5) — An orgasm feels extremely pleasurable, yet it can be so violent that the feeling of uncontrol is frightening. It also is hard to describe because it is as if I am in limbo – only conscious of release.

(6) — To me an orgasmic experience is the most satisfying pleasure that I have experienced in relation to any other type of satisfaction or pleasure that I've had which was nonsexually oriented.

(7) — The period when the orgasm takes place – a loss of a real feeling for the surroundings except for the other person. The movements are spontaneous and intense.

(8) — They vary a great deal depending on circumstances. If it's just a physical need or release it's OK, but it takes more effort to 'get there'. If you're really very much in love (at least in my case) it's so close at hand that the least physical expression by your partner, or slightest touch on the genitals brings it on. And then if the lovemaking is continued it repeats again and again. It's about 90 per cent cortical or emotional and the rest physical. But one has to have the emotion or (in my case) I don't even want to begin or try.

(9) — Obviously, we can't explain what it feels 'like' because it feels 'like' nothing else in human experience. A poetic description may well describe the emotions that go with it, but the physical 'feeling' can only be described with very weak mechanical terminology. It is a release that occurs after a period of manipulation has sufficiently enabled internal, highly involuntary spasms that are pleasurable due to your complete involuntary control (no control).

(10) — It's like shooting junk on a sunny day in a big, green, open field.

(11) — It is like turning a water faucet on. You notice the oncoming flow but it can be turned on or off when desired. You feel the valves open and close and the fluid flow. An orgasm makes your head and body tingle.

(12) — An orgasm . . . located (originating) in the genital area, capable of spreading out further . . . legs, abdomen. A sort of pulsating feeling – very nice if it can extend itself beyond the immediate genital area.

(13) — A build-up of tension which starts to pulsate very fast, and there is a sudden release from the tension and desire to sleep.

(14) — Begins with tensing and tingling in anticipation, rectal contractions starting series of chills up spine. Tingling and buzzing sensations grow suddenly to explosion in genital area, some sensation of dizzying and weakening – almost loss of conscious sensation, but not really. Explosion sort of flowers out to varying distance from genital area, depending on intensity.

(15) — A heightened feeling of excitement with severe muscular tension especially through the back and legs, rigid straightening of the entire body for about five seconds, and a strong and general relaxation and very tired relieved feeling.

(16) — A tremendous release of built-up tension all at once lasting around five to ten seconds where a particular 'pulsing' feeling is felt throughout my body along with a kind of tickling and tingling feeling.

## *Group B*

(1) — I really think it defies description by words. Combination of waves of very pleasurable sensations and mounting of tensions culminating in a fantastic sensation and release of tension.

(2) — Physical tension and excitement climaxing and then a feeling of sighing, a release of tensionlike feelings.

(3) — It is a pleasant, tension-relieving muscular contraction. It relieves physical tension and mental anticipation.

(4) — It is a very pleasurable sensation. All my tensions have really built to a peak and are suddenly released. It feels like a great upheaval; like all of the organs in the stomach area have turned over. It is extremely pleasurable.

(5) — Orgasm gives me a feeling of unobstructed intensity of satisfaction. Accompanied with the emotional feeling and love one has for another, the reality of the sex drive, and our culturally conditioned status on sex, an orgasm is the only experience that sends my whole body and mind into a state of beautiful oblivion.

(6) — Tension builds to an extremely high level – muscles are tense, etc. There is a sudden expanding feeling in the pelvis and muscle spasms throughout the body followed by release of tension. Muscles relax and consciousness returns.

(7) — A release of a very high level of tension, but ordinarily tension is unpleasant whereas the tension before orgasm is far from unpleasant.

(8) — Basically it's an enormous build-up of tension, anxiety, strain followed by a period of total oblivion to sensation then a tremendous expulsion of the build-up with a feeling of wonderfulness and relief.

(9) — Intense excitement of entire body. Vibrations in stomach – mind can consider only your own desires at the moment of climax. After, you feel like you're floating – a sense of joyful tiredness.

(10) — It is a great release of tension followed by a sense of electriclike tingling which takes over all control of your senses.

(11) — A building up of tensions – like getting ready for takeoff from a launching pad, then a sudden blossoming relief that extends all over the body.

(12) — The feeling of orgasm in my opinion is feeling of utmost relief of any type of tension. It is the most fulfilling experience I have ever had of enjoyment. The feeling is exuberant and the most enjoyable feeling I have ever experienced.

(13) — I think that there are a variety of orgasms that I experience. I have noted a shallow 'orgasm' which consists of a brief period which is characterized by an urge to thrust but which passes quickly. On the other hand, I have also experienced what I call a hard climax, characterized by a mounting, building tension and strong thrusting movements which increase in strength and frequency until the tension is relieved.

(14) — An orgasm is a very quick release of sexual tension which results in a kind of flash of pleasure.

(15) — An orgasm is a great release of tension with spasmodic reaction at the peak.

(16) — A building of tension, sometimes, and frustration until the climax. A tightening inside, palpitating rhythm, explosion, and warmth and peace.

*Group C*

(1) — An orgasm feels like heaven in the heat of hell; a tremendous build-up within of pleasure that makes the tremendous work of releasing that pleasure worthwhile.

(2) — There is a building up of 'tension' (poor description) to a very high stage. There is then a surging release which is exhilarating, leaving me in a totally relaxed, exhausted state.

(3) — Spasm of the abdominal and groin area, tingling sensation in limbs, and throbbing at the temples on each side of my head.

(4) — Experience of a build-up of tension, uncoordination of movement – to a few seconds of amazing feeling, to a release of tension and a period of satisfaction and relaxation.

(5) — Often loss of contact with reality. All senses acute. Sight becomes patterns of colour, but often very difficult to explain because words were made to fit in the real world.

(6) — A feeling where nothing much else enters the mind other than that which relates to the present, oh sooo enjoyable and fulfilling sensation. It's like jumping into a cool swimming pool after hours of sweating turmoil. 'Ahh Relief!' What a great feeling it was, so ecstatically wild and alright!

(7) — A feeling of intense physical and mental satisfaction. The height of a sexual encounter. Words can hardly describe a feeling so great.

(8) — Stomach muscles get 'nervous' causing a thrusting movement with hips or pelvis. Muscular contraction all over the body.

(9) — Building of tenseness to a peak where it seems as if everything is going to drain out of you. It's almost like a complete physical drain.

(10) — Starts with hot-cold tingles up in the back of the thighs. What happens from there depends on the strength of the stimulation. Usually, shuddery contractions and the same sort of hot-cold feeling only in the genital area. Sometimes, with really strong stimulation, there's more of a blackout of complete mental awareness of what's happening, then a gradual letting down.

(11) — An orgasm is a heightening relief of tension wherein the muscles are flexing and a great deal of tension is relieved in an extremely short period. It's a feeling of incurring climax and enjoyment due to the acute sensual nerve feelings and consciousness (kind of two opposing dialectics).

(12) — Building up of a good type of tension. With the release of all this build-up in one great rush that makes your whole body tingle and feel very pleasurable. Feeling is weakening and is great. Just want to stay still for a long time.

(13) — Has a build-up of pressure in genitals with involuntary thrusting of hips and twitching of thigh muscles. Also contracting and releasing of the genital muscles. The pressure becomes quite intense – like there is something underneath the skin of the genitals pushing out. Then there is a sudden release of the tension with contraction of genitals with a feeling of release and relaxation.

(14) — I have had orgasm at times under certain conditions. I also have had it during intercourse. It is more relaxing with less mental duress during intercourse. It is a tensing of the whole body and a bright sensual feeling of release after.

(15) — Orgasm amounts to a build-up of muscle tension accompanied by an increase in respiration rate. A sudden release of the build-up constitutes an orgasm. All in all, a highly pleasurable physical sensation.

(16) — A complete relief of all tensions. Very powerful and filled with ecstasy. Contraction of stomach and back muscles.

### *Answer Key for Sex of Orgasm Questionnaire*

Group A: 1-F, 2-F, 3-F, 4-M, 5-F, 6-M, 7-F, 8-F, 9-M, 10-F, 11-F, 12-F, 13-F, 14-M, 15-F, 16-M.

Group B: 1-M, 2-M, 3-M, 4-F, 5-M, 6-F, 7-M, 8-M, 9-F, 10-F, 11-M, 12-F, 13-F, 14-M, 15-M, 16-F.

Group C: 1-M, 2-M, 3-M, 4-F, 5-M, 6-M, 7-F, 8-M, 9-M, 10-F, 11-M, 12-M, 13-F, 14-M, 15-F, 16-M.

Tally up the number you got right using the key above and you will have a score somewhere in the range of nought to forty-eight. If you are very much higher than twenty-four you either cheated or you know a lot more than the experts, for Vance and Wagner found that none of the professional groups were able to distinguish male and female orgasm on the basis of these descriptions. This could mean they don't know their job, or that we cannot properly describe our orgasmic experiences in words, but the most probable meaning is that men and women actually do obtain nearly identical thrills in orgasm.

There was one item that was consistently identified as female by the experts. This was Group A Item 8, which refers to multiple orgasm. Apparently this is one way in which orgasms are different for women. Some women are able to have several orgasms in quick succession; men are generally supposed not to.

But is it really impossible for men to have multiple orgasms? Research by Masters and Johnson and others suggests that, contrary to widespread belief, orgasm and ejaculation are actually separable processes in man. In a recent paper delivered at the 1975 International Congress of Sexology in Montreal, Californian sexologist Mina Robbins described her efforts to train men in recognizing this distinction so that they could enjoy several orgasms before ejaculation. She began by testing a number of men who claimed to have multi-orgasmic capacity, monitoring their heart rate, respiration rate and anal sphincter activity (the three best indicators of orgasm) to see whether their claims were justified. Of the initial list of volunteers, a short-list of thirteen men survived this screening. They tended to be in their late thirties and had experience of more than one partner but favoured long term affairs. Their techniques for delaying ejaculation took many forms, but most included staying still and breathing slowly but regularly. Robbins took these and certain other features of their performance as the basis of her training programme. This programme was administered to thirty-three men who brought their partners along to the clinic and engaged in intercourse with them. The three prime indicators of orgasm were converted into tracings on moving graph-paper positioned so that the female partner could follow her man's progress. When his orgasm was getting close she would give him a warning and he would call into play the prescribed techniques for avoiding ejaculation. According to Robbins, most of these men learned within about twelve sessions how to control their ejaculations but at the same time let their orgasms proceed. Thereafter it was found that the biofeedback machinery could be dispensed with. A portable version of this apparatus is apparently now being constructed by an Oxford electronics firm, so that it may soon be possible to transfer the training method from laboratory to bedroom. Just how reliable and practical the programme will turn out to be remains to be seen, but if Robbins' faith is justified women's only major sexual privilege may soon be encroached upon by a new breed of multi-orgasmic males.

Women are often said to have two different kinds of orgasm, one clitoral and one vaginal. To some extent, this distinction is based on the location of the stimulation which leads to orgasm, but most women also describe the sensations as different. Clitoral orgasms are more likely to be described as intense, sharp or 'electrical', while vaginal orgasms are more likely to be described as throbbing, deep, diffused and spiritual. Physiologically, the two types of orgasm are not distinguished (although orgasms obtained through masturbation of the clitoris are on average more intense) and there is now good evidence that all orgasms are mediated via the clitoris even though the primary stimulation is in the vagina.

S. Fisher asked a sample of 500 married women, 'If you had the choice of receiving only clitoral or vaginal stimulation, which would you select?' Nearly two-thirds chose clitoral stimulation, while less than one-third voted vaginal. A few women reported that stimulation in the non-preferred area was unpleasant or actually painful, but most enjoyed stimulation in both places. Women who expressed a clitoral preference were more likely to describe their orgasms as 'ecstatic' when given a list of adjectives to choose from, and the impression was that vaginal orgasms were relatively muted in their impact. Also, contrary to the Freudian assertion that clitoral sex is an immature, if not pathological, outlet, the vaginally oriented women showed greater signs of tension, anxiety and depersonalization (lack of awareness of their own bodies). There was, however, no difference between clitoral and vaginal women in terms of their reported frequency of orgasm. Apparently, sexual satisfaction can be obtained by either attack. Perhaps it is this superior versatility that women allude to when they criticize men as only being able to think of 'one thing'.

When it comes to the ease and reliability with which orgasms are obtained, men certainly have the edge over women. In Victorian days it was regarded as indelicate for a woman to enjoy sex at all, let alone have orgasms. Sex was endured in order to please the husband or produce children. Respectable ladies were advised to 'shut their eyes and think of England'. Today the double standard concerning the desirability of sexual pleasure has largely dissolved but the orgasm remains relatively elusive for women. The graph below is based on a fairly representative sample of British men and women and shows reported rates of orgasm in relation to age. Of course there was a great deal of variation within each sex and overlap between them, but the typical (median) rates are quite divergent. There is a fairly steady decline with age for both men and women (due to declining sex activity) but at every age level the men are reporting about twice as many orgasms per week as the women. The graph includes orgasms due both to intercourse and masturbation so that part of the difference may be due to a greater frequency of masturbation in men. But for the most part, the difference is due to failure of orgasm during the act of intercourse for some of the women some of the time, compared to an almost 100 per cent orgasm rate for men. Estimates of the number of nonorgasmic women vary, but up to 10 per cent never experience an orgasm, and at least another 50 per cent have more or less unreliable orgasms.

What determines whether or not a girl will have orgasms? A study of the feelings, attitudes and personality characteristics of girls who have and do not have orgasms was made by D. Shope of Pennsylvania State University. Surveying forty girls who were 'coitally orgasmic'

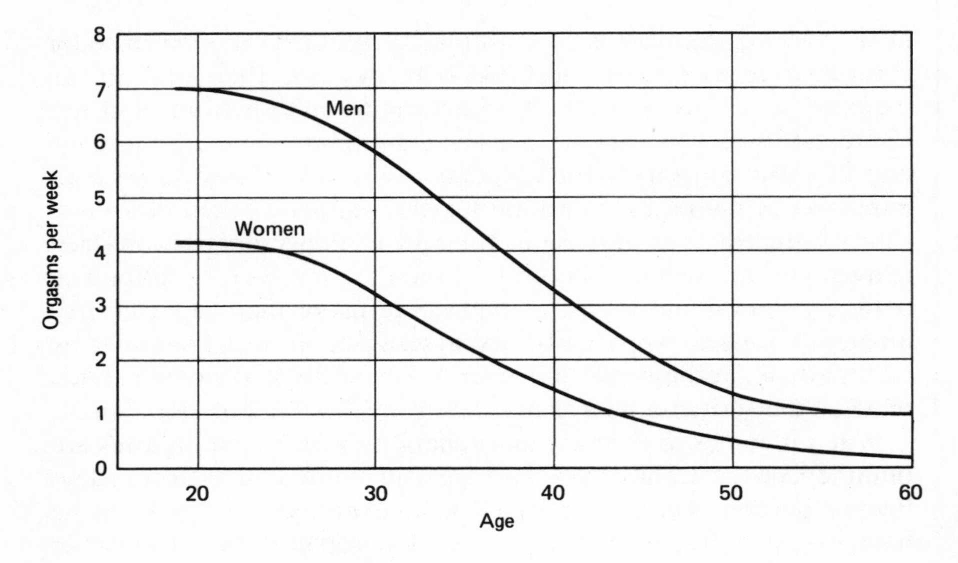


Figure 11 Weekly rates of orgasm reported by British men and women

and forty girls who had intercourse but not orgasm, he found that the orgasmic girls were much more aware of physiological changes taking place in their genitals, such as erection and pulsation of the clitoris, and softening and enlarging of the vaginal walls. Non-orgasmic women reported greater control over their pelvic contractions, were more likely to express feelings of sexual inhibition, to perceive their man as having a higher sex drive than themselves, and to feel that they were 'giving in' to him by having sex.

Only one personality difference between the two groups emerged; the girls who had orgasms were less emotionally 'stable' than those who did not. It is difficult to interpret this finding, particularly in view of other clinical and questionnaire findings to the effect that orgasm difficulties are associated with general neuroticism. Since few details are available concerning the measure of emotionality used by Shope, it is possible that it would be better described as 'expressiveness', which is more an extraverted characteristic than a neurotic one.

Another finding to emerge from Shope's study was that orgasmic and non-orgasmic girls did not differ in terms of the amount or kind of sexual experience that they had. The two groups engaged in about the same amount of fellatio, cunnilingus and masturbation, and were similar as regards number of partners, age at first intercourse and frequency of intercourse. This was despite the fact that the groups were not matched for sexual experience, with the exception of the selection requirement that they should have engaged in intercourse at least fifteen times over the last two months. It seems, then, that a girl's chances of orgasm are much more strongly related to *who* she is than *what* she does. This is bad news for those who think that learning a few new techniques is bound to solve the problem of anorgasmia. Also, since all the girls in the study were unmarried, it is clear that mere experience of premarital intercourse is not going to be sufficient to guarantee sexual responsiveness in marriage, as some champions of the permissive society have maintained.

It is popularly supposed that religious training and upper class morality are antithetical to female orgasm because they impose certain inhibitions. If that were the case we would expect the more 'earthy' working classes, and primitive people, the 'happy savages', to experience orgasm more consistently. This is not so – female orgasms need to be worked at in all societies. And within our own society it appears that the higher social classes have higher rates of orgasm. Although there are many individual case reports that seem to implicate overly strict religious principles in orgasm difficulty, survey research finds only slight associations at best between religious affiliation and orgasmic capacity. Religion is influential in reducing sexual activity before marriage, but has little influence on rates of intercourse or orgasm after marriage. Nor is the capacity for orgasm lost with age. Although the graph above might seem to suggest a decline in orgasmic capacity with age, the orgasm rate expressed as a proportion of occasions of intercourse remains fairly steady. Altogether, these social and demographic factors are poor predictors of orgasmic capacity in women.

Another common belief is that certain traumatic incidents in a girl's development, such as being raped or having an abortion, will permanently impair her sexual responsiveness. Many investigations have sought such links, but they have failed to turn up any convincing evidence. Shope actually found that orgasmic girls had had *more* shocking sexual encounters before the age of sixteen than girls unable to achieve orgasm. Other studies which have focused on premarital abortions and unpleasant honeymoon experiences have failed to adduce evidence of any lasting harm attributable to these events. It is possible that a few individuals suffer long-term sexual impairment as a result of one terrifying incident, but overall it seems that the importance of such experiences has been overrated.

Certain less obvious traumas may, however, be involved. The work of Fisher revealed that non-orgasmic women were more preoccupied about loss or separation than orgasmic women. For example, they were more likely to recall the death of a relative or the loss of a favourite pet. Their father was more frequently unavailable to them, either because he had died or because work responsibilities caused him to be absent from home a great deal. (Unavailability of the mother was not so implicated.) In writing fictional stories the non-orgasmic women were more likely to include themes of separation, desertion and loneliness. Fisher's interpretation is that the low-orgasm women feels insecure about the dependability of the relationships that matter most to her. He goes on to suggest that the blurring of vision and reality experienced during the build-up of sexual excitement becomes threatening to these women and prevents them from 'letting go'. 'The fading of objects signifies losing them, and (the non-orgasmic woman) cannot tolerate such loss. Her alarm interferes with the process of accumulating enough excitement to reach orgasm.' This explanation seems to us rather obtuse. A better idea is thrown in later by Fisher, almost as an afterthought. This is that a woman's orgasm is facilitated by any conditions which increase her feeling that the man she is having sex with can be counted upon as loyal and likely to stay around afterwards. This would mean that she would be better able to obtain orgasms in the context of a happy, stable marriage than a transitory, illicit relationship (probably true); it would also mean that her entire life history as regards experiences of male dependancy would have an influence.

Another finding coming from Fisher's study was that orgasmic women showed more persistence or endurance as a personality characteristic. It appears that, for a woman, orgasm is a task that has to be worked at and concentrated upon for completion to occur. The orgasmic women were also distinguished in terms of voice quality – high-orgasm voices being judged by independent observers as less constricted, more natural, and more often using emphatic or dramatizing sounds like sighs and deep breaths. By contrast, the low-orgasm woman's voice seemed to be very controlled, narrow in tonal range, and mechanical in quality. This could be an indication that the low-orgasmic woman is generally 'uptight' and unemotional, consistent with the Shope finding, or it might simply mean that the more vocally agile woman makes more noise at climax and is therefore more likely to apply the label of 'orgasm' to her experience, knowing that this is one of its prime defining characteristics.

Some evidence for physical differences between orgasmic and non-orgasmic women has been reported by New York biochemist S. Deutsch. The patients were all attending the Human Sexuality Clinic at Queens Hospital, Long Island, and the comparison was between women who did not experience orgasms but whose husbands had little difficulty and women who had no sexual problems but were attending the clinic because their husbands had difficulties. The clearest finding to emerge from this comparison was that non-orgasmic women had higher glucose and insulin levels in their blood. Since it is well known that diabetes often produces sexual problems in both men and women, it is possible that what was observed in this study was a slight tendency towards diabetes. Other differences were also observed. The non-orgasmic women showed lower levels of phosphorus, cholesterol, calcium and urea nitrogen in the blood. What these differences mean, and whether they are a cause or an effect of the lack of orgasm, is not clear, but they do suggest that a woman's biochemical condition may be connected with her orgasmic capacity.

A group of chemicals that do have a direct influence on sexual desire, and probably also orgasm, are the steroid hormones. Both libido and performance in women appear to be dependent upon the 'male' hormone testosterone which is produced in small amounts by the adrenal cortex. (In men, of course, it is produced in much larger quantities by the testes.) If women are given injections of testosterone their clitoris becomes enlarged and more sensitive and, probably as a result, they are more sexually responsive. This is logical when it is considered that they are becoming temporarily more like men, who typically have a higher sex drive and little difficulty with orgasm. Progesterone, on the other hand, seems to have a depressing effect on women's sex drive and their ability to achieve orgasm. This lowering of sexual responsiveness is seen in the post-ovulatory part of the menstrual cycle, during pregnancy, and when a woman is taking contraceptive pills of the 'combination' type. All these conditions have in common high levels of progesterone. The third major group of sex hormones, the oestrogens, do not seem to have any marked or predictable effects on libido or orgasmic capacity (Kane, Lipton & Ewing, 1969).

The fact that there may be biological factors impeding orgasm in some women does not mean that their chances cannot be improved by appropriate training. Many programmes have been set up for this purpose, most of them more or less derivative of the pioneering work of Masters and Johnson. Usually they stress the need for the male partner to be gentle and considerate and to bear in mind the likelihood that his woman will need a longer period of stimulation and foreplay than himself in order to obtain orgasm. They also commonly point out the importance of relaxation and freedom from current and past anxieties for a woman to get the best out of a sexual encounter.

Since Chapter 8 is entirely devoted to the topic of sex therapy we will not go into it deeply here, but we should pause to consider the allegation that has often been made to the effect that female orgasm difficulties can be attributed to male insensitivity and incompetence as lovers. At present there is no evidence that the husbands of non-orgasmic women are any different from those of orgasmic women, or that their techniques of love-making are different in any way. Research suggests that the husbands of these two types of women are similar in personality, upbringing, sex education and sexual experience, and also, surprisingly, that a woman's responsiveness is not correlated with how long her husband stimulates her before or during intercourse. In another study it was found that a group of alcoholic husbands were just as capable of producing orgasms in their wives as non-alcoholic men. All the evidence concerning the role of the husband in female orgasmic difficulties is negative, and while retraining and therapy involving the husband is often helpful, the onus seems to be largely upon the wife herself to discover the source of the difficulty. Blaming the male partner for clumsiness and selfishness is not only unproductive, it is usually also unfair.

Increasingly, it is being recognized that women may need to discover orgasm through self-stimulation and then transfer what they have learned about the way their body responds to intercourse with a partner. Julia Heiman and colleagues at the State University of New York at Stony Brook have produced a book which is designed to train women in how to become orgasmic. Among their many suggestions are the following list of 'triggers' to orgasm that have been reported as useful by some women and which therefore might prove to be helpful hints to other women with difficulties:

(1) During sexual arousal, try deliberately tensing your legs, stomach, arms, or feet or exaggerating these things if you find yourself doing them. Body tension (such as pointing your toes or clenching your hands) is sometimes an automatic response, and increasing this tension often triggers orgasm.
(2) Practise vaginal muscle contractions. The squeeze and release movements often enhance arousal and will keep you focused on your genital sensations.
(3) As you get aroused, change position so that your head is hanging back over the edge of the bed or couch. This increases blood flow to your head and changes your breathing, both of which seem to add to feelings of tension and arousal in some women.
(4) Try really letting go. Begin to role-play an orgasm. Move your hips. Say some exciting words to yourself as though you were encouraging your body – 'come' or 'more', whatever seems right to you at the time.
(5) When you feel some arousal, try teasing yourself. Move away from the area you're concentrating on and then come back to it. Move your fingers over your breasts, nipples and stomach as well as your clitoris. Or change the pressure of your touch or your tempo as you touch your clitoris.
(6) You might try arranging a mirror so that you can watch while you're pleasuring yourself.
(7) Read a favourite passage from an erotic book after you've spent some time stimulating yourself. Or try really imagining yourself in your most intense fantasy. Really get into it. Let yourself go.
(8) Pick a sensual or sexy nightgown, bra, slip or underpants. Begin your session with this on. Feel the texture of this with your fingers. How does it feel to touch your breasts or genitals through this material? Undress yourself after a while or continue partially dressed if you like the feeling.
(9) Try touching yourself in a different position. If you've always pleasured yourself while on your back, turn over. You might try just having your rear up and your head and chest resting on a pillow. Or lie on your side or on your back with your legs up if you've always kept them stretched out flat. Try some body movements, such as moving your pelvis.
(10) Try holding your breath for a short while or breathing heavily (panting).

These exercises are mainly intended for use in connection with masturbation rather than intercourse. Certainly it is not necessary for a woman to have a penis inside her to experience orgasm. In intercourse the mechanism by which orgasm is achieved is a rhythmic pulling on the labia at the outer part of the vagina which indirectly stimulates the clitoris, usually by movement of the hood over the top of it. As we have noted, all female orgasms are mediated through stimulation of the clitoris (which is the penis analogue in women) even if 'vaginal orgasms' feel different because of the presence of a penis inside the vagina. Masters and Johnson have shown that in terms of physiological reactions orgasm achieved by masturbation is much the same as that achieved through intercourse and, if anything, more intense. Although, ultimately, the satisfaction obtained through intercourse is usually greater, there is no doubt that self-manipulation of the clitoris is often a more effective way for a woman to begin tackling her orgasmic difficulties, perhaps with the aid of a vibrator and erotic materials. The work of S. Hite, among others, has revealed a sizeable group of women who find it very much easier to achieve orgasm through masturbation than through sex with a man, and some can only get an orgasm in this way. Thus many therapists such as Heiman begin their treatment for anorgasmia with exercises in masturbation, and in parts of California there are lunchtime meetings of women in prestigious hotels to discuss techniques of masturbation as a way of dealing with orgasm difficulties – the modern equivalent of the pottery, yoga and flower-arrangement classes that used to absorb the spare time of suburban housewives.

The stress on female orgasm that is to be found in these classes and in the love manuals implies that intercourse without climax is unsatisfactory to women. Others go further and suggest that if a woman is sexually aroused and not brought to climax she will be left in a near-painful state of neuromuscular tension. Research indicates that orgasm is not a necessary condition to a woman's enjoyment of intercourse. P. Wallin of Stanford University surveyed 540 wives in the early years of marriage. He did find a general association between orgasm and sexual satisfaction but some wives, who said they seldom or never had orgasm, nevertheless experienced complete sexual relief. A smaller number of wives rated themselves as usually or always having orgasm but obtaining less than complete sexual release. The preferred monthly rate of intercourse was associated with sexual release but not with orgasm frequency. Thus it seems that while intercourse without orgasm often leads to some degree of frustration, some women are capable of having enjoyable intercourse which gives them release from sexual desire without climax.

Wallin found that highly educated women were less likely to report sexual release without orgasm. He interpreted this as meaning that expectation of orgasm (which is presumably raised through education) is one determinant of the extent of enjoyment of intercourse without orgasm. This may be so, but in view of the caution given in Chapter 1 we would need to be certain that women of different educational levels were interpreting key words such as 'orgasm' in the same way.

Two German researchers, V. Sigusch and G. Schmidt, asked a hundred women who sometimes missed orgasm during intercourse how they felt on those occasions. Two-thirds said they were disappointed and unsatisfied when this occurred. Many of these experienced considerable frustration, and anger directed at their male partner whom they felt was responsible for the omission. Most of the other women reacted to non-achievement of orgasm with calm or indifference. In about 4 per cent of cases this seemed to be an expression of general lethargy, but 9 per cent felt it was unimportant because it happened so rarely. Six per cent found intercourse pleasant even without orgasm, and another 5 per cent felt that the difficulty occurred only if they were not in the mood for sex at the time and were having intercourse just to please their man.

It seems, then, that orgasm is not an absolute necessity for female enjoyment of intercourse, but the majority of women need to experience it on a reasonable proportion of occasions at least. One could surmise that the extent of frustration felt by a woman who misses orgasm would depend upon the length of time over which her excitement has been escalating. Many women find a 'quickie' in the bathroom or the back seat of a car exciting and pleasurable at times, and this may leave them with a warm and pleasant feeling if not complete satisfaction. However, a long period of foreplay in which the woman is brought to the threshold of orgasm, at which point stimulation is abruptly withdrawn (usually because the man has ejaculated and satisfied himself) is likely to engender intense feelings of lack of fulfilment. At the extreme she may feel pain in the pelvis, equivalent to the 'sore balls' sensation experienced by most teenage boys in their early abbreviated amorous adventurers, as well as some less fortunate adult men.

Does orgasm in the female increase the chances that conception will occur? This is a question of great interest to gynaecologists and family planners, but so far there is no strong evidence either way. There are, however, two observations which indirectly suggest that female orgasm might facilitate conception. One was a study of physiological changes taking place in the uterus during intercourse using an implanted radio capsule to monitor pressure inside the uterus. This study by C. Fox of St Bartholomew's Hospital, London, showed that at orgasm itself there is a contraction of the uterus which increases the pressure inside it. This contraction moves down the uterus like the contractions occurring during labour and would therefore be more inclined to expel sperm than suck them in. However, immediately after orgasm, during the so-called resolution phase, there is a marked drop in uterine pressure which might be sufficient to assist the passage of sperm from the vagina through the cervix and into the uterus. Therefore, orgasm may help fertilization by creating a steep drop in uterine pressure giving rise to suction just at the time when sperm is available for transport.

The other piece of evidence that might bear on the connection between orgasm and conception is a report that girls who have been raped are very much more likely to get pregnant than could be accounted for on the basis of the usual chances (Parkes, 1976). One interpretation of this finding was that rape is so much more exciting than run-of-the-mill intercourse with a legitimate and gentle partner that it is more likely to result in orgasm, and the orgasm in turn facilitates pregnancy. This is a fairly weak theory, however, given then women who have had been raped usually deny any experience remotely resembling orgasm. Another explanation is that, as with many non-human animals, copulation might induce ovulation, especially if it is close to happening anyway. Orgasm could accelerate this tendency, but the fear and horror of being raped might have a similar effect. Finally, since this study was made some time ago (1947) and does not appear to have been replicated, we should consider the more mundane possibility that the results were due to some methodological error. For example, some of the girls may have decided that they had been raped only after discovering they were pregnant, thus to account for their unwelcome condition to irate parents.

Why should women have greater difficulty in achieving orgasm than men? A currently popular theory puts it down to the repressive history of attitudes towards female sexuality, the cultural double-standard that has caused women to be sexually inhibited. Feminists in particular are inclined to argue that a shift from a male dominated society could result in an equalization of orgasmic potential between men and women.

Certainly, there is great cultural variation in the extent to which female orgasms are recognized and regarded as desirable (Mead, 1961). Some primitive tribes view the female climax as essential to satisfactory sex; others have no word for it in their language and seem to be unaware of it as a possibility. Other cultures again, such as classical India, have favoured long-term maintenance of intercourse before ejaculation for the sake of female erotic pleasure, but without any emphasis on climax. It seems that there is no great biological imperative as regards the status of human female orgasm. In this case the individual variation among women in propensity for having orgasms is probably so great as to allow social norms and expectations to determine the majority experience.

This is not the same thing as saying that orgasm difficulties in women are due to repressive upbringing and sex-role stereotypes. If that were so then these social factors would have to operate progressively more powerfully down the evolutionary scale, for female orgasms are even more rare in the animal world than they are in human society. While male orgasms are easily observed, excitement in female animals tends to dissipate slowly and they remain responsive to sexual stimulation for a long time after coitus. The male, of course, has lost all interest immediately after ejaculation. On the other hand, some kind of female orgasm is suggested by the observation of parallel patterns of physiological build-up and release in male and female chimpanzees monitored during intercourse. Orgasm probably evolved late in females, whereas in males it is the continuation of mechanisms present in much earlier species (Katchadourian & Lunde, 1975).

E. Elkan (1948) supposes that female orgasm is unnecessary in any species in which the male has a mechanism for restraining the female in a copulatory position until he has ejaculated into her, thus implying that rape is the natural order of the animal kingdom. One wonders if human arms represent such a mechanism for holding down the female, in which case our species would have no need for orgasm either. Perhaps our evolutionary need for female orgasms arose out of our strange, civilized convention of requesting from a woman some form of consent, verbal or otherwise acceptable to a court of law, before proceeding to have intercourse with her. A more sensible suggestion is that the face-to-face intercourse so commonly practised by human beings, but which appears only as a perversion in other primates, might have something to do with the ability of the human female to share the delights of orgasm with her male partner. After all, the clitoris is round the front side of a woman and is therefore more directly contacted by the male partner in this position than is the case with rear-entry intercourse.

Finally, we might look at the evolutionary function, or survival value, of male and female orgasms as they appear in our society today. Orgasm serves two main functions – termination of intercourse, and reward for having begun it. Considering termination first, it is important that we have a mechanism for letting the parties know when to stop, otherwise the coitus would go on forever (or at least until they reached exhaustion). It is quite reasonable that this termination point should be soon after the ejaculation of the male, for then the seed is implanted. If the female were to have an identical orgasm to the male, she would be terminating coitus on 50 per cent of the occasions before any sperm had been deposited in her vagina. Clearly, this would not maximize the chances of conception occurring, and would therefore be disadvantageous from an evolutionary point of view.

On the other hand, if women were never to experience the pleasure of an orgasm and the feeling of complete and utter contentment which follows, they might be less motivated to engage in sex. Nature, in her wisdom, has arranged it so that the female has a slower and less reliable orgasm. She seldom in the normal course of events has her orgasm before that of her male partner, so at least one ejaculation has usually taken place before she is contented. In terms of B.F. Skinner's learning theory, she is on an 'intermittent reinforcement schedule'. Being rewarded on some occasions and not others makes for a habit that is particularly persistent. Also, if a woman is sometimes left frustrated because she does not obtain orgasm on a particular occasion she might be able to make up for it by having multiple orgasms on another. Altogether, the human system for distributing orgasms is a very good one from the evolutionary point of view, even though it may not be quite equitable within the terms of the Sex Discrimination Act.

## References

COMFORT, A., *The Joy of Sex.* New York: Crown Publishers, 1972.

ELKAN, E., 'The evolution of female orgastic capacity', *International Journal of Sex*, 1948, **84**, August 1.

FISHER, S., *Understanding the Female Orgasm.* Harmondsworth: Penguin, 1973.

FOX, C.A., WOLFF, H. & BAKER, J.A., 'Measurement of intra-vaginal and intra-uterine pressures during human coitus by radio telemetry', *Journal of Reproduction and Fertility*, 1970, **22**, 243–51.

HEIMAN, J., LOPICCOLO, L., & LOPICCOLO, J., *Becoming orgasmic: A Sexual Growth Program for Women.* Englewood Cliffs, N.J.: Prentice-Hall, 1976.

KANE, F.J., LIPTON, M.A. & EWING, J.A., 'Hormonal influences in female sexual response', *Archives of General Psychiatry,* 1969, **20**, 202–9.

KATCHADOURIAN, H.A. & LUNDE, D.T., *Fundamentals of Human Sexuality* (2nd Edition). New York: Holt, Rinehart and Winston, 1975.

MASTERS, W.H. & JOHNSON, V.E., *Human Sexual Response.* Boston: Little, Brown and Co., 1966.

MEAD, M., 'Cultural Determinants of Sexual Behaviour', in W.C. Young (ed), *Sex and Internal Secretions*, Vol. II. Baltimore: Williams and Wilkins, 1961.

PARKES, A.S., *Patterns of Sexuality and Reproduction.* London: Oxford University Press, 1976.

SIGUSCH, V. & SCHMIDT G., 'Lower class sexuality: Some emotional and social aspects of West German males and females', *Archives of Sexual Behaviour*, 1971, **1**, 29–44.

SHOPE, D.F., 'The orgastic responsiveness of selected college females', *The Journal of Sex Research*, 1968, **4**, 204–19.

VANCE, E.B. & WAGNER, N.N., 'Written descriptions of orgasm: A study of Sex differences', *Archives of Sexual Behaviour*, 1976, **5**, 87–98.

WALLIN, P., 'A study of orgasm as a condition of Women's enjoyment of intercourse', *Journal of Social Psychology*, 1960, **51**, 191–8.

# 8 The new sex therapies

It is well known that man is subject to many physical disabilities and diseases; it is becoming equally well known that man is also subject to numerous mental disorders, which sometimes disguise themselves as physical in nature, but for which nevertheless there is no known physical cause. Neurotic disorders in particular are extremely widespread: it is calculated that something like one person in three will suffer some form of neurotic breakdown in the course of his or her life, and that one person in six will seek active psychiatric help. This has led many people to believe that neurotic disorders are more frequent now than they used to be in days gone by, and the manifold stresses of modern life are often blamed.

This is almost certainly untrue. Estimates dating from three hundred years ago suggest that then also about one person in three was subject to neurotic disorders of one kind or another, and it would certainly be untrue to say that the stresses of life were less then than they are now; if anything the opposite is true. A few hundred years ago medicine did not know of the existence of anaesthetics: teeth were pulled out and limbs amputated with the victim conscious of all that was going on. Large numbers of infants died in the first year of life, as did their mothers, due to lack of medical knowledge and simple hygiene. Famine, war and plagues were endemic, and poverty extreme. If neuroses seem to be more prevalent now than ever before, this is no doubt due to the fact that we make more provision for neurotic patients; by a kind of Parkinson's law, the more mental hospitals are built, the more patients will throng to fill them! (Eysenck, 1977).

Sexual disorders make up a large portion of the neurotic disabilities which cause so much unhappiness to men and women in our time. Impotence, premature ejaculation, frigidity, lack of orgasmic capacity, fetishism, transvestism (cross dressing), pedophilia (sexual liking for small children), and the manifold perversions which, though they seem natural to some people, are abhorrent to others, such as bestialism (intercourse with animals) – these are only some of the many odd and often grotesque ways in which the sexual instinct can be disguised or rechannelled in human beings. All give rise to considerable emotional difficulties, anxieties and depressive reactions, and all cause a great deal of suffering in the men and women who experience them. Sadism and masochism, i.e. the infliction or suffering of pain in order to experience sexual fulfilment, are other unusual and probably neurotic forms of sexual behaviour; indeed, the list is almost endless.

Why do human beings behave in such an odd fashion? Why, to add to the confusion, do some people prefer persons of their own sex as sexual objects, as in male homosexuality or female lesbianism? And can anything be done to relieve these unwilling victims of an eccentric sex drive of their unwanted aberrations? Some, of course, do not wish to be relieved of what to them is the perfectly sensible and acceptable form of behaviour, and if their behaviour does not interfere with the rights of others, and does not give rise to public scandal, there is no reason to regard their actions as neurotic, or to impose on them a course of therapy which they do not themselves desire. Historically, of course, the law has taken an active interest in these matters, and it is only comparatively recently that homosexuality, for instance, ceased to be regarded as a criminal act. Even nowadays, sodomy (buggery) is regarded as a crime punishable with life imprisonment by the English law – even though the act may be carried out between husband and wife! In addition to being excessively inhumane in regard to sex practices, the law is also an ass, as we all know. It decreed that only men can in general commit buggery, but legally a woman can commit buggery with an animal! The mind boggles. The whole notion that men can be made moral by law, particularly in the sexual sphere where the concepts of normality are particularly subjective and ambiguous, is of course of doubtful value; in relation to such an act between consenting adults one would imagine that it had no place in a modern, civilized society. However, the great majority of sufferers from these many disorders do desperately wish to be cured of them, and it would be cruelty to withhold treatment from them, provided such treatment could be shown to be effective. We will in this chapter look at the causes of the deviant sexual behaviours, and go on to discuss some of the methods that have been used successfully to cure those patients who express a wish to be cured.

Let us first of all deal quite briefly with psychoanalysis. To most lay readers the theories advanced by Freud at the turn of the century to explain neurotic disorders and sexual dysfunctions are probably better known than any psychological explanations and methods of treatment, and they may still labour under the misapprehension that psychoanalysis is a useful and accepted theory, giving rise to methods of treatment that actually work. Unfortunately the facts show otherwise. As far as neurosis in general is concerned, Freudian methods of treatment not only take an inordinate length of time (the usual length of psychoanalysis is between two and four years, with treatment often taking even longer than that!), but are also on the whole quite ineffective in alleviating the manifold symptoms of which the patient complains. Such a statement is often hotly contested by psychoanalysts who claim to have been successful in a number of cases, and quote these as evidence. Such evidence, however, is quite inconclusive, for a very simple reason: neurotic disorders tend to disappear on their own (i.e. without explicit psychiatric help) in a very large number of cases; several studies have shown that spontaneous remission (as this process is called) leads to a cure or a very marked improvement in something like 80 per cent of all severely neurotic patients in the length of time that is typically taken by psychoanalytic treatment. In other words, to demonstrate that the treatment works it would be necessary to show that the percentage of cures is greater than that which could be explained by spontaneous remission; the evidence shows that if anything it is smaller! This is now pretty universally agreed, even by leading psychoanalysts. What they now claim is that their treatment, while not curing the disorder, enables the patient to accept it with a better heart, or that in fact the treatment makes them a 'better person' in some unspecified manner. Such vague claims cannot of course be tested, and in any case would be small help to the patient who wishes to be rid of the symptoms (Rachman, 1971).

It may be interesting just to look at some of the psychoanalytic theories about sexual difficulties in order to contrast them with the biologically oriented theories to be considered later. Let us look first at male impotence. The psychoanalysts believe that between the third and fifth year of life the boy wants to have intercourse with his mother and kill his father, who has come to represent a hated rival. On the other hand, he also fears that the detection of these incestuous impulses by his father will result in severe punishment, i.e. castration. Thus, in the interest of self-preservation, these infantile sexual aims are repressed and preserved in the unconscious; this is the course of evolution of the famous Oedipus complex.

According to this theory, then, the pre-eminent cause of impotence is unconscious castration anxiety. The early incestuous wishes, together with the anxiety and guilt feelings they engendered, are re-evoked whenever sexual excitement is experienced and result in disturbances of potency. Impotence can thus be understood within this conceptual framework as a neurotic defence against the emergence of unbearable emotions. According to this theory, potency can only be restored if these unconscious conflicts are resolved by analytic treatment.

Psychoanalytic theories about the causes of premature ejaculation are even more remote from reality. According to Freudian theory, the premature ejaculator experiences intense, but unconscious, sadistic feelings towards women. The unconscious purpose of the rapid ejaculation is to defile and soil the woman and, incidentally, to deprive her of pleasure. In some odd way, the sex partner is identified with the mother, towards whom the patient has ambivalent feelings which later transfer to all women. As the Duke of Wellington once replied when, striding along Pall Mall in his Field Marshal's uniform, he was addressed by a gentleman who said to him: 'Mr Smith, I believe?' 'If you believe that, you'll believe anything' (Kaplan, 1974).

Needless to say, methods of treatment based on such insubstantial and quite unproven theories have not led to any notable cures, and other methods have been found to be not only much shorter but also much more effective. We will next turn to a consideration of these methods (Gillan & Gillan, 1976).

Before discussing these methods and theories in any detail, however, we must first of all look at man as he emerges through the process of evolution. It is impossible to arrive at any sensible way of looking at neurotic disorders, or indeed any human activity, without bearing in mind that man, through evolution, has evolved from lowly animal origins, and still carries the marks of these origins with him. Man is indeed a rational being, but he is also irrational; he is characterized by a cortex supremely able to indulge in rational activities, but his cortex is superimposed on other brain structures which are more primitive. The rational man of the enlightenment, or the economic man of Victorian times, was not supposed to act in an irrational manner; they are bad psychological models which do not represent reality in any way. What has happened is that we suffer from a generation gap on a truly gigantic scale – not on an *ontogenetic* scale, like that due to our growing older and not maintaining contact with the younger people in our society, but rather on a *phylogenetic* scale, i.e. related to our whole evolutionary development.

Paul MacLean, Chief of the Laboratory of Brain Evolution and Behaviour at the National Institute of Mental Health in the USA, has put it very clearly:

> In evolution (see Figure 12) the primate forebrain expands along the lines of three basic patterns characterized as reptilian, palaeomammalian and neomammalian. The result is a remarkable linkage of three brain types which are radically different in structure and chemistry, and which, in an evolutionary sense, are countless generations apart. We possess, so to speak, a hierarchy of three-brains-in-one – a triune brain. Or, stated another way, we have a linkage of three biocomputers, each with its own special kind of intelligence, sense of time, memory, motor and other functions. Although my proposed scheme for sub-dividing the brain may seem simplistic, the fact remains that the three basic formations are there for anyone to see, and, thanks to improved anatomical, chemical, and physiological techniques, stand out in clearer detail than ever before.

What do these three 'brains' do that sets them apart from each other? According to MacLean, the reptilian brain is basic for such genetically constituted behaviour as selecting home sites, establishing and defending territory, hunting, homing, mating, forming social hierarchies and the like. In humans especially, he believes that the reptilian brain is involved with compulsive, repetitive, ritualistic, deceptive and imitative forms of behaviour. Essentially, much of our more primitive, instinctive behaviour is built on these physiological foundations, reaching back through 250 million years of history, to the age of the reptiles. As he points out:

> It is traditional to belittle the role of instincts in human behaviour, but how should we categorize those actions that stem from a predisposition to compulsive and ritualistic behaviour; a proclivity to prejudice and deception; the propensity to seek and follow precedent as in legal and other matters; and a natural tendency to imitation? All these propensities have survival value, but they are double-edged and can cut both ways.

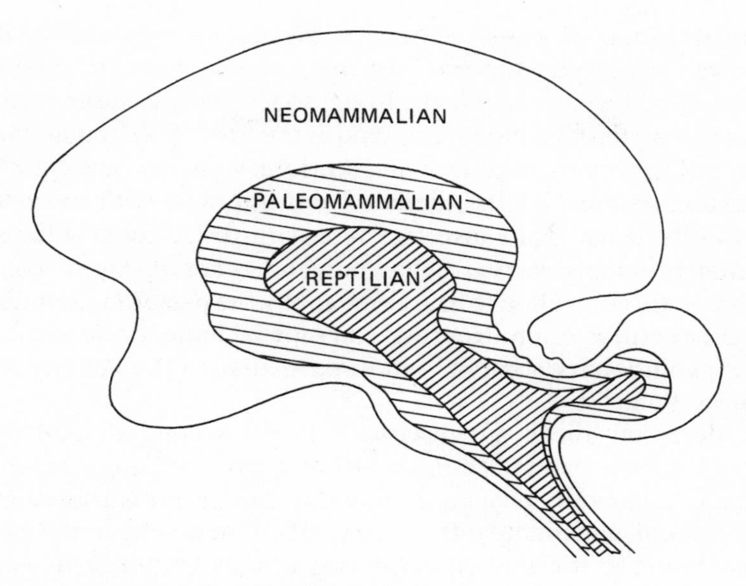


Figure 12 Three evolutionary brain mechanisms

Reptiles have only a rudimentary cortex, and in the transition to mammals it is thought that this was expanded and elaborated, providing the animal with a better means of viewing the environment and learning to survive. In both lower and higher mammals the old cortex occupies a large convolution (the limbic lobe) which surrounds the brain stem. This primitive limbic cortex is concerned with emotional behaviour such as is observed in fear and anger, and with feeding, fighting and self-protection. Genital and other forms of sexual behaviour have also recently been found related to this palaeomammalian brain, suggesting that it is concerned with expressive and feeling states which promote the procreation of the species. There are also suggestions that this system may be concerned fundamentally with the development of the feeling of individuality and personal identity. These are all important functions, but they are clearly still differentiated from cognitive behaviour, inductive and deductive reasoning, and other peculiarly human behaviour patterns. 'Compared with the limbic cortex, the new cortex is like an expanding numerator. It mushrooms late in evolution, culminating in man to become the brain of reading, writing, and arithmetic. Mother of invention and father of abstract thought, it promotes the preservation and procreation of ideas.' Science is the natural expression of the neocortex in its purest form. As the neocortex is the apogee of evolutionary development in the brain, so science is a cultural expression of this highest development. And as the lower palaeomammalian and reptilian brains interact and interfere with the activity of the neocortex, so they set the limits to and interfere with the natural growth of science. They also interfere with the rational solution of personal problems, sexual behaviour and other forms of conduct which are still controlled to a large extent by the palaeomammalian or even the reptilian brain. Neurosis can only be understood in relation to this evolutionary context, and in particular to the activity of the limbic system.

Readers may recall our discussion in the second chapter of the personality dimension of emotionality or neuroticism, and its relation to sexual behaviour; physiologically this dimension is rooted in the limbic system, and innate differences in the functioning of this system are responsible for the different degrees of emotionality shown characteristically by some types of people. The limbic system governs and coordinates the activities of the autonomic system, which in turn activates the various peripheral expressions of the emotions with which we are familiar. This system is not completely independent of the neocortex, of course, but it is largely so, and rational thought will not help us to reduce our emotional disturbances, or help us to adjust to inappropriate emotional reactions.

The emotional system, the limbic cortex, the autonomic system – wherever you want to designate this emotional complex, it clearly has an important function to play in life – otherwise evolution would not have ensured its survival. What is this function? It is essentially that of mobilizing bodily resources for fight and flight. When the sympathetic parts of the autonomic system are aroused, adrenalin flows through the body, increasing its capacity for energy output; blood rushes faster through the system, supplying vital oxygen to the various organs of the body, including the brain; the pupil of the eye is enlarged, so that it can all the better see the enemy, and the opportunities for escape. These and many other changes have been vital for millions of years for the survival of man and his animal ancestors; they have now largely ceased to fulfil this function – the kinds of problems which face us nowadays are seldom soluble in terms of bodily combat, or flight. Hence strong emotions of fear and anger are largely inappropriate in our lives, and merely serve to complicate it. It is for this reason that emotions play a predominant part in maladaptive neurotic disorders.

Just as the cortex has its special organs, like the eyes, the ears, and the receptors of the skin, which warn us of approaching danger, and which signal future encounters long before they happen, so the emotional system also has its own warning system. And just as the neocortex enables us to learn from experience, so the emotional system also has a means of turning past experience to good account. This is done by means of *conditioning*. The principles of conditioning were first uncovered by I. Pavlov at the time of the First World War, and they are of particular importance in looking at sexual dysfunctions. Most people are familiar with the defining experiment that Pavlov carried out. He measured the rate of salivation of a dog when confronted with a bell ringing; usually dogs do not respond at all. When a hungry dog is presented with food, however, he salivates copiously. We can now make the dog salivate to the bell by pairing it a number of times with the food: first the bell is rung, then the food is presented. When this has been done some ten or twenty times, the dog will salivate to the bell even when no food is presented. This is the so-called conditioned response; the bell is called the conditioned stimulus, and the food is the unconditioned stimulus, i.e. a stimulus that produces the effects without prior learning. Conditioning essentially associates the previously neutral conditioned stimulus with a response that previously only occurred to the unconditioned stimulus. This is clearly of biological significance; we need saliva to digest our food, and even to swallow it, and to begin to produce saliva early on, before the food is actually presented, in response to extraneous stimuli associated with feeding, makes the process all the more effective.

This biological importance of conditioning is even more important when we consider the formation of conditioned emotional responses. Suppose you put a dog in a shuttlebox, i.e. a large box divided into two compartments, (a) and (b); both of these have a metal floor which can be electrified such that the dog receives an electric shock through its paws. The two parts of the box are divided by a hurdle over which the dog can easily jump. Let us now see how the dog reacts to a flickering light; the answer is that he will disregard it. Let this flickering light now become the conditioned stimulus for electrifying the floor, and giving the dog a shock. Upon receiving the shock he will jump over the hurdle into the safe compartment, and when the flickering light is put on again, and a shock is given to him in this second compartment, he will jump back to the first. After a few jumps he learns that the flickering light precedes shock, and he will start jumping to the flickering light, without waiting for the shock. In other words, through the process of conditioning he has learned to avoid the shock, which is biologically of considerable value to him. It is easy to translate this whole process into the kinds of conditions that obtain in wild life, and it will be seen that conditioning is an extremely valuable adjunct to the other energy-producing properties of the limbic system.

How is all this relevant to sexual dysfunctions? The simple answer is that sexual behaviour is very easily conditioned to various previously neutral stimuli, and consequently can be manipulated and sidetracked very easily from its natural or usual functioning. A simple example will illustrate what we have in mind. In fetishism, the sufferer requires some object (a slipper, or whatever it might be) to be present whenever he has sexual intercourse; without the slipper no sexual arousal takes place, and the slipper by itself produces sexual arousal. How does this come about? The obvious suggestion is that in the past the sight and/or feel of slippers has preceded sexual satisfaction, and has thus become a conditioned stimulus which by itself produces sexual arousal. How could one prove such a theory?

In an experiment carried out in our laboratories by Dr S. Rachman, an attempt was made artificially to induce a (very mild) form of shoe fetishism in quite normal subjects. The reaction measured was the erection of the penis, which can easily be recorded through a penis plethysmograph which is connected to an ink writing device. This instrument simply measures the volume of the penis, which increases with sexual excitement; what is measured is the amount of increase produced by the stimuli presented to the subject.

The subjects were presented with slides of boots; these produced no sexual reaction of any kind. They were then presented with slides of nude females; these produced quite a marked reaction. Next, slides of boots were shown preceding slides of nude females, until after a while the conditioned stimuli (the slides showing the boots) produced a penile reaction even without any further showing of the slides with the nude females. Thus it is quite easy to condition sexual reactions to previously neutral and meaningless stimuli. The experiment also showed another property which is well known from laboratory studies of conditioning with both animals and men, namely *generalization*. Conditioning is to a particular stimulus, but stimuli similar to the conditioned one also produce the same effect, although to a slightly lesser extent. Thus it was not only boots that produced the sexual reaction, but also slides of shoes, slippers, Wellingtons, etc.! We can thus demonstrate experimentally the plausibility of a theory which attributes fetishism to events in the patient's past which involve the formation of conditioned responses.

How can we conceptualize the growth of other forms of sexual dysfunction? Conditioning will serve well as a causal factor in transvestism, in various of the so-called perversions, and indeed in most of the behaviours we have enumerated previously. In some cases there is undoubtedly also a genetic factor involved: there seems to be no doubt that many homosexuals have developed in that way because of strong hereditary factors; we have already looked at some of the hormonal and other influences involved.

It would be quite wrong to look for unicausal theories for such a complex behaviour as homosexuality; it is not at all necessary to postulate that there is one single cause which is responsible for all homosexual behaviour, equally in all homosexuals. It is quite possible that homosexual behaviour is largely innate in some, produced by social conditions (life on board ship, or in prison, or boarding schools, or in some other entirely male company) in others. There may be, and often are, other complicating features. Many homosexuals have been found to be actively afraid of women, in other words to respond with flight and fright to the presence of women in their lives; this again may be largely innate, or due to conditioning, e.g. through unfortunate experiences with stepmothers or other threatening female figures. Once a fear is present, it makes sexual advances to women difficult or impossible, and the person in question makes do with the less threatening semi-equivalent, namely a male sex object. Clearly if a homosexual wishes to be cured of his particular sexual preference, it is important to know the cause of the disorder. If a fear of women is prominently involved, then one would proceed to *desensitize* him of this fear. As desensitization is very important for all aspects of sex therapy, a few words concerning it may be useful at this point.

As we have already mentioned, the autonomic system mediates the emotions, but it is itself divided into two largely antagonistic parts. The sympathetic part produces emotional arousal; the parasympathic part has the opposite function of calming down emotional upheaval. What we have to deal with in most neurotics is the fact that some conditioned stimuli has become associated with sympathetic arousal, and what we have to do in order to cure the disorder is to attach parasympathetic responses to these stimuli, to counteract the sympathetic ones. If we can do this, then two will cancel out, and the person will not experience any emotional reaction to the originally fear-producing object.

In practice we would do this by first of all training the patient in relaxation, i.e. training the various muscles of his body to become relaxed whenever he wishes to reduce tension. Most people learn this quite easily in three or four lessons, and of course a state of relaxation is related to parasympathic activity, and is incompatible with emotional arousal. Next, having instructed the patient to relax as completely as he can, the therapist would then instruct him to try to visualize in his mind's eye a relatively non-fearful female, such as a little girl. When this is done without arousing any great emotion, the therapist proceeds up a kind of hierarchy of emotion-producing females, always going from the bottom of the hierarchy to the next in line, until he finally reaches the top of the fear-producing hierarchy, which might be an image of a nude, large-breasted female making excessive sexual demands on the patient! Having gone through all the steps of the hierarchy without experiencing any undue emotion, and at each step conditioning parasympathetic responses to the female conditioned stimuli presented, the patient would now be enabled to encounter living women in a state of relaxation, and thus extend the hierarchy to everyday life situations. There are many studies to show that his method actually works very well, and can cure homosexuality in patients where the prime cause is fear of women. In others, where the situation is more complicated and where fear of women only plays a contributory part, this would nevertheless be one part of the total cure (Annon, 1975).

In other cases what has been used is a technique often referred to as *aversion therapy*. In this technique what is attempted is to form an aversive conditioned reaction to male sex objects in the patient. This is done by showing him photographs of nude males, and giving him a relatively mild electric shock after the exposure of the photograph. The longer he keeps looking at the photograph the stronger the shock gets, until finally he pushes a button which removes the picture, stops the electric shock, and produces in front of him the picture of a nude female. In this way we associate nude males with electric shock, pain, fear and anxiety, and nude women with relaxation and the removal of anxiety. This method, though far from perfect, has been shown to work in many cases, and has been found superior to psychoanalytic and other 'talking' methods.

The reader will no doubt share our own feelings about aversion therapy methods of this kind, namely that they look inhumane, appear to reduce a human being to the status of a robot and seem unworthy of civilized human beings. These objections are well taken, but they should be looked at in the light of certain facts which may alter our opinion. Let us assume, as we believe is in fact the case, that this method works better than other methods, such as psychotherapy and psychoanalysis, and that indeed these other methods do not produce much change in the homosexual patient. Let us also assume, as is often the case, that the patient is very highly motivated to undergo treatment and to change his position. Indeed, as the therapy is only administered to patients who voluntarily seek it out, there is here no question of the therapist violating the privacy or the psychological independence of the patient; his wholehearted consent has been secured before any kind of therapy is undertaken. Under these conditions, would it be humane to withhold treatment from the patient, although he himself desires it, and has had the exact details of what is going to be done explained to him? We recall a particular case in which a QC came to us, having heard one of us give a lecture on behaviour therapy; he was a homosexual and urgently wanted to be treated by these methods. It was impossible at the time to accommodate him as no properly equipped treatment rooms were available. Three weeks later he committed suicide. Would it have been less humane, granted the possibility of carrying out treatment at the time, to have afforded him the opportunity for rechannelling his sexual energy?

It is of course true in some sense that the treatment is an insult to human dignity, but the insult is presented not so much by the therapist as by nature itself. The neocortex contains what is generally regarded as specifically human in us, but we cannot disguise the presence of the palaeocortex and the reptile brain, to use MacLean's terminology. It is these that render us less-than-human, and the problems presented by this sub-human aspect of our nature can probably only be dealt with by methods which themselves are adapted to this level. The whole question is a social and ethical one on which we do not wish to lay down the law; the reader must make up his own mind. We have merely mentioned the case of aversion therapy to illustrate the methods that have been used, and have been found more effective than others, although of course much less than 100 per cent effective. Much further research is obviously needed in order to improve them to the point where failures are very much the exception.

Some homosexual groups have objected altogether that homosexuality is not a disease, just as it is no longer a crime in England, and that consequently there is no need for any form of therapy. Up to a point we agree with this; homosexuality is not a disease in any meaningful sense, and homosexuals who wish to live as such, and who do not offend against the law in other ways, such as by the perversion of minors, have a perfect right to do so. However, we have encountered many homosexuals who, for one reason or another, wish to change their sexual affiliation and become heterosexual. Should they be prevented from achieving this aim simply because other homosexual people or groups have objections to the methods used, or to the desirability of the aim itself? We believe that the only reasonable and ethical principle is the desire of the patient himself; the wishes and opinions of outside groups should carry very little weight with the therapist responsible.

Aversion therapy has been used successfully not only with homosexuality (that is male homosexuality; we know of no case of lesbianism being treated in this way), but also fetishism, tranvestism and other practices regarded by the patient as undesirable for one reason or another. A particular form of aversion therapy is used for the treatment of premature ejaculation, and as the method is extremely successful (nearly 100 per cent so!) it deserves to be discussed in some detail.

Premature ejaculation essentially results because the male gets too excited to control his ejaculatory process, and this happens before he is able to attempt coitus, or so shortly thereafter that the woman remains completely unsatisfied. Aversive conditioning would seem to imply that the stimuli associated normally with sexual excitement should become conditioned to some counter-stimuli which oppose the sexual excitement. This is done by the female squeezing the penis of the male when he signals to her that ejaculation is imminent. Immediately this state occurs, and the signal is given, the female squeezes her partner's penis by firmly placing her thumb on his frenulum and her first two fingers on either side of the coronal sulcus; this simply means the tip of the penis, and any encyclopaedia or textbook will demonstrate the position of these parts.

After the penis has been firmly squeezed for a few seconds, the man loses his desire to ejaculate and experiences a partial loss of erection. Love play is initiated again at this point, and when the desire to ejaculate occurs again, the female again applies the squeeze. It is possible for partners to enjoy fifteen to twenty minutes of sex play without ejaculation by using this technique during genital stimulation. As already said, the method works extremely well in practically all cases; the only warning one might feel inclined to give is of course that if the whole thing is continued for too long, it might lead to impotence or other undesirable consequences! This, however, is extremely unlikely, and no cases have been reported of this occurring; in all cases where it has been used the male has been only too pleased with his new-found freedom, and has been eager to use it at the first occasion, thus making it unlikely that the squeezing would be continued for such a long period of time that untoward consequences would occur! (Hartman & Fithian, 1972).

Another technique, sometimes used in conjunction with the squeeze technique, is the so-called stop and start method; here the woman stops the stimulation of her partner's penis when he signals her to do so. The man is advised to focus his attention on the erotic sensations he feels when his penis is stimulated, and instruct his partner to stop stimulating him when he feels he is approaching ejaculation. When excitement has subsided, stimulation may recommence. In this way the male notices and learns that the sensation disappears in a few seconds after stimulation has ceased, and this increases his ejaculatory control.

For the treatment of impotence quite powerful methods are now available. These depend mainly on the reduction of anxiety, and in order to understand their function we must go back to the distinction we made between the sympathetic and the parasympathetic parts of the autonomic nervous system. The erection of the male penis is produced by the parasympathetic system, while male orgasm is produced by the sympathetic system. We have already mentioned that the sympathetic system is also concerned with fear, anxiety and other strong emotions; it is obvious therefore that when a person is anxious, or afraid, his sympathetic will be aroused and make it difficult if not impossible for the parasympathetic system to produce a penile erection. Thus anxiety and fear are emotions directly opposed to sexual potency, and the person who is anxious or fearful is unlikely to be able to experience a proper erection (Belliveau & Richter, 1971).

This often leads to a circular accelerating process of growing impotence. A male may experience impotence because he has been drinking too much, or because he has been working too hard, or because of some other purely physical and external reason. Next time he attempts to have intercourse he will remember his previous impotence and get worried and anxious that it might happen again; this worry and anxiety, of course, will have the very effect the male is trying to prevent. Thus we get a positive feedback system in which the original case of impotence produces worry, and the worry produces subsequent impotence, which in turn increases the worry and anxiety! This vicious circle can only be broken by reducing the anxiety through some form of desensitization.

In this desensitization the therapist actually instructs the patient not to try to have intercourse, or to think about an erection, but simply to have some quiet fun lying in bed unclothed with his sex partner, kissing and cuddling, and not attempting anything more demanding or serious. As no demands are made upon the male, there is no anxiety as to what he might fail to produce, and consequently he has a perfectly normal erection. Very gradually slight demands are imposed on him, never sufficient to produce anxiety, and after a series of sessions of this course he is finally allowed to have intercourse in the normal way. His sex partner is also instructed to increase his pleasure, and sexual excitement, by indulging in all sorts of stimulating practices. Impotence is a more difficult disorder to treat than premature ejaculation, and indeed there are different types of impotence which may require different treatment; nevertheless, the method of desensitization has proved its value without any question, although success has still not reached the 100 per cent level (Brecher & Brecher, 1969).

Frigidity and anorgasm in females can also be treated with considerable success by an adaptation of this mode of therapy. Often women have been brought up to feel disgust and other negative emotions with regard to sex, and this feeling has to be overcome by discussion and demonstration of the error of this method of viewing sexual intercourse. Many women have had little experience with sexual arousal, and have to be introduced to the positive delights of the bodily feelings accompanying it. The therapist often has to instruct such women in the art of masturbation, and may even have to prescribe pornographic reading matter or films in order to help them on their way. Once orgasm has been achieved through masturbation, and sexual fantasies have become centred on the type of behaviour that the woman is wishing to practise, she is instructed to indulge in sex play with her lover on the same lines as we have discussed before in relation to impotence, i.e. in an undemanding situation where the emphasis is entirely on happy, pleasurable sensory feelings. By proceeding in this step by step way the fears of such women are desensitized, and orgasmic capacity is produced in quite a high percentage of sufferers.

Considering the importance of sex in our lives, and the untold unhappiness suffered by impotent men and anorgasmic women, the demonstration by behaviour therapists that these new methods can and do work extremely quickly and extremely effectively is one of the most reassuring indications that psychology can be practically useful as well as academically respectable. It is unfortunate that very few medical practitioners, consultants, and psychiatrists are trained in these methods; a great deal of human suffering and misery could be eliminated if only more psychologists were trained to give practical sex therapy (Masters & Johnson, 1970; Cauthery & Cole, 1971).

There are a number of ethical points which arise in connection with sex therapy. We will discuss some of these, without wishing to provide any kind of definitive answer to them. Here too readers will have to come to their own decision; we will merely outline the arguments and the problems which arise. The first and most obvious of these problems, of course, is that sex therapy only works when you have a man and a woman; the problems can usually not be solved by simply dealing with one or the other by themselves. It is perfectly all right, and no difficulty is involved, when you are dealing with a married couple, both of whom are willing to cooperate; what is one going to do, however, with single males or females, or with married couples where one or other of the partners is unwilling to take part in the therapy? Some

American investigators have provided 'surrogates' for such missing partners, i.e. women who are willing to play the part of wives in the therapy, and who become very skilled in taking the part of the 'wife'. Critics have sometimes slated these 'surrogates' as nothing better than prostitutes, but this is untrue as well as unkind. Such women play an extremely important role in sex therapy, and without them many males would be condemned to continued suffering without any hope of relief. An ethical problem obviously arises, but this is produced more by the sexual intolerance so characteristic of our society, than by the actual circumstances of the case itself.

Another difficulty arises in the case of many homosexuals who are cured of their preference for male partners, but who are then faced with the unusual and difficult task of acquiring, seducing and making love to a female sex partner. Most heterosexual males have learned these techniques from childhood onwards, and have little difficulty in carrying out the necessary steps. The newly converted homosexual, however, has had no such training, and may have the greatest difficulty in understanding these tasks. In order to get him out of this difficulty, some American psychologists have taken to instructing such patients in the art of seduction; here again there seem to be some moral and ethical problems which may be difficult to resolve, even in our present more permissive climate. The same teaching in the techniques of seduction has become necessary in the case of many heterosexual males whose sexual difficulties may seem ridiculous and absurd to most normal people, but they do afflict quite a sizeable proportion of men, particularly younger ones.

Many interesting and important questions remain. To what extent can sex education in schools act as a prophylactic against later sex problems? To what extent does it produce such problems? To what extent does the present availability of pornographic films and magazines influence the sexual mores and habits of our society? Is permissiveness really producing better adjusted, less neurotic and sexually more satisfied people than did an earlier, more inhibited type of society? We do not know the answers to most of these questions, although there is a good deal of evidence at least on the effectiveness of sex and violence in the media in changing the habits of viewers, listeners and readers (Eysenck & Nias, 1978). But apart from this we are faced with a great sea of ignorance surrounding us, and unfortunately advocates on both sides refuse to carry out the necessary research which alone could tell us what we want to know. Advocates of permissiveness want to introduce large-scale sex education into our schools, but puritans reject the whole notion out of hand. Yet neither side has ever produced any evidence whatsoever to indicate that sex education in schools has positive or negative effects of any kind. Even if such effects could be demonstrated, we would still not know what type of sex education produces what kind of effects, or on what types of children – there is every reason to believe that introverted children and extraverted children will react quite differently to the same type of teaching, as would highly emotional and highly unemotional children. Individual differences are so marked in everything that we do that it would be quite absurd to imagine that one particular mode of sex teaching would affect all children in the same way.

It is unfortunate that our society is oriented along political, religious and ethical lines, and impervious to the need for scientific proof. We believe what we want to believe; this is the opposite to the point of view of the scientist who asks for evidence before accepting any belief, however tentatively. The fact that we have now learned to cure most of the sexual dysfunctions which men and women suffer from on such a large scale should not make us oblivious of the fact that it would be much better to take prophylactic action and avoid the origins of these sexual dysfunctions in the first place. How this can be done only further research will show; we already have a number of good theories to tell us at least in which direction to look. Until such research is carried out we will have to remain content with the knowledge that most of the disorders people complain of in the sexual field can now be cured, and cured quickly, cheaply and effectively. That at least is something, and psychologists can rightly be pleased with the success of the methods developed so far – even though much may still remain to be done in order to improve these methods, make them more effective and allow them to be applied to a greater number of people.

So far we have been talking about sexual difficulties and disorders which affect a particular person. It is interesting to note, however, that there are now also psychological methods for dealing with problems of interaction between people, as in marriage. Between one-third and a half of all marriages in Great Britain and the United States break down, and it may be useful to consider whether there may not be ways and means of dealing with the problems that cause these breakups. The analysis of the problem begins with certain assumptions. The first of these is that the husband and the wife both expect certain rewards from the marriage, using the term 'reward', to combine financial, social and sexual satisfactions. The second assumption is that most married adults expect to enjoy reciprocal relations with their partners, i.e. they expect that each party has rights and duties, and that these in turn result in a form of interaction which leads each partner to dispense social reinforcement at an equitable rate. In other words, the husband should aim to please the wife, and do the things she wishes him to do, just as the wife should try and please her husband in a similar manner. There is thus an expectation of reciprocity, each partner handing out rewards to the other, and expecting to receive rewards in turn. In the technical language of the psychologists such rewards are usually called 'reinforcements', because rewards reinforce (strengthen) the kind of behaviour that precedes them, just as in the tale of the donkey trotting along because you dangle a carrot in front of his nose.

Analysis of disordered marriages in the light of this reinforcement-attraction hypothesis show that in most cases the partners reinforce each other at a low rate, and each is therefore relatively unattractive to, and unreinforced by the other. We might write this as an equation:

Happy marriage = plenty of mutual reinforcement.
Unhappy marriage = little mutual reinforcement.

This leads to the suggestion that in order to modify an unsuccessful marital interaction, it is essential to develop the power of each partner to administer rewards to the other, in the hope that the other will reciprocate, thus leading to a higher degree of interchange of rewards or reinforcements, and thus (hopefully!) to a happier marriage.

Unhappy marriages, i.e. marriages where there is too low a level of reward, tend to lead to one of two consequences. One is coercion, where one partner seeks to gain rewards from the other, not by in turn rewarding the spouse, but by force, blackmail or other means of coercion. Thus a husband who wants his wife to show more affection and sexual compliance, but who is unable or unwilling to behave in a manner pleasing to his wife, and thus rewarding for her, may respond to her refusals by becoming abusive, by beating her, or by cutting down her housekeeping money. This is not a good method, and it merely leads to a quicker breakup of the marriage.

So does the other method often used, namely withdrawal. While coercion is used mainly by men, withdrawal is used mainly by women, who may refuse to give any rewards to their husbands, and withdraw from the union completely. Withdrawal usually leads to the discovery, on the part of the spouse, of other sources of reinforcement, such as drink, mistresses, drugs, etc.

We may say that in the unhappy marriage, each partner requires reinforcements or rewards from the other, but is unwilling to provide them. Both need to realize that before the partner is likely to behave in a satisfactory manner, each person must himself or herself invest in reinforcing behaviour. It is usually difficult for people involved in an unsatisfactory marriage to take the first step, because of the obvious emotional entanglements, and it is the task of the psychologist to break this deadlock, and to lead the married partners back to a set of behaviours which are mutually rewarding.

To achieve this, the psychologist will usually begin by explaining the situation to the couple and to introduce what is sometimes called a 'token economy', in which tokens are given for reinforcing behaviour, and can be exchanged for other types of reinforcing behaviour. Thus a wife may want her husband to talk to her in the morning rather than read the paper, or to help with the washing up rather than watching television. Conversely, the husband may wish the wife to be more responsive sexually at night, or to stop asking her mother into the house so frequently. A list would then be drawn up of all the desired behaviours on both sides, with points or tokens awarded on an agreed basis for each of these different behaviours. If the husband would thus start talking to his wife in the morning, she in turn would cut down the invitations to her mother, and in return for helping with the dishes the husband might receive a warmer welcome in bed! This whole method may seem completely mechanistic and even somewhat ridiculous to the outsider, but with shy, tongue-tied, badly educated and rather dull people (and even with some not so dull, tongue-tied and poorly educated!) the method seems to work well, and has in many cases led to a marked improvement in the marital situation. Most married people don't want their marriage to break up; they do not realize the mistakes they are making in their behaviour, and indeed the situation is one involving a positive feedback action – the husband in some way, possibly quite unwittingly, annoys the wife; the wife in return annoys the husband, in revenge and the husband then purposely does something which will annoy the wife even more. In this way quarrels escalate and spiral up into emotional conflicts which the participants find very difficult to resolve (Knox, 1971).

The criticism that this method of dealing with the problem is mechanistic is one that has been made of all the other methods of therapy we have discussed so far. It is indeed true, and to some extent even tautological, that the outsider views the emotional troubles and eternal difficulties of other people from the outside, and this inevitably means that he takes a more objective and possibly 'mechanistic' view of the whole situation. This, it is said, does not do justice to our common humanity, and leads to the treating of human beings as automated robots or machines. There are two answers to such criticisms. In the first place, if it can be shown that the treatment based on these hypotheses works, then it seems possible or even likely that the hypotheses are in fact correct, and that part at least of our behaviour is mediated by fairly definitive laws and rules which have a somewhat mechanical character. Secondly, to demonstrate that some of our actions are thus mechanical does not mean that all of them are, or that we are complete puppets, governed only by the laws of the conditioned reflex. Some behaviourist psychologists have indeed suggested such an unlikely generalization, but in doing so they have stepped outside the realm of science into that of speculative philosophy; the fact that certain actions are governed by the laws of conditioning does not mean that all actions are thus governed. It is more useful to remain in the realm of fact and simply note that certain possibly rigid and mechanistic methods of treatment do seem to work rather better than others based on more high-falutin' ideas and notions; there is no need to generalize from these observations to wide-ranging statements about human nature as a whole! If we bear this limitation in mind we may be more patient in both understanding the troubles which are caused in human beings by the remnants of their animal ancestry, and more willing to accept methods of treatment which are based on a proper understanding of the structures mediating much of our emotional behaviour, and giving rise to our neurotic and sexual problems.

## References

ANNON, J., *The Behavioral Treatment of Sexual Problems*. Honolulu: Kapiolani Health Series, 1975.

BELLIVEAU, F. & RICHTER, L., *Understanding Human Sexual Inadequacy*. London: Hodder and Stoughton, 1971.

BRECHER, R. & BRECHER, E., *An Analysis of Human Sexual Response*. London: Panther, 1969.
CAUTHERY, O. & COLE, M., *The Fundamentals of Sex*. London: W.H. Allen, 1971.
EYSENCK, H.J., *You and Neurosis*. London: Temple Smith, 1977.
EYSENCK, H.J. & NIAS, D., *Sex, Violence and the Media*. London: Temple Smith, 1978.
GILLAN, P. & GILLAN, R., *Sex Therapy Today*. London: Open Books, 1976.
HARTMAN, W.E. & FITHIAN, M.A., *Treatment of Sexual Dysfunction*. Long Beach: Center for Marital and Sexual Studies, 1972.
KAPLAN, H.S., *The New Sex Therapy*. New York: Brunner/Mazel, 1974.
KNOX, D., *Marital Happiness. A Behavioural Approach to Counselling*. Champagne, Illinois: Research Press, 1971.
MASTERS, W.H. & JOHNSON, V.E., *Human Sexual Inadequacy*. London: Churchill Livingstone, 1970.
RACHMAN, S., *The Effects of Psychotherapy*. London: Pergamon, 1971.

# Index